VOICES OF FREEDOM

A Documentary History

Fifth Edition

Volume 1

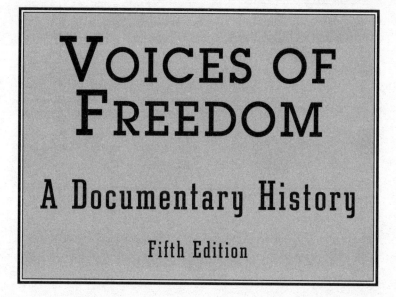

VOICES OF FREEDOM

A Documentary History

Fifth Edition

EDITED BY

ERIC FONER

Volume 1

W.W. NORTON & COMPANY · NEW YORK · LONDON

W. W. Norton & Company has been independent since its founding in 1923, when William Warder Norton and Mary D. Herter Norton first published lectures delivered at the People's Institute, the adult education division of New York City's Cooper Union. The firm soon expanded its program beyond the Institute, publishing books by celebrated academics from America and abroad. By midcentury, the two major pillars of Norton's publishing program—trade books and college texts—were firmly established. In the 1950s, the Norton family transferred control of the company to its employees, and today—with a staff of four hundred and a comparable number of trade, college, and professional titles published each year—W. W. Norton & Company stands as the largest and oldest publishing house owned wholly by its employees.

Copyright © 2017, 2014, 2011, 2008, 2005 by W. W. Norton & Company, Inc.

Printed in the United States of America

Manufacturing by Maple Press
Book design by Antonina Krass
Composition by Westchester Book Group

Library of Congress Cataloging-in-Publication Data

Names: Foner, Eric, 1943– editor.
Title: Voices of freedom: a documentary history / edited by Eric Foner.
Description: Fifth edition. | New York: W.W. Norton & Company, 2016. |
    Includes bibliographical references.
Identifiers: LCCN 2016045203 | ISBN 9780393614497 (pbk., v. 1) |
    ISBN 9780393614503 (pbk., v. 2)
Subjects: LCSH: United States—History—Sources. | United States—Politics
    and government—Sources.
Classification: LCC E173 .V645 2016 | DDC 973—dc23 LC record available at
https://lccn.loc.gov/2016045203

ISBN: 978-0-393-61449-7 (pbk.)

W. W. Norton & Company, Inc., 500 Fifth Avenue, New York, NY 10110
    wwnorton.com
W. W. Norton & Company Ltd., 15 Carlisle Street, London W1D 3BS
    1 2 3 4 5 6 7 8 9 0

ERIC FONER is DeWitt Clinton Professor of History at Columbia University, where he earned his B.A. and Ph.D. In his teaching and scholarship, he focuses on the Civil War and Reconstruction, slavery, and nineteenth-century America. Professor Foner's publications include *Free Soil, Free Labor, Free Men: The Ideology of the Republican Party Before the Civil War*; *Tom Paine and Revolutionary America*; *Politics and Ideology in the Age of the Civil War*; *Nothing but Freedom: Emancipation and Its Legacy*; *Reconstruction: American's Unfinished Revolution, 1863–1877*; *Freedom's Lawmakers: A Directory of Black Officeholders During Reconstruction*; *The Story of American Freedom*; *Who Owns History? Rethinking the Past in a Changing World*; and *Forever Free: The Story of Emancipation and Reconstruction*. His history of Reconstruction won the *Los Angeles Times* Book Award for History, the Bancroft Prize, and the Parkman Prize. He served as president of the Organization of American Historians, the American Historical Association, and the Society of American Historians. His most recent trade publications include *The Fiery Trial: Abraham Lincoln and American Slavery*, which won numerous awards including the Lincoln Prize, the Bancroft Prize, and the Pulitzer Prize, and *Gateway to Freedom: The Hidden History of the Underground Railroad*.

Contents

3

Creating Anglo-America, 1660–1750

4

Slavery, Freedom, and the Struggle for Empire to 1763

5

The American Revolution, 1763–1783

6

The Revolution Within

7

Founding a Nation, 1783–1791

8

Securing the Republic, 1790–1815

9

The Market Revolution, 1800–1840

10

Democracy in America, 1815–1840

11

The Peculiar Institution

12

An Age of Reform, 1820–1840

13

A House Divided, 1840–1861

14

A New Birth of Freedom: The Civil War, 1861–1865

15

"What Is Freedom?": Reconstruction, 1865–1877

Preface

Voices of Freedom is a documentary history of American freedom from the earliest days of European exploration and settlement of the Western Hemisphere to the present. I have prepared it as a companion volume to *Give Me Liberty!*, my survey textbook of the history of the United States centered on the theme of freedom. This fifth edition of *Voices of Freedom* is organized in chapters that correspond to those in the fifth edition of the textbook. But it can also stand independently as a documentary introduction to the history of American freedom. The two volumes include more than twenty documents not available in the third edition.

No idea is more fundamental to Americans' sense of themselves as individuals and as a nation than freedom, or liberty, with which it is almost always used interchangeably. The Declaration of Independence lists liberty among mankind's inalienable rights; the Constitution announces as its purpose to secure liberty's blessings. "Every man in the street, white, black, red or yellow," wrote the educator and statesman Ralph Bunche in 1940, "knows that this is 'the land of the free' . . . 'the cradle of liberty.'"

The very universality of the idea of freedom, however, can be misleading. Freedom is not a fixed, timeless category with a single unchanging definition. Rather, the history of the United States is, in part, a story of debates, disagreements, and struggles over freedom. Crises such as the American Revolution, the Civil War, and the Cold

War have permanently transformed the idea of freedom. So too have demands by various groups of Americans for greater freedom as they understood it.

In choosing the documents for *Voices of Freedom*, I have attempted to convey the multifaceted history of this compelling and contested idea. The documents reflect how Americans at different points in our history have defined freedom as an overarching idea, or have understood some of its many dimensions, including political, religious, economic, and personal freedom. For each chapter, I have tried to select documents that highlight the specific discussions of freedom that occurred during that time period, and some of the divergent interpretations of freedom at each point in our history. I hope that students will gain an appreciation of how the idea of freedom has expanded over time, and how it has been extended into more and more areas of Americans' lives. But at the same time, the documents suggest how freedom for some Americans has, at various times in our history, rested on lack of freedom—slavery, indentured servitude, the subordinate position of women—for others.

The documents that follow reflect the kinds of historical developments that have shaped and reshaped the idea of freedom, including war, economic change, territorial expansion, social protest movements, and international involvement. The selections try to convey a sense of the rich cast of characters who have contributed to the history of American freedom. They include presidential proclamations and letters by runaway slaves, famous court cases and obscure manifestos, ideas dominant in a particular era and those of radicals and dissenters. They range from advertisements in colonial newspapers seeking the return of runaway indentured servants and slaves to debates in the early twentieth century over the definition of economic freedom, the controversy over the proposed Equal Rights Amendment for women, and recent Supreme Court decisions dealing with the balance between liberty and security in wartime.

I have been particularly attentive to how battles at the boundaries of freedom—the efforts of racial minorities, women, and others to secure greater freedom—have deepened and transformed the concept and extended it into new realms. In addition, in this fifth edition I have included a number of new documents that illustrate how the history of the western United States, and more particularly the borderlands area of the Southwest, have affected the evolution of the idea of freedom. These include the Texas Declaration of Independence of 1836, a reminiscence about homesteading in the West in the late nineteenth century, a report on the status of Mexican-Americans in the aftermath of World War II, and an explanation of the so-called Sagebrush Rebellion of the 1970s.

All of the documents in this collection are "primary sources"— that is, they were written or spoken by men and women enmeshed in the events of the past, rather than by later historians. They therefore offer students the opportunity to encounter ideas about freedom in the actual words of participants in the drama of American history. Some of the documents are reproduced in their entirety. Most are excerpts from longer interviews, articles, or books. In editing the documents, I have tried to remain faithful to the original purpose of the author, while highlighting the portion of the text that deals directly with one or another aspect of freedom. In most cases, I have reproduced the wording of the original texts exactly. But I have modernized the spelling and punctuation of some early documents to make them more understandable to the modern reader. Each document is preceded by a brief introduction that places it in historical context and is followed by two questions that highlight key elements of the argument and may help to focus students' thinking about the issues raised by the author.

A number of these documents were suggested by students in a U.S. history class at Juniata College in Huntingdon, Pennsylvania, taught by Professor David Hsiung. I am very grateful to these students, who responded enthusiastically to an assignment by Professor Hsiung that asked them to locate documents that might be included in this edition of *Voices of Freedom* and to justify their choices with historical arguments. Some of the documents are included in the online exhibition, "Preserving American Freedom," created by the Historical Society of Pennsylvania.

Taken together, the documents in these volumes suggest the ways in which American freedom has changed and expanded over time. But they also remind us that American history is not simply a narrative of continual progress toward greater and greater freedom. While freedom can be achieved, it may also be reduced or rescinded. It can never be taken for granted.

Eric Foner

VOICES OF FREEDOM

A Documentary History

Fifth Edition

Volume 1

CHAPTER 1

A New World

1. Adam Smith, The Results of Colonization (1776)

Source: Adam Smith, An Inquiry into the Nature and Causes of the Wealth of Nations *(London, 1776), Vol. 2, pp. 190–91, 235–37.*

"The discovery of America," the Scottish writer Adam Smith announced in his celebrated work *The Wealth of Nations,* published in 1776, was one of "the two greatest and most important events recorded in the history of mankind." Smith is regarded as the founder of modern economics. It is not surprising that looking back nearly three centuries after the initial voyage of Christopher Columbus in 1492, Smith focused primarily on the economic results of the conquest and colonization of North and South America. The influx of goods from the New World, he insisted, greatly increased the "enjoyments" of the people of Europe and the market for European goods. Nonetheless, Smith did not fail to note the price paid by the indigenous population of the New World, who suffered a dramatic decline in population due to epidemics, wars of conquest, and the exploitation of their labor. "Benefits" for some, Smith observed, went hand in hand with "dreadful misfortunes" for others—a fitting commentary on the long encounter between the Old and New Worlds.

OF THE ADVANTAGES which Europe has derived from the Discovery of America, and from that of a Passage to the East Indies by the Cape of Good Hope

1

What are [the advantages] which Europe has derived from the discovery and colonization of America?

The general advantages which Europe, considered as one great country, has derived from the discovery and colonization of America, consist, first, in the increase of its enjoyments; and, secondly, in the augmentation of its industry.

The surplus produce of America, imported into Europe, furnishes the inhabitants of this great continent with a variety of commodities which they could not otherwise have possessed; some for conveniency and use, some for pleasure, and some for ornament, and thereby contributes to increase their enjoyments.

The discovery and colonization of America, it will readily be allowed, have contributed to augment the industry, first, of all the countries which trade to it directly, such as Spain, Portugal, France, and England; and, secondly, of all those which, without trading to it directly, send, through the medium of other countries, goods to it of their own produce; such as Austrian Flanders, and some provinces of Germany, which, through the medium of the countries before mentioned, send to it a considerable quantity of linen and other goods. All such countries have evidently gained a more extensive market for their surplus produce, and must consequently have been encouraged to increase its quantity....

• • •

The discovery of America, and that of a passage to the East Indies by the Cape of Good Hope, are the two greatest and most important events recorded in the history of mankind. Their consequences have already been very great; but, in the short period of between two and three centuries which has elapsed since these discoveries were made, it is impossible that the whole extent of their consequences can have been seen. What benefits or what misfortunes to mankind may hereafter result from those great events, no human wisdom can foresee. By uniting, in some measure, the most distant parts of the world, by enabling them to relieve one another's wants, to increase one another's enjoyments, and to encourage one another's industry, their general tendency would seem to be beneficial. To the natives however, both of the East and West Indies, all the commercial benefits which can have resulted from those events have been sunk and lost in the dreadful misfortunes which they have occasioned. . . .

• • •

In the meantime one of the principal effects of those discoveries has been to raise the mercantile system to a degree of splendour and glory which it could never otherwise have attained to. It is the object of that system to enrich a great nation rather by trade and manufactures than by the improvement and cultivation of land, rather by the industry of the towns than by that of the country. But, in consequence of those discoveries, the commercial towns of Europe, instead of being the manufacturers and carriers for but a very small part of the world (that part of Europe which is washed by the Atlantic Ocean, and the countries which lie round the Baltic and Mediterranean seas), have now become the manufacturers for the numerous and thriving cultivators of America, and the carriers and in some respects the manufacturers too, for almost all the different nations of Asia, Africa, and America. Two new worlds have been opened to their industry, each of them much greater and more extensive than the old one, and the market of one of them growing still greater and greater every day.

Questions

1. According to Adam Smith, how did the "discovery and colonization" of America affect the economic development of Europe?

2. Why does Smith believe that the "benefits" of colonization outweigh the "misfortunes"?

2. Giovanni da Verrazano, Encountering Native Americans (1524)

Source: Giovanni da Verrazano: from The Voyages of Giovanni da Verrazano, *1524–1528, Lawrence C. Wroth, ed., Susan Tarrow, trans. (New Haven, 1970). Reprinted by permission of Yale University Press.*

One of the first European explorers to encounter the Indians of eastern North America, Giovanni da Verrazano was an Italian-born navigator who sailed in 1524 under the auspices of King Philip I of France. His voyage took him from modern-day Cape Fear, North Carolina, north to the coast of Maine. In the following excerpt from his diary, which he included in a letter to the king, Verrazano tries to describe the appearance, economic life, customs, and beliefs of some of the region's various Native American groups. Some, he reports, were friendly and generous; others warlike and hostile. He is particularly interested in their spiritual beliefs, concluding that they have "no religion." Verrazano found the east coast thickly populated. By the time English settlement began in the early seventeenth century, many of the groups he encountered had been all but destroyed by epidemic diseases.

————

SINCE THE STORM that we encountered in the northern regions, Most Serene King, I have not written to tell your majesty of what happened to the four ships which you sent over the Ocean to explore new lands, as I thought you had already been informed of everything—how we were forced by the fury of the winds to return in distress to Brittany with only the *Normandy* and the *Dauphine*, and that after undergoing repairs there, began our voyage with these two ships, equipped for war, following the coasts of Spain, Your Most Serene Majesty will have heard; and then according to our new plan, we continued the original voyage with only the *Dauphine*; now on our return from this voyage I will tell Your Majesty of what we found. . . .

Seeing that the land continued to the south, we decided to turn and skirt it toward the north, where we found the land we had

sighted earlier. So we anchored off the coast and sent the small boat
in to land. We had seen many people coming to the seashore, but
they fled when they saw us approaching; several times they stopped
and turned around to look at us in great wonderment. We reassured
them with various signs, and some of them came up, showing great
delight at seeing us and marveling at our clothes, appearance, and
our whiteness; they showed us by various signs where we could
most easily secure the boat, and offered us some of their food. We
were on land, and I shall now tell Your Majesty briefly what we were
able to learn of their life and customs.

They go completely naked except that around their loins they
wear skins of small animals like martens, with a narrow belt of
grass around the body, to which they tie various rails of other animals which hang down to the knees; the rest of the body is bare, and
so is the head. Some of them wear garlands of birds' feathers. They
are dark in color, not unlike the Ethiopians, with thick black hair,
not very long, tied back behind the head like a small tail. As for
the physique of these men, they are well proportioned, of medium
height, a little taller than we are. They have broad chests, strong
arms, and the legs and other parts of the body are well composed.
There is nothing else, except that they tend to be rather broad in the
face; but not all, for we saw many with angular faces. They have big
black eyes, and an attentive and open look. They are not very strong,
but they have a sharp cunning, and are agile and swift runners.
From what we could tell from observation, in the last two respects
they resemble the Orientals. . . .

We reached another land 15 leagues from the island, where we
found an excellent harbor; before entering it, we saw about 20 boats
full of people who came around the ship uttering various cries of
wonderment. They did not come nearer than fifty paces, but stopped
to look at the structure of our ship, our persons, and our clothes;
then all together they raised a loud cry which meant that they were
joyful. We reassured them somewhat by imitating their gestures,
and they came near enough for us to throw them a few little bells

and mirrors and many trinkets, which they took and looked at, laughing, and then they confidently came on board ship.... These people are the most beautiful and have the most civil customs that we have found on this voyage. They are taller than we are; they are a bronze color, some tending more toward whiteness, others to a tawny color; the face is clear-cut; the hair is long and black, and they take great pains to decorate it; the eyes are black and alert, and their manner is sweet and gentle, very like the manner of the ancients....

Their women are just as shapely and beautiful; very gracious, of attractive manner and pleasant appearance; their customs and behavior follow womanly custom as far as befits human nature; they go nude except for stag skin embroidered like the men's, and some wear rich lynx skins on their arms; their bare heads are decorated with various ornaments made of braids of their own hair which hang down over their breasts on either side.... Both men and women have various trinkets hanging from their ears as the Orientals do; and we saw that many had sheets of worked copper which they prize more than gold. They do not value gold because of its color; they think it the most worthless of all, and rate blue and red above all other colors. The things we gave them that they prized the most were little bells, blue crystals, and other trinkets to put in the ear or around the neck. They did not appreciate cloth of silk and gold, nor even of any other kind, nor did they care to have them; the same was true for metals like steel and iron, for many times when we showed them some of our arms, they did not admire them, nor ask for them, but merely examined the workmanship. They did the same with mirrors; they would look at them quickly, and then refuse them, laughing.

They are very generous and give away all they have. We made great friends with them, and one day before we entered the harbor with the ship, when we were lying at anchor one league out to sea because of unfavorable weather, they came out to the ship with a great number of their boats; they had painted and decorated their faces with various colors, showing us that it was a sign of happiness. They brought us some of their food, and showed us by signs where we should anchor in the port for the ship's safety, and then accompanied us all the way until we dropped anchor...

At a distance of fifty leagues, keeping more to the north, we found high country full of very dense forests, composed of pines, cypresses, and similar trees which grow in cold regions.

The people were quite different from the others, for while the previous ones had been courteous in manner, these were full of crudity and vices, and were so barbarous that we could never make any communication with them, however many signs we made to them. They were clothed in skins of bear, lynx, sea-wolf and other animals. As far as we could judge from several visits to their houses, we think they live on game, fish, and several fruits which are a species of root which the earth produces itself.... We saw no sign of cultivation, nor would the land be suitable for producing any fruit or grain on account of its sterility. If we wanted to trade with them for some of their things, they would come to the seashore on some rocks where the breakers were most violent, while we remained in the little boat, and they sent us what they wanted to give on a rope, continually shouting at us not to approach the land; they gave us the barter quickly, and would take in exchange only knives, hooks for fishing and sharp metal. We found no courtesy in them, and when we had nothing more to exchange and left them, the men made all the signs of scorn and shame that any brute creature would make. Against their wishes, we penetrated two or three leagues inland with 25 armed men, and when we disembarked on the shore, they shot at us with their bows and uttered loud cries before fleeing into the woods....

Due to a lack of [a common] language, we were unable to find out by signs or gestures how much religious faith these people we found possess. We think they have neither religion nor laws, that they do not know of a First Cause or Author, that they do not worship the sky, the stars, the sun, the moon, or other planets, nor do they even practice any kind of idolatry; we do not know whether they offer any sacrifices or other prayers, nor are there any temples or churches of prayer among their peoples. We consider that they have no religion and that they live in absolute freedom, and that everything they do proceeds from Ignorance; for they are very easily persuaded, and they imitated everything that they saw us Christians do with regard to divine worship, with the same fervor and enthusiasm that we had.

Questions

1. How much do Verrazano's observations seem to the affected by his own beliefs and experiences?

2. Why does he write that Indians live in "absolute freedom," and why does he consider this a criticism rather than a compliment?

---

3. Bartolomé de las Casas on Spanish Treatment of the Indians, from *History of the Indies* (1528)

Source: Bartolomé de las Casas: "History of the Indies (1528)," excerpt from History of the Indies, *trans. and ed. by Andrée Collard. (New York: Harper and Row, 1971), pp. 82, 112–115. Copyright © 1971 by Andrée Collard, renewed 1999 by Joyce J. Contrucci. Reprinted by permission of Joyce Contrucci.*

Known as the "Apostle of the Indians," Bartolomé de las Casas, a Catholic priest, was the most eloquent critic of Spanish mistreatment of the New World's native population. Las Casas took part in the exploitation of Indian labor on Hispaniola and Cuba. But in 1514, he freed his Indian slaves and began to preach against the injustices of Spanish rule. In his *History of the Indies*, Las Casas denounced Spain for causing the deaths of millions of innocent people. The excerpt that follows details events on

Hispaniola, the Caribbean island first conquered and settled by Spain. Las Casas called for the Indians to enjoy the rights of other subjects of Spain.

Largely because of Las Casas's efforts, in 1542 Spain promulgated the New Laws, ordering that Indians no longer be enslaved. But Spain's European rivals seized upon Las Casas's criticisms to justify their own ambitions. His writings became the basis for the Black Legend, the image of Spain as a uniquely cruel empire. Other nations would claim that their imperial ventures were inspired by the desire to rescue Indians from Spanish rule.

IN THAT YEAR of 1500, ... the King determined to send a new governor to Hispaniola, which at the time was the only seat of government in the Indies. The new governor was fray Nicolás de Ovando, Knight of Alcántara, and at that time comendador of Lares.

• • •

At first, the Indians were forced to stay six months away at work; later, the time was extended to eight months and this was called a shift, at the end of which they brought all the gold for minting. The King's part was subtracted and the rest went to individuals, but for years no one kept a single peso because they owed it all to merchants and other creditors, so that the anguish and torments endured by the Indians in mining that infernal gold were consumed entirely by God and no one prospered. During the minting period, the Indians were allowed to go home, a few days' journey on foot. One can imagine their state when they arrived after eight months, and those who found their wives there must have cried, lamenting their condition together. How could they even rest, since they had to provide for the needs of their family when their land had gone to weeds? Of those who had worked in the mines, a bare 10 per cent survived to start the journey home. Many Spaniards had no scruples about making them work on Sundays and holidays, if not in the mines then on minor tasks such as building and repairing houses, carrying firewood, etc. They fed them cassava bread, which is adequate nutrition only when supplemented with meat, fish or other more substantial food. The

minero killed a pig once a week but he kept more than half for himself and had the leftover apportioned and cooked daily for thirty or
forty Indians, which came to a bite of meat the size of a walnut per
individual, and they dipped the cassava in this as well as in the broth.

• • •

The comendador arranged to have wages paid as follows, which
I swear is the truth: in exchange for his life of services, an Indian
received 3 *maravedís* every two days, less one-half a *maravedí* in order
not to exceed the yearly half gold peso, that is, 225 *maravedís*, paid
them once a year as pin money or *cacona*, as Indians call it, which
means bonus or reward. This sum bought a comb, a small mirror and
a string of green or blue glass beads, and many did without that consolation for they were paid much less and had no way of mitigating
their misery, although in truth, they offered their labor up for nothing, caring only to fill their stomachs to appease their raging hunger
and find ways to escape from their desperate lives. For this loss of body
and soul, then, they received less than 3 *maravedís* for two days; many
years later their wages were increased to 1 gold peso by the order of
King Hernando, and this was no less an affront, as I will show later.

I believe the above clearly demonstrates that the Indians were
totally deprived of their freedom and were put in the harshest, fierc-
est, most horrible servitude and captivity which no one who has not
seen it can understand. Even beasts enjoy more freedom when they
are allowed to graze in the fields. But our Spaniards gave no such
opportunity to Indians and truly considered them perpetual slaves,
since the Indians had not the free will to dispose of their persons but
instead were disposed of according to Spanish greed and cruelty, not
as men in captivity but as beasts tied to a rope to prevent free movement. When they were allowed to go home, they often found it
deserted and had no other recourse than to go out into the woods to
find food and to die. When they fell ill, which was very frequently
because they are a delicate people unaccustomed to such work, the
Spaniards did not believe them and pitilessly called them lazy dogs,
and kicked and beat them; and when illness was apparent they sent
them home as useless, giving them some cassava for the twenty- to

eighty-league journey. They would go then, falling into the first stream and dying there in desperation; others would hold on longer but very few ever made it home. I sometimes came upon dead bodies on my way, and upon others who were gasping and moaning in their death agony, repeating "Hungry, hungry." And this was the freedom, the good treatment and the Christianity that Indians received.

• • •

About eight years passed under the comendador's rule and this disorder had time to grow; no one gave it a thought and the multitude of people who originally lived on this island . . . was consumed at such a rate that in those eight years 90 per cent had perished. From here this sweeping plague went to San Juan, Jamaica, Cuba and the continent, spreading destruction over the whole hemisphere.

• • •

Questions

1. What do you think Las Casas hoped to accomplish by writing so critically about Spanish treatment of the Indians?

2. Why, after describing illness and starvation among the Indians, does Las Casas write, "this was the freedom, the good treatment and the Christianity that Indians received"?

---

4. The Pueblo Revolt (1680)

Source: Charles W. Hackett: "Declarations of Josephe and Pedro Naranjo," Revolt of the Pueblo Indians of New Mexico and Otermín's Attempted Reconquest 1680–1682, Volume 2, *pp. 238–48, 1942. Reprinted with permission of the University of New Mexico Press.*

In 1680, the Pueblo Indians of modern-day New Mexico revolted against Spanish rule. During the seventeenth century, governors, settlers, and missionaries had sought to exploit the labor of an Indian population that declined from about 60,000 in 1600 to some 17,000 eighty years later. Franciscan friars worked diligently, often violently, to convert Indians to Catholicism. Some natives accepted baptism. But the friars' efforts to stamp out traditional religious ceremonies in New Mexico—they burned Indian idols, masks, and other sacred objects—alienated far more Indians than they converted. Under the leadership of Popé, a local religious leader, the rebelling Indians killed 400 colonists, including twenty-one Franciscan missionaries. The Pueblo Revolt was the most complete victory for Native Americans over Europeans and the only wholesale expulsion of settlers in the history of North America. The uprising, concluded a royal attorney who interviewed survivors in Mexico City, arose from the "many oppressions" the Indians had suffered. In 1692, the Spanish launched an invasion that reconquered New Mexico.

Declaration of Josephe, Spanish-speaking Indian.
[Place of the Rio del Norte, December 19, 1681.]

Asked what causes or motives the said Indian rebels had for renouncing the law of God and obedience to his Majesty, and for committing so many kinds of crimes, and who were the instigators of the rebellion, and what he had heard while he was among the apostates, he said that the prime movers of the rebellion were two Indians of San Juan, one named El Popé and the other El Taqu, and another from Taos named Saca, and another from San Ildefonso named Francisco. He knows that these were the principals, and the causes they gave were alleged ill treatment and injuries received from the present secretary, Francisco Xavier, and the maestre de campo, Alonso García, and from the sargentos mayores, Luis de Quintana and Diego López, because they beat them, took away what they had, and made them work without pay. Thus he replies.

Asked if he has learned or it has come to his notice during the time that he has been here the reason why the apostates burned the images, churches, and things pertaining to divine worship, making a mockery and a trophy of them, killing the priests and doing the other things they did, he said that he knows and has heard it generally stated that while they were besieging the villa the rebellious traitors burned the church and shouted in loud voices, "Now the God of the Spaniards, who was their father, is dead, and Santa Maria, who was their mother, and the saints, who were pieces of rotten wood," saying that only their own god lived. Thus they ordered all the temples and images, crosses and rosaries burned, and this function being over, they all went to bathe in the rivers, saying that they thereby washed away the water of baptism. For their churches, they placed on the four sides and in the center of the plaza some small circular enclosures of stone where they went to offer flour, feathers, and the seed of maguey, maize, and tobacco, and performed other superstitious rites, giving the children to understand that they must all do this in the future. The captains and chiefs ordered that the names of Jesus and of Mary should nowhere be uttered, and that they should discard their baptismal names, and abandon the wives whom God had given them in matrimony, and take the ones that they pleased. He saw that as soon as the remaining Spaniards had left, they ordered all the estufas erected, which are their houses of idolatry, and danced throughout the kingdom the dance of the cazina, making many masks for it in the image of the devil. Thus he replied to this question. . . .

Asked if he knows, or whether it has come to his notice, that the said apostates have erected houses of idolatry which they call estufas in the pueblos, and have practiced dances and superstitions, he said there is a general report throughout the kingdom that they have done so and he has seen many houses of idolatry which they have built, dancing the dance of the cachina, which this declarant has also danced. Thus he replied to the question.

DECLARATION OF PEDRO NARANJO OF THE QUERES NATION.
[PLACE OF THE RÍO DEL NORTE, DECEMBER 19, 1681.]

Asked for what reason they so blindly burned the images, temples, crosses, and other things of divine worship, he stated that the said

Indian, Popé, came down in person, and with him El Saca and El
Chato from the pueblo of Los Taos, and other captains and leaders
and many people who were in his train, and he ordered in all the
pueblos through which he passed that they instantly break up
and burn the images of the holy Christ, the Virgin Mary and the
other saints, the crosses, and everything pertaining to Christianity, and that they burn the temples, break up the bells, and separate from the wives whom God had given them in marriage and
take those whom they desired. In order to take away their baptismal names, the water, and the holy oils, they were to plunge into
the rivers and wash themselves with amole, which is a root native
to the country, washing even their clothing, with the understanding that there would thus be taken from them the character
of the holy sacraments. They did this, and also many other things
which he does not recall, given to understand that this mandate
had come from the Caydi and the other two who emitted fire from
their extremities in the said estufa of Taos, and that they thereby
returned to the state of their antiquity, as when they came from
the lake of Copala; that this was the better life and the one they
desired, because the God of the Spaniards was worth nothing and
theirs was very strong, the Spaniards's God being rotten wood.
These things were observed and obeyed by all except some who,
moved by the zeal of Christians, opposed it, and such persons the
said Popé caused to be killed immediately. He saw to it that they
at once erected and rebuilt their houses of idolatry which they
call estufas, and made very ugly masks in imitation of the devil
in order to dance the dance of the cacina; and he said likewise
that the devil had given them to understand that living thus in
accordance with the law of their ancestors, they would harvest a
great deal of maize, many beans, a great abundance of cotton,
calabashes, and very large watermelons and cantaloupes; and
that they could erect their houses and enjoy abundant health and
leisure.

Questions

1. What actions did Indians take during the Pueblo Revolt to demonstrate their new freedom from Spanish rule?

2. Why do you think religion played such a large role in the Pueblo Revolt?

---

5. Father Jean de Brébeuf on the Customs and Beliefs of the Hurons (1635)

Source: Reuben G. Thwaites, ed., The Jesuit Relations and Allied Documents: Travels and Explorations of the Jesuit Missionaries in New France, 1610–1791 *(Cleveland, 1896–1901), Vol. 12, pp. 117–24.*

With its small white population and emphasis on the fur trade rather than agricultural settlement, the viability of New France depended on friendly relations with local Indians. The French neither appropriated substantial amounts of Indian land like the English nor conquered native inhabitants militarily and set them to forced labor, as in Spanish America. The Jesuits, a missionary religious order, sought to convert Indians to Catholicism. One of the Jesuit missionaries to the Huron people in modern-day Quebec, Jean de Brébeuf, left a vivid description of the lives and customs of the Indians. In the following excerpt, he dwells upon their religious beliefs, marriage customs, and gender relations—all aspects of Indian life that seemed very alien to Europeans—and describes how he tried to convert them. De Brébeuf was killed after being captured during a war between Hurons and Iroquois in 1649.

IT REMAINS NOW to say something of the country, of the manners and customs of the Hurons, of the inclination they have to the Faith, and of our insignificant labors.

As to the first, the little paper and leisure we have compels me to say in a few words what might justly fill a volume. The Huron country is not large, its greatest extent can be traversed in three or four days. Its situation is fine, the greater part of it consisting of plains. It is surrounded and intersected by a number of very beautiful lakes or rather seas, whence it comes that the one to the North and to the Northwest is called "fresh-water sea" [Lake Huron]... There are twenty Towns, which indicate about 30,000 souls speaking the same tongue, which is not difficult to one who has a master. It has distinctions of genders, number, tense, person, moods; and, in short, it is very complete and very regular, contrary to the opinion of many....

It is so evident that there is a Divinity who has made Heaven and earth that our Hurons cannot entirely ignore it. But they misapprehend him grossly. For they have neither Temples, nor Priests, nor Feasts, nor any ceremonies.

They say that a certain woman called *Eataensic* is the one who made earth and man. They give her an assistant, one named *Jouskeha*, whom they declare to be her little son, with whom she governs the world. This *Jouskeha* has care of the living, and of the things that concern life, and consequently they say that he is good. *Eataensic* has care of souls; and, because they believe that she makes men die, they say that she is wicked. And there are among them mysteries so hidden that only the old men, who can speak with authority about them, are believed.

This God and Goddess live like themselves, but without famine; make feasts as they do, are lustful as they are; in short, they imagine them exactly like themselves. And still, though they make them human and corporeal, they seem nevertheless to attribute to them a certain immensity in all places.

They say that this *Eataensic* fell from the Sky, where there are inhabitants as on earth, and when she fell, she was with child. If you ask them who made the sky and its inhabitants, they have no other reply than that they know nothing about it. And when we preach to them of one God, Creator of Heaven and earth, and of all things, and even when we talk to them of Hell and Paradise and of our other mysteries, the headstrong reply that this is good for our Country and not for theirs; that every Country has its own fashions. But having pointed out to them, by means of a little globe that we had brought, that there is only one world, they remain without reply.

I find in their marriage customs two things that greatly please me; the first, that they have only one wife; the second, that they do not marry their relatives in a direct or collateral line, however distant they may be. There is, on the other hand, sufficient to censure, were it only the frequent changes the men make of their wives, and the women of their husbands.

They believe in the immortality of the soul, which they believe to be corporeal. The greatest part of their Religion consists of this point. We have seen several stripped, or almost so, of all their goods, because several of their friends were dead, to whose souls they had made presents. Moreover, dogs, fish, deer, and other animals have, in their opinion, immortal and reasonable souls. In proof of this, the old men relate certain fables, which they represent as true; they make no mention either of punishment or reward, in the place to which souls go after death. And so they do not make any distinction between the good and the bad, the virtuous and the vicious; and they honor equally the interment of both, even as we have seen in the case of a young man who poisoned himself from the grief he felt because his wife had been taken away from him. Their superstitions are infinite, their feast, their medicines, their fishing, their hunting, their wars,—in short almost their whole life turns upon this pivot; dreams, above all have here great credit.

As regards morals, the Hurons are lascivious, although in two leading points less so than many Christians, who will blush some day in their presence. You will see no kissing nor immodest caressing; and in marriage a man will remain two or three years apart from his wife, while she is nursing. They are gluttons, even to disgorging; it is true, that does not happen often, but only in some superstitious feasts,—these, however, they do not attend willingly. Besides they

endure hunger much better than we,—so well that after having
fasted two or three entire days you will see them still paddling,
carrying loads, singing, laughing, bantering, as if they had dined
well. They are very lazy, are liars, thieves, pertinacious beggars. Some
consider them vindictive; but, in my opinion, this vice is more notice-
able elsewhere than here.

We see shining among them some rather noble moral virtues. You
note, in the first place, a great love and union, which they are careful to
cultivate by means of their marriages, of their presents, of their feasts,
and of their frequent visits. On returning from their fishing, their
hunting, and their trading, they exchange many gifts; if they have
thus obtained something unusually good, even if they have bought it,
or if it has been given to them, they make a feast to the whole village
with it. Their hospitality towards all sorts of strangers is remarkable;
they present to them, in their feasts, the best of what they have prepared, and, as I have already said, I do not know if anything similar, in
this regard, is to be found anywhere. They never close the door upon a
Stranger, and, once having received him into their houses, they share
with him the best they have; they never send him away, and when he
goes away of his own accord, he repays them by a simple "thank you."

• • •

About the month of December, the snow began to lie on the ground,
and the savages settled down into the village. For, during the whole
Summer and Autumn, they are for the most part either in their rural
cabins, taking care of their crops, or on the lake fishing, or trading;
which makes it not a little inconvenient to instruct them. Seeing
them, therefore, thus gathered together at the beginning of this year,
we resolved to preach publicly to all, and to acquaint them with the
reason of our coming into their Country, which is not for their furs,
but to declare to them the true God and his son, Jesus Christ, the universal Saviour of our souls.

The usual method that we follow is this: We call together the people
by the help of the Captain of the village, who assembles them all in
our house as in Council, or perhaps by the sound of the bell. I use the

surplice and the square cap, to give more majesty to my appearance. At the beginning we chant on our knees the *Pater noster*, translated into Huron verse. Father Daniel, as its author, chants a couplet alone, and then we all together chant it again; and those among the Hurons, principally the little ones, who already know it, take pleasure in chanting it with us. That done, when every one is seated, I rise and make the sign of the Cross for all; then, having recapitulated what I said last time, I explain something new. After that we question the young children and the girls, giving a little bead of glass or porcelain to those who deserve it. The parents are very glad to see their children answer well and carry off some little prize, of which they render themselves worthy by the care they take to come privately to get instruction. On our part, to arouse their emulation, we have each lesson retraced by our two little French boys, who question each other,—which transports the Savages with admiration. Finally the whole is concluded by the talk of the Old Men, who propound their difficulties, and sometimes make me listen in my turn to the statement of their belief.

Two things among others have aided us very much in the little we have been able to do here, by the grace of our Lord; the first is, as I have already said, the good health that God has granted us in the midst of sickness so general and so widespread. The second is the temporal assistance we have rendered to the sick. Having brought for ourselves some few delicacies, we shared them with them, giving to one a few prunes, and to another a few raisins, to others something else. The poor people came from great distances to get their share.

Questions

1. Which aspects of Indian practices and beliefs does de Brébeuf find admirable and which does he criticize most strongly?

2. How do Huron gender and family relations seem to differ from those of Europeans?

6. Jewish Petition to the Dutch West India Company (1655)

Source: Samuel Oppenheim, "The Early History of the Jews in New York City, 1654–1664," Publications of the American Jewish Historical Society *(1909), pp. 9–11.*

Among European colonies in the seventeenth century, New Netherland was noted for religious toleration, although its rulers made a careful distinction between private worship in a home, which was allowed, and public worship, which was confined to the established Dutch Reformed church. In 1655, a group of Jews arrived from Brazil, from which they had been expelled after the Portuguese wrested control of the colony from the Dutch. When Governor Petrus Stuyvesant ordered them to leave, Jews in Amsterdam asked the Dutch West India Company to reverse the decision. The company granted the request, so long as the newcomers did not become a public "charge"—that is, require financial assistance.

———

To the Honorable Lords, Directors of the Chartered West India Company, Chamber of the City of Amsterdam.

The merchants of the Portuguese Nation residing in this City respectfully remonstrate to your Honors that it has come to their knowledge that your Honors raise obstacles to the giving of permits or passports to the Portuguese Jews to travel and to go to reside in New Netherland, which if persisted in will result to the great disadvantage of the Jewish nation. It also can be of no advantage to the general Company but rather damaging.

There are many of the nation who have lost their possessions at Pernambuco [Brazil] and have arrived from there in great poverty, and part of them have been dispersed here and there. So that your petitioners had to expend large sums of money for their necessaries of life, and through lack of opportunity all cannot remain here to live. And as they cannot go to Spain or Portugal because of the

Inquisition, a great part of the aforesaid people must in time be obliged to depart for other territories of their High Mightinesses the States-General and their Companies, in order there, through their labor and efforts, to be able to exist under the protection of the administrators of your Honorable Directors, observing and obeying your Honors' orders and commands.

It is well known to your Honors that the Jewish nation in Brazil have at all times been faithful and have striven to guard and maintain that place, risking for that purpose their possessions and their blood.

Yonder land is extensive and spacious. The more of loyal people that go to live there, the better it is in regard to the population of the country as in regard to the payment of various excises and taxes which may be imposed there, and in regard to the increase of trade, and also to the importation of all the necessaries that may be sent there.

Your Honors should also consider that the Honorable Lords, the Burgomasters of the City and the Honorable High Illustrious Mighty Lords, the States-General, have in political matters always protected and considered the Jewish nation as upon the same footing as all the inhabitants and burghers. Also it is conditioned in the treaty of perpetual peace with the King of Spain that the Jewish nation shall also enjoy the same liberty as all other inhabitants of these lands.

Your Honors should also please consider that many of the Jewish nation are principal shareholders in the Company. They having always striven their best for the Company, and many of their nation have lost immense and great capital in its shares and obligations.

The Company has by a general resolution consented that those who wish to populate the Colony shall enjoy certain districts of land gratis. Why should now certain subjects of this State not be allowed to travel thither and live there? The French consent that the Portuguese Jews may traffic and live in Martinique, Christopher and others of their territories, whither also some have gone from here, as your

Honors know. The English also consent at the present time that the Portuguese and Jewish nation may go from London and settle at Barbados, whither also some have gone.

As foreign nations consent that the Jewish nation may go to live and trade in their territories, how can your Honors forbid the same and refuse transportation to this Portuguese nation who reside here and have been settled here well on to about sixty years, many also being born here and confirmed burghers, and this to a land that needs people for its increase?

Therefore the petitioners request, for the reasons given above (as also others which they omit to avoid prolixity), that your Honors be pleased not to exclude but to grant the Jewish nation passage to and residence in that country; otherwise this would result in a great prejudice to their reputation. Also that by an Apostille and Act the Jewish nation be permitted, together with other inhabitants, to travel, live and traffic there, and with them enjoy liberty on condition of contributing like others, &c.

Questions

1. What does the petition tell us about the extent of religious toleration in the seventeenth century?

2. How do the petitioners argue that allowing Jews to settle will benefit New Netherland?

CHAPTER 2

Beginnings of English America, 1607–1660

7. Exchange between John Smith and Powhatan (1608)

Source: John Smith, The Generall Historie of Virginia . . . *(London, 1624), pp. 74–76.*

When English colonists arrived in Virginia in 1607, they landed in an area inhabited by more than 15,000 Indians, members of some thirty tribes loosely united in a confederacy whose leader the settlers called Powhatan, the native word for both his tribe and the title of paramount chief. In a history written in 1624, the English leader John Smith recalled his exchange with Powhatan sixteen years earlier. Of course, Powhatan's words are filtered through Smith's memory. But the exchange seems to capture differences in outlook between the two leaders.

━━━━━

THE 12 OF JANUARY we arrived at Werowocomoco.... Quartering in the next houses we found, we sent to Powhatan for provision, who sent us plenty of bread, turkeys, and venison; the next day having feasted us after his ordinary manner, he began to ask us when we would be gone, saying he sent not for us, neither had he any corn; and his people much less, yet for forty swords he would procure us forty baskets.... The King concluded the matter with a merry laughter, asking for our commodities, but none he liked without guns and swords, valuing a basket of corn more precious than a basket of copper, saying he would rate his corn, but not the copper.

Captain Smith seeing the intent of this subtle savage began to deal with him after this manner.

Powhatan, though I had many courses to have made my provision, yet believing your promises to supply my wants, I neglected all to satisfy your desire, and to testify my life, I sent you my men for your building, neglecting my own. What your people had you have engrossed, forbidding them our trade, and now you think by consuming the time, we shall consume for want, not having to fulfill your strange demands. As for swords and guns, I told you long ago I had none to spare, and you must know those I have can keep me from want, yet steal or wrong you I will not, nor dissolve that friendship we have mutually promised, except you constrain me by our bad usage.

The King having attentively listened to this discourse, promised that both he and his country would spare him what he could, which within two days they should receive. Yet Captain Smith, said the King, some doubt I have of your coming hither, that makes me not so kindly seek to relieve you as I would, for many do inform me, your coming hither is not for trade, but to invade my people, and possess my country, who dare not come to bring you corn, seeing you thus armed with your men. To free us of this fear, leave abroad your weapons, for here they are useless, we being all friends, and for ever Powhatan's. . . .

While we expected the coming in of the country, we wrangled out of the King ten quarters of corn for a copper kettle. . . . Wherewith each seemed well contented, and Powhatan began to expostulate the difference of Peace and War after this manner.

Captain Smith, you may understand that I having seen the death of all my people thrice, and not any one living of these three generations but myself, I know the difference of Peace and War better than any in my country. But now I am old and ere long must die, my brethren, namely Opichapam, Opechancanough, and Kekataugh, my two sisters, and their two daughters, are distinctly each others successors. I wish their experience no less than mine, and your love to them no less than mine to you. But this [rumor] that you are come to destroy my country, so much frightens all my people as they dare not visit you. What will it avail you to take that by force you may quickly have by love, or to destroy them that provide you food? What can you get by war, when we can hide our provisions and fly to the woods, whereby you must famish by wronging us your friends. And why are you thus jealous of our loves seeing us unarmed, and both do and are willing still to feed you, with that you cannot get but by our laborers? Think you I am so simple, not to know it is better to eat good meat, lie well, and sleep quietly with my women and children, laugh and be merry with you, have copper, hatchets, or what I want being your friend, than be forced to fly from all, to lie cold in the woods, feed upon acorns, roots, and such trash, and be so hunted by you, that I can neither rest, eat, not sleep, but my tired men must watch, and if a twig but break, every one cries there comes Captain Smith. Then I must fly I know not where, and thus with miserable fear, end my miserable life, leaving my pleasures to such youths as you.... Let this therefore assure you of our love, and every year our friendly trade shall furnish you with corn, and now also, if you would come in friendly manner to see us, and not this with your guns and swords as to invade your foes.

To this subtle discourse, [Smith] replied.

Seeing you will not rightly conceive of our words, we strive to make you know our thoughts by our deeds; the vow I made you of my love, both myself and my men have kept. As for your promise I find it every day violated by some of your subjects, yet we finding your love and kindness, our custom is so far from being ungrateful, that for your sake only we have curbed our thirsting desire of revenge, else had they known as well the cruelty we use to out enemies, as out true love and courtesy to our friends. And I think your judgment sufficient to conceive, as well by the adventures we have undertaken, as by the advantage we have (by our arms) of yours, that had we intended you any hurt, long ere this we could have effected it.

Questions

1. What goods does each leader seek from the other?

2. How does the exchange illuminate some of the roots of conflict between settlers and Indians?

---

8. Sending Women to Virginia (1622)

Source: Susan Myra Kingsbury, ed., **The Records of the Virginia Company of London** *(Washington, D.C., 1906–1935), Vol. I, pp. 256–57.*

Early Virginia lacked one essential element of English society—stable family life. Given the demand for male servants to work in the tobacco fields, for most of the seventeenth century men in the Chesapeake outnumbered women by four or five to one. The Virginia Company avidly promoted the immigration of women, sending "tobacco brides" to the colony in 1620 and 1621 for arranged marriages (so-called because the husband was ordered to give a payment in tobacco to his wife). The company preferred that the women marry only free, independent colonists. Unlike these women, however, the vast majority of women who emigrated to the region in the seventeenth century came as indentured servants. Since they usually had to complete their terms of service before marrying, they did not begin to form families until their mid-twenties. Virginia remained for many years a society with large numbers of single men, widows, and orphans rather than the family-oriented community the company desired.

WE SEND YOU in this ship one widow and eleven maids for wives for the people in Virginia. There hath been especial care had in the choice of them; for there hath not any one of them been received but upon good commendations, as by a note herewith sent you may perceive. We pray you all therefore in general to take them into your care; and more especially we recommend them to you Master Pountis, that at their first landing they may be housed, lodged and provided for of diet till they be married, for such was the haste of sending them away, as that straitened with time we had no means to put provisions aboard, which defect shall be supplied by the magazine ship. And in case they cannot be presently married, we desire they may be put to several householders that have wives till they can be provided of husbands. There are near fifty more which are shortly to come, are sent by our most honorable Lord and Treasurer the Earl of Southampton and certain worthy gentlemen, who taking into their consideration that the Plantation can never flourish till families be planted and the respect of wives and children fix the people on the soil, therefore have given this fair beginning, for the reimbursing of whose charges it is ordered that every man that marries them give 120 lbs. weight of the best leaf tobacco for each of them, and in case any of them die, that proportion must be advanced to make it up upon those that survive.... And though we are desirous that marriage be free according to the law of nature, yet would we not have these maids deceived and married to servants, but only to freemen or tenants as have means to maintain them. We pray you therefore to be fathers to them in this business, not enforcing them to marry against their wills; neither send we them to be servants, save in case of extremity, for we would have their condition so much bettered as multitudes may be allured thereby to come unto you. And you may assure such men as marry those women that the first servants sent over by the Company shall be consigned to them, it being our intent to preserve families and to prefer married men before single persons.

Questions

1. What advantages does the Virginia Company see in the promotion of family life in the colony?

2. Why does the company prefer that the women marry landowning men rather than servants?

---

9. Maryland Act Concerning Religion (1644)

Source: William H. Browne et al., eds., **Archives of Maryland,** *Vol. 1 (Baltimore, 1883), pp. 244–46.*

Religious liberty in a modern sense existed in very few parts of the Atlantic world of the seventeenth century. Most nations and colonies had established churches, supported by public funds, and outlawed various religious groups that rulers deemed dangerous or disruptive. Among the early English colonies in North America, Maryland stood out as an exception. It was established in 1632 as a grant of land and government authority to Cecilius Calvert, a Catholic who hoped to demonstrate that Protestants and Catholics could live in a harmony unknown in Europe. Protestants made up a majority of the settlers, but the early colonists included a number of Catholic gentlemen and priests, and Calvert appointed many Catholics to public office.

With the religious-political battles of the English Civil War echoing in the colony, Maryland in the 1640s verged on total anarchy. To help reestablish order, in 1649 Maryland adopted an Act Concerning Religion, which institutionalized the principle of toleration that had prevailed from the colony's beginning. It provided punishment for anyone who "troubled or molested" a Christian for religious reasons. Repealed and reenacted several times in the decades that followed, the act was a milestone in the early history of religious freedom in America.

FORASMUCH AS IN a well governed and Christian Commonwealth matters concerning religion and the honor of God ought in the first place to be taken into serious consideration and endeavored to be settled, be it therefore ordered and enacted....

That whatsoever person or persons within the Province ... shall from henceforth blaspheme God, that is curse Him, or deny our Savior Jesus Christ to be the son of God, or shall deny the Holy Trinity, the father, son, and Holy Ghost, or the Godhead of any of the said three persons of the Trinity or the unity of the Godhead, or shall use or utter any reproachful speeches, words, or language concerning the same Holy Trinity, or any of the said three persons thereof, shall be punished with death and confiscation or forfeiture of all his or her lands and goods to the Lord Proprietary and his heirs....

And whereas the enforcing of the conscience in matters of religion has frequently fallen out to be of dangerous consequence in those commonwealths where it has been practiced, and for the more quiet and peaceable government of this Province, and the better to preserve mutual love and amity among the inhabitants thereof. Be it therefore ... enacted (except as in this present Act is before declared and set forth) that no person or persons whatever in the Province ... professing to believe in Jesus Christ, shall from henceforth be any ways troubled, molested, or discountenanced for or in respect of his or her religion nor in the free exercise thereof within the Province ... nor any way compelled to the belief or exercise of any other religion against his or her consent, so [long] as they be not unfaithful to the Lord Proprietary, or molest or conspire against the civil government established or to be established in this Province under him or his heirs.

And that all and every person and persons that shall presume contrary to this Act and the true intent and meaning thereof directly or indirectly either in person or estate willfully to wrong, disturb, trouble, or molest any person whatsoever within this Province professing to believe in Jesus Christ for or in respect of his or her religion or the free exercise thereof within this Province other than is provided for in this Act, that such person or persons so offending shall be compelled to pay triple damages to the party so wronged or molested, and for every such offense shall also forfeit £20 sterling in money or the value thereof, half thereof for the use of the Lord Proprietary ... and the other half for the use of the party so wronged or molested as aforesaid. Or, if the party so offending as aforesaid shall refuse or be unable to recompense the party so wronged, or to satisfy such fine or forfeiture, then such offender shall be severely punished by public whipping and imprisonment.

Questions

1. Members of which religious groups would be excluded from toleration under the Maryland law?

2. What does the law refer to as the major reasons for instituting religious toleration?

---

10. John Winthrop, Speech to the Massachusetts General Court (1645)

Source: John Winthrop, Speech to the General Court of Massachusetts, July 3, 1645, in James Savage, The History of New England from 1630 to 1649 by John Winthrop *(Boston, 1825–1826), Vol. 2, pp. 279–82.*

The early settlers of New England were mainly Puritans, English Protestants who believed that the Church of England in the early seventeenth century retained too many elements of Catholicism. Like other emigrants to America, Puritans came in search of liberty, especially the right to worship and govern themselves in what they deemed a Christian manner. Freedom for Puritans had nothing to do with either religious toleration or unrestrained individual behavior. In a 1645 speech to the Massachusetts legislature explaining the Puritan conception of freedom, Governor John Winthrop distinguished sharply between two kinds of liberty. "Natural"

liberty, or acting without restraint, suggested "a liberty to [do] evil."
"Moral" liberty meant "a liberty to [do] that only which is good." It meant
obedience to religious and governmental authority—following God's law
and the law of rulers like Winthrop himself.

Winthrop's distinction between "moral" and "natural" liberty has been
invoked many times by religious groups who feared that Americans were
becoming selfish and immoral and who tried to impose their moral standards on society as a whole.

• • •

THE GREAT QUESTIONS that have troubled the country, are about
the authority of the magistrates and the liberty of the people. It is
yourselves who have called us to this office, and being called by you,
we have our authority from God, in way of an ordinance, such as
hath the image of God eminently stamped upon it, the contempt
and violation whereof hath been vindicated with examples of divine
vengeance. I entreat you to consider, that when you choose magistrates, you take them from among yourselves, men subject to like
passions as you are. Therefore when you see infirmities in us, you
should reflect upon your own, and that would make you bear the
more with us, and not be severe censurers of the failings of your
magistrates, when you have continual experience of the like infirmities in yourselves and others. We account him a good servant,
who breaks not his covenant. The covenant between you and us is
the oath you have taken of us, which is to this purpose, that we
shall govern you and judge your causes by the rules of God's laws
and our own, according to our best skill. When you agree with a
workman to build you a ship or house, etc., he undertakes as well
for his skill as for his faithfulness, for it is his profession, and you
pay him for both. But when you call one to be a magistrate, he doth
not profess nor undertake to have sufficient skill for that office, nor
can you furnish him with gifts, etc., therefore you must run the hazard of his skill and ability. But if he fail in faithfulness, which by his
oath he is bound unto, that he must answer for. If it fall out that the

case be clear to common apprehension, and the rule clear also, if he transgress here, the error is not in the skill, but in the evil of the will: it must be required of him. But if the case be doubtful, or the rule doubtful, to men of such understanding and parts as your magistrates are, if your magistrates should err here, yourselves must bear it.

For the other point concerning liberty, I observe a great mistake in the country about that. There is a twofold liberty, natural (I mean as our nature is now corrupt) and civil or federal. The first is common to man with beasts and other creatures. By this, man, as he stands in relation to man simply, hath liberty to do what he lists; it is a liberty to evil as well as to good. This liberty is incompatible and inconsistent with authority, and cannot endure the least restraint of the most just authority. The exercise and maintaining of this liberty makes men grow more evil, and in time to be worse than brute beasts. . . . This is that great enemy of truth and peace, that wild beast, which all the ordinances of God are bent against, to restrain and subdue it. The other kind of liberty I call civil or federal, it may also be termed moral, in reference to the covenant between God and man, in the moral law, and the politic covenants and constitutions, amongst men themselves. This liberty is the proper end and object of authority, and cannot subsist without it; and it is a liberty to that only which is good, just, and honest. This liberty you are to stand for, with the hazard (not only of your goods, but) of your lives, if need be. Whatsoever crosseth this, is not authority, but a distemper thereof. This liberty is maintained and exercised in a way of subjection to authority; it is of the same kind of liberty wherewith Christ hath made us free. The woman's own choice makes such a man her husband; yet being so chosen, he is her lord, and she is to be subject to him, yet in a way of liberty, not of bondage; and a true wife accounts her subjection her honor and freedom, and would not think her condition safe and free, but in her subjection to her husband's authority. Such is the liberty of the church under the authority of Christ, her king and husband; his yoke is so easy and sweet to her as a bride's ornaments; and if through forwardness or wantonness, etc., she shake it off, at any time, she is at no rest in her spirit, until she take it up again; and whether her lord smiles upon her, and embraceth her in his arms, or whether he frowns, or rebukes, or smites her, she apprehends the sweetness of his love in all, and is refreshed, supported, and instructed by every such dispensation of his authority over her. On the other side, ye know who they are that complain of this yoke and say, let us break their bands, etc., we will not have this man to rule over us. Even so, brethren, it will be between you and your magistrates. If you stand for your natural corrupt liberties, and will do what is good in your own eyes, you will not endure the least weight of authority, but will murmur, and oppose, and be always striving to shake off that yoke; but if you will be satisfied to enjoy such civil and lawful liberties, such as Christ allows you, then will you quietly and cheerfully submit unto that authority which is set over you, in all the administrations of it, for your good. Wherein, if we fail at anytime, we hope we shall be willing (by God's assistance) to hearken to good advice from any of you, or in any other way of God; so shall your liberties be preserved, in upholding the honor and power of authority amongst you.

Questions

1. Why does Winthrop use an analogy to the status of women within the family to explain his understanding of liberty?

2. Why does Winthrop consider "natural" liberty dangerous?

---

11. The Trial of Anne Hutchinson (1637)

Source: Thomas Hutchinson: "The Examination of Mrs. Ann Hutchinson at the Court of Newtown." Reprinted by permission of the publisher from The History of the Colony and Province of Massachusetts Bay, *Vol. II, by Thomas Hutchinson, edited by Lawrence Shaw Mayo, pp. 366–91, Cambridge, Mass.:*

A midwife and the daughter of a clergyman, Anne Hutchinson arrived in Massachusetts with her husband in 1634. She began holding meetings in her home where she led discussions of religious issues. Hutchinson charged that most of the ministers in Massachusetts were guilty of faulty preaching by distinguishing "saints" predestined to go to Heaven from the damned through activities such as church attendance and moral behavior rather than by an inner state of grace.

In 1637, Hutchinson was placed on trial before a civil court for sedition (expressing opinions dangerous to authority). Hutchinson's examination by John Winthrop and deputy governor Thomas Dudley, excerpted below, is a classic example of the collision between established power and individual conscience. For a time, Hutchinson more than held her own. But when she spoke of divine revelations, of God speaking to her directly rather than through ministers or the Bible, she violated Puritan doctrine and sealed her own fate. Hutchinson and a number of her followers were banished.

―――――

TRIAL AT THE COURT AT NEWTON. 1637

GOV. JOHN WINTHROP: Mrs. Hutchinson, you are called here as one of those that have troubled the peace of the commonwealth and the churches here; you are known to be a woman that hath had a great share in the promoting and divulging of those opinions that are the cause of this trouble, and to be nearly joined not only in affinity and affection with some of those the court had taken notice of and passed censure upon, but you have spoken divers things, as we have been informed, very prejudicial to the honour of the churches and ministers thereof, and you have maintained a meeting and an assembly in your house that hath been condemned by the general assembly as a thing not tolerable nor comely in the sight of God nor fitting for your sex, and notwithstanding that was cried down you have continued the same. Therefore we have thought good to send for you to understand how things are, that if you be in an erroneous way we may reduce you that so you may become a profitable member here among us. Otherwise if you be obstinate in your course that then the court may take such course that you may trouble us no further. Therefore I would intreat you to express whether you do assent and hold in practice to those opinions and factions that have been handled in court already, that is to say, whether you do not justify Mr. Wheelwright's sermon and the petition.

MRS. ANNE HUTCHINSON: I am called here to answer before you but I hear no things laid to my charge.

GOV. JOHN WINTHROP: I have told you some already and more I can tell you.

MRS. ANNE HUTCHINSON: Name one, Sir.

GOV. JOHN WINTHROP: Have I not named some already?

MRS. ANNE HUTCHINSON: What have I said or done?

GOV. JOHN WINTHROP: Why for your doings, this you did harbor and countenance those that are parties in this faction that you have heard of.

MRS. ANNE HUTCHINSON: That's matter of conscience, Sir.

GOV. JOHN WINTHROP: Your conscience you must keep, or it must be kept for you.

MRS. ANNE HUTCHINSON: Must not I then entertain the saints because I must keep my conscience.

GOV. JOHN WINTHROP: Say that one brother should commit felony or treason and come to his brother's house, if he knows him guilty and conceals him he is guilty of the same. It is his conscience to entertain him, but if his conscience comes into act in giving countenance and entertainment to him that hath broken the law he is guilty too. So if you do countenance those that are transgressors of the law you are in the same fact.

MRS. ANNE HUTCHINSON: What law do they transgress?

GOV. JOHN WINTHROP: The law of God and of the state.

MRS. ANNE HUTCHINSON: In what particular?

GOV. JOHN WINTHROP: Why in this among the rest, whereas the Lord doth say honour thy father and thy mother.

MRS. ANNE HUTCHINSON: Ey Sir in the Lord.

GOV. JOHN WINTHROP: This honour you have broke in giving countenance to them.

MRS. ANNE HUTCHINSON: In entertaining those did I entertain them against any act (for there is the thing) or what God has appointed?

GOV. JOHN WINTHROP: You knew that Mr. Wheelwright did preach this sermon and those that countenance him in this do break a law.

MRS. ANNE HUTCHINSON: What law have I broken?

GOV. JOHN WINTHROP: Why the fifth commandment.

MRS. ANNE HUTCHINSON: I deny that for he (Mr. Wheelwright) saith in the Lord.

GOV. JOHN WINTHROP: You have joined with them in the faction.

MRS. ANNE HUTCHINSON: In what faction have I joined with them?

GOV. JOHN WINTHROP: In presenting the petition.

MRS. ANNE HUTCHINSON: Suppose I had set my hand to the petition. What then?

GOV. JOHN WINTHROP: You saw that case tried before.

MRS. ANNE HUTCHINSON: But I had not my hand to (not signed) the petition.

GOV. JOHN WINTHROP: You have councelled them.

MRS. ANNE HUTCHINSON: Wherein?

GOV. JOHN WINTHROP: Why in entertaining them.

MRS. ANNE HUTCHINSON: What breach of law is that, Sir?

GOV. JOHN WINTHROP: Why dishonouring the commonwealth, Mrs. Hutchinson.

MRS. ANNE HUTCHINSON: But put the case, Sir, that I do fear the Lord and my parents. May not I entertain them that fear the Lord because my parents will not give me leave?

GOV. JOHN WINTHROP: If they be the fathers of the commonwealth, and they of another religion, if you entertain them then you dishonour your parents and are justly punishable.

MRS. ANNE HUTCHINSON: If I entertain them, as they have dishonoured their parents I do.

GOV. JOHN WINTHROP: No but you by countenancing them above others put honor upon them.

MRS. ANNE HUTCHINSON: I may put honor upon them as the children of God and as they do honor the Lord.

GOV. JOHN WINTHROP: We do not mean to discourse with those of your sex but only this: you so adhere unto them and do endeavor to set forward this faction and so you do dishonour us.

MRS. ANNE HUTCHINSON: I do acknowledge no such thing. Neither do I think that I ever put any dishonour upon you.

. . .

GOV. JOHN WINTHROP: Your course is not to be suffered for. Besides that we find such a course as this to be greatly prejudicial to the state. Besides the occasion that it is to seduce many honest persons that are called to those meetings and your opinions and your opinions being known to be different from the word of God may seduce many simple souls that resort unto you. Besides that the occasion which hath come of late hath come from none but such as have frequented your meetings, so that now they are flown off from magistrates and ministers and since they have come to you. And besides that it will not well stand with the commonwealth that families should be neglected for so many neighbors and dames and so much time spent. We see no rule of God for this. We see not that any should have authority to set up any other exercises besides what authority hath already set up and so what hurt comes of this you will be guilty of and we for suffering you.

MRS. ANNE HUTCHINSON: Sir, I do not believe that to be so.

GOV. JOHN WINTHROP: Well, we see how it is. We must therefore put it away from you or restrain you from maintaining this course.

MRS. ANNE HUTCHINSON: If you have a rule for it from God's word you may.

GOV. JOHN WINTHROP: We are your judges, and not you ours and we must compel you to it.

MRS. ANNE HUTCHINSON: If it please you by authority to put it down I will freely let you for I am subject to your authority. . . .

• • •

DEPUTY GOV. THOMAS DUDLEY: I would go a little higher with Mrs. Hutchinson. About three years ago we were all in peace. Mrs. Hutchinson, from that time she came hath made a disturbance, and some that came over with her in the ship did inform me what she was as soon as she was landed. I being then in place dealt with the pastor and teacher of Boston and desired them to enquire of her, and then I was satisfied that she held nothing different from us. But within half a year after, she had vented divers of her strange opinions and had made parties in the country, and at length it comes that Mr. Cotton and Mr. Vane were of her judgment, but Mr. Cotton had cleared himself that he was not of that mind.

• • •

But now it appears by this woman's meeting that Mrs. Hutchinson hath so forestalled the minds of many by their resort to her meeting that now she hath a potent party in the country. Now if all these things have endangered us as from that foundation and if she in particular hath disparaged all our ministers in the land that they have preached a covenant of works, and only Mr. Cotton a covenant of grace, why this is not to be suffered, and therefore being driven to the foundation and it being found that Mrs. Hutchinson is she that hath depraved all the ministers and hath been the cause of what is fallen out, why we must take away the foundation and the building will fall.

MRS. ANNE HUTCHINSON: I pray, Sir, prove it that I said they preached nothing but a covenant of works.

DEP. GOV. THOMAS DUDLEY: Nothing but a covenant of works. Why a Jesuit may preach truth sometimes.

MRS. ANNE HUTCHINSON: Did I ever say they preached a covenant of works then?

DEP. GOV. THOMAS DUDLEY: If they do not preach a covenant of grace clearly, then they preach a covenant of works.

MRS. ANNE HUTCHINSON: No, Sir. One may preach a covenant of grace more clearly than another, so I said. . . .

DEP. GOV. THOMAS DUDLEY: When they do preach a covenant of works do they preach truth?

MRS. ANNE HUTCHINSON: Yes, Sir. But when they preach a covenant of works for salvation, that is not truth.

DEP. GOV. THOMAS DUDLEY: Ask you this: when the ministers do preach a covenant of works do they preach a way of salvation?

MRS. ANNE HUTCHINSON: I did not come hither to answer questions of that sort.

DEP. GOV. THOMAS DUDLEY: Because you will deny the thing.

MRS. ANNE HUTCHINSON: Ey, but that is to be proved first.

DEP. GOV. THOMAS DUDLEY: I will make it plain that you did say that the ministers did preach a covenant of works.

MRS. ANNE HUTCHINSON: I deny that.

DEP. GOV. THOMAS DUDLEY: And that you said they were not able ministers of the New Testament, but Mr. Cotton only.

MRS. ANNE HUTCHINSON: If ever I spake that I proved it by God's word.

• • •

MRS. ANNE HUTCHINSON: If you please to give me leave I shall give round of what I know to be true. Being much troubled to see the falseness of the constitution of the Church of England, I had like to have turned Separatist. Whereupon I kept a day of solemn humiliation and pondering of the thing; this scripture was brought unto me—he that denies Jesus Christ to be come in the flesh is antichrist. This I considered of and in considering found that the papists did not deny him to be come in the flesh, nor we did not deny him— who then was antichrist? Was the Turk antichrist only? The Lord knows that I could not open scripture; he must by his prophetical office open it unto me. So after that being unsatisfied in the thing, the Lord was pleased to bring this scripture out of the Hebrews.

He that denies the testament denies the testator, and in this did open unto me and give me to see that those which did not teach the new covenant had the spirit of antichrist, and upon this he did discover the ministry unto me; and ever since, I bless the Lord, he hath let me see which was the clear ministry and which the wrong.

Since that time I confess I have been more choice and he hath left me to distinguish between the voice of my beloved and the voice of Moses, the voice of John the Baptist and the voice of antichrist, for all those voices are spoken of in scripture. Now if you do condemn me for speaking what in my conscience I know to be truth I must commit myself unto the Lord.

MR. NOWEL (ASSISTANT TO THE COURT): How do you know that was the spirit?

MRS. ANNE HUTCHINSON: How did Abraham know that it was God that bid him offer his son, being a breach of the sixth commandment?

DEP. GOV. THOMAS DUDLEY: By an immediate voice.

MRS. ANNE HUTCHINSON: So to me by an immediate revelation.

DEP. GOV. THOMAS DUDLEY: How! an immediate revelation.

• • •

GOV. JOHN WINTHROP: Mrs. Hutchinson, the sentence of the court you hear is that you are banished from out of our jurisdiction as being a woman not fit for our society, and are to be imprisoned till the court shall send you away.

Questions

1. What seem to be the major charges against Anne Hutchinson?

2. What does the Hutchinson case tell us about how Puritan authorities understood the idea of religious freedom?

12. Roger Williams, Letter to the Town of Providence (1655)

Source: Perry Miller and Thomas H. Johnson, eds., **The Puritans** *(2 vols.: New York, 1963), vol. 1, p. 225.*

Roger Williams, the son of a London merchant, studied at Cambridge University and emigrated to New England in 1631. He is considered one of the founders of the principle of religious toleration. Williams was banished from the Massachusetts Bay Colony after preaching that the colonists must not occupy Indian land without first purchasing it, and that the government had no right to punish individuals for their religious beliefs. He went on to found the community of Providence, Rhode Island. After traveling to England and returning to Providence in 1654, he found it torn by dissension, with some settlers refusing to accept civil authority at all. Williams published the following letter, explaining his view of the extent and limits of liberty. He made it clear that while no one should be forced to follow any particular religious belief, this did not lessen the requirement that all members of a community must obey the "masters and officers" in charge of civil matters.

THAT EVER I SHOULD SPEAK or write a tittle, that tends to ... an infinite liberty of conscience, is a mistake, and which I have ever disclaimed and abhorred. To prevent such mistakes, I shall at present only propose this case: There goes many a ship to sea, with many hundred souls in one ship, whose weal or woe is common, and is a true picture of a commonwealth, or a human combination or society. It hath fallen out sometimes, that both papists and Protestants, Jews and Turks [Muslims], may be embarked in one ship; upon which supposal I affirm, that all the liberty of conscience, that ever I pleaded for, turns upon these two hinges—that none of the papists, Protestants, Jews, or Turks, be forced to come to the ship's prayers or worship, nor compelled from their own particular prayers or worship, if they practice any. I further add, that I never denied, that notwithstanding this liberty, the commander of this ship ought to command the ship's course, yea, and also command that justice, peace and sobriety, be kept and practiced, both among the seamen and all the passengers. If any of the seamen refuse to perform their services, or passengers to pay their freight; if any refuse to help, in person or purse, towards the common charges or defense; if any refuse to obey the common laws and orders of the ship, concerning their common peace or preservation; if any shall mutiny and rise up against their commanders and officers; if any should preach or write that there ought to be no commanders or officers, because all are equal in Christ, therefore no masters nor officers, no laws nor orders, nor corrections nor punishments;—I say, I never denied, but in such cases, whatever is pretended, the commander or commanders may judge, resist, compel and punish such transgressors, according to their deserts and merits. This if seriously and honestly minded, may, if it so please the Father of lights, let in some light to such as willingly shut not their eyes.

Roger Williams

Questions

1. In what ways does Williams place limits on liberty?

2. What are the strengths and weaknesses of Williams's analogy between civil society and a group of people aboard a ship?

———

13. The Levellers, The Agreement of the People Presented to the Council of the Army (1647)

Source: The Agreement of the People Presented to the Council of the Army *(London, 1647).*

During the 1640s, the battle for political supremacy in England between the Stuart monarchs James I and Charles I and Parliament culminated in civil war, the temporary overthrow of the monarchy, and, in 1649, the execution of Charles I. This struggle produced an intense public debate over the concept of English freedom. In 1647, the Levellers, history's first democratic political movement, proposed a written constitution, The Agreement of the People, which began by proclaiming "at how high a rate we value our just freedom." At a time when "democracy" was still widely seen as the equivalent of anarchy and disorder, the document proposed to abolish the monarchy and House of Lords and greatly expand the right to vote. It called for religious freedom and equality before the law for all Englishmen.

The Levellers were soon suppressed. But the Agreement of the People offered a glimpse of the modern, democratic definition of freedom as a universal entitlement in a society based on equal rights, rather than the traditional idea of "liberties" as a collection of limited rights defined by social class, with some groups enjoying far more than others.

AN AGREEMENT OF the People for a firm and present peace upon grounds of common right.

Having by our late labors and hazards made it appear to the world at how high a rate we value our just freedom, and God having so far owned our cause as to deliver the enemies thereof into our hands, we do now hold ourselves bound in mutual duty to each other to take the best care we can for the future to avoid both the danger of returning into a slavish condition and the chargeable remedy of another war; for, as it cannot be imagined that so many of our countrymen would have opposed us in this quarrel if they had understood their own good, so may we safely promise to ourselves that, when our common rights and liberties shall be cleared, their endeavors will be disappointed that seek to make themselves our masters. Since, therefore, our former oppressions and scarce-yet-ended troubles have been occasioned, either by want of frequent national meetings in Council, or by rendering those meetings ineffectual, we are fully agreed and resolved to provide that hereafter our representatives be neither left to an uncertainty for the time nor made useless to the ends for which they are intended. In order whereunto we declare:

I

That the people of England, being at this day very unequally distributed by Counties, Cities and Boroughs for the election of their deputies in Parliament, ought to be more indifferently proportioned, according to the number of the inhabitants; the circumstances whereof for number, place, and manner are to be set down before the end of this present Parliament.

II

That, to prevent the many inconveniences apparently arising from the long continuance of the same persons in authority, this present Parliament be dissolved upon the last day of September which shall be in the year of our Lord 1648.

III

That the people do, of course, choose themselves a Parliament once in two years, viz. upon the first Thursday in every second March, after the manner as shall be prescribed before the end of this Parliament, to begin to sit upon the first Thursday in April following, at Westminster or such other place as shall be appointed from time to time by the preceding Representatives, and to continue till the last day of September then next ensuing, and no longer.

IV

That the power of this, and all future Representatives of this Nation, is inferior only to theirs who choose them, and doth extend, without the consent or concurrence of any other person or persons, to the enacting, altering, and repealing of laws; to the erecting and abolishing of offices and courts; to the appointing, removing, and calling to account magistrates and officers of all degrees; to the making war and peace; to the treating with foreign states; and, generally, to whatsoever is not expressly or impliedly reserved by the represented to themselves:

Which are as followeth,

1. That matters of religion and the ways of God's worship are not at all entrusted by us to any human power, because therein we cannot remit or exceed a title of what our consciences dictate to be the mind of God, without wilful sin; nevertheless the public way of instructing the nation (so it be not compulsive) is referred to their discretion.

2. That the matter of impressing and constraining any of us to serve in the wars is against our freedom; and therefore we do not allow it in our Representatives; the rather, because money (the sinews of war), being always at their disposal, they can never want numbers of men apt enough to engage in any just cause.

3. That after the dissolution of this present Parliament, no person be at any time questioned for anything said or done in reference to the late public differences, otherwise than in execution of the judgments of the present Representatives, or House of Commons.

4. That in all laws made or to be made every person may be bound alike, and that no tenure, estate, charter, degree, birth, or place do confer any exemption from the ordinary course of legal proceedings whereunto others are subjected.

5. That as the laws ought to be equal, so they must be good, and not evidently destructive to the safety and well-being of the people.

These things we declare to be our native rights, and therefore are agreed and resolved to maintain them with our utmost possibilities against all opposition whatsoever; being compelled thereunto not only by the examples of our ancestors, whose blood was often spent in vain for the recovery of their freedoms, suffering themselves through fraudulent accommodations to be still deluded of the fruit of their victories, but also by our own woeful experience, who, having long expected and dearly earned the establishment of these certain rules of government, are yet made to depend for the settlement of our peace and freedom upon him that intended our bondage and brought a cruel war upon us.

Questions

1. What are the Levellers criticizing when they propose that "in all laws made or to be made every person may be bound alike"?

2. What are the main rights that the Levellers are aiming to protect?

CHAPTER 3

Creating Anglo-America, 1660–1750

14. William Penn, Pennsylvania Charter of Privileges and Liberties (1701)

Source: Francis N. Thorpe, The Federal and State Constitutions, Colonial Charters, and Other Organic Laws ... *(7 vols.: Washington, D.C., 1909), vol. 5, pp. 3076–81.*

The last English colony to be established in the seventeenth century was Pennsylvania, founded in 1680 by William Penn. A devout member of the Society of Friends, or Quakers, Penn envisioned the colony as a place where those facing religious persecution in Europe could enjoy spiritual freedom. Quakers held that the spirit of God dwelled within all people, not just the elect, and that this "inner light," rather than the Bible or teachings of the clergy, offered the surest guidance in spiritual matters. Thus, the government had no right to enforce any particular form of religious worship.

Penn drew up a Frame of Government in 1682 but it proved unworkable and in 1701 was replaced with a Charter of Liberties that established a political system that lasted until the American Revolution. Its first clause restated Penn's cherished principle of religious toleration, although it limited officeholding to Christians. It also established an elected legislature and promised that colonists would enjoy the same rights as "free-born subjects of England."

KNOW YE . . . That for the further Well-being and good Government of the said Province, and Territories; . . . I the said William Penn do declare, grant and confirm, unto all the Freemen, Planters and Adventurers, and other Inhabitants of this Province and Territories, these following Liberties, Franchises and Privileges . . .

Because no People can be truly happy, though under the greatest enjoyment of civil liberties, if abridged of the freedom of their consciences, as to their religious profession and worship: And Almighty God being the only Lord of Conscience, Father of Lights and Spirits; and the Author as well as object of all divine knowledge, faith and worship, who only doth enlighten the Minds, and persuade and convince the understandings of people, I do hereby grant and declare, that no person or persons, inhabiting in this Province or Territories, who shall confess and acknowledge One almighty God, the Creator, Upholder and Ruler of the World; and profess him or themselves obliged to live quietly under the Civil Government, shall be in any case molested or prejudiced, in his or their person or estate, because of his or their conscientious persuasion or practice, nor be compelled to frequent or maintain any religious worship, place or ministry, contrary to his or their mind, or to do or suffer any other act or thing, contrary to their religious persuasion.

And that all persons who also profess to believe in Jesus Christ, the Savior of the World, shall be capable (notwithstanding their other persuasions and practices in point of conscience and religion) to serve this Government in any capacity, both legislatively and executively. . . .

For the well governing of this Province and Territories, there shall be an Assembly yearly chosen, by the freemen thereof, to consist of four persons out of each county, of most note for virtue, wisdom and ability, . . . which Assembly shall have power to choose a Speaker and other officers; . . . prepare Bills in order to pass into Laws; impeach criminals, and redress grievances; and shall have all other powers and privileges of an Assembly, according to the rights of the free-born subjects of England.

Questions

1. What are Penn's arguments in favor of religious liberty?

2. Why does the document refer to "the rights of the free-born subjects of England"?

---

15. Nathaniel Bacon on Bacon's Rebellion (1676)

Source: **Virginia Magazine of History and Biography,** *Vol. I (1894), pp. 55–61.*

The largest popular revolt in the early English colonies was Bacon's Rebellion, which occurred in Virginia in 1676. For thirty years, Governor William Berkeley had run a corrupt regime in alliance with an inner circle of tobacco planters, while heavy taxes reduced the prospects of small farmers. His refusal to allow white settlement in areas reserved for Indians angered colonists who saw landownership as central to freedom.

After a minor confrontation between Indians and settlers on Virginia's western frontier, settlers demanded that the governor authorize the extermination or removal of the colony's Indians to open more land for whites. Berkeley refused. An uprising began that quickly grew into a full-fledged rebellion. The leader, Nathaniel Bacon, was himself a wealthy and ambitious planter. But his call for the removal of all Indians from the colony, a reduction of taxes, and an end to rule by "grandees" rapidly gained support from small farmers, landless men, indentured servants, and even some slaves. Bacon's "manifesto," which follows, outlined the rebels' complaints against the governor and the colony's "protected and darling Indians." The uprising failed. But the frightened authorities reduced taxes and adopted a more aggressive Indian policy, opening western areas to small farmers. They also accelerated the shift from indentured white labor to African slaves.

IF VIRTUE BE a sin, if piety be guilt, all the principles of morality, goodness and justice be perverted, we must confess that those who are now called rebels may be in danger of those high imputations. Those loud and several bulls would affright innocents and render the defence of our brethren and the inquiry into our sad and heavy oppressions, treason. But if there be, as sure there is, a just God to appeal to; if religion and justice be a sanctuary here; if to plead the cause of the oppressed; if sincerely to aim at his Majesty's honour and the public good without any reservation or by interest; if to stand in the gap after so much blood of our dear brethren bought and sold; if after the loss of a great part of his Majesty's colony deserted and dis-peopled, freely with our lives and estates to endeavour to save the remainders be treason; God Almighty judge and let guilty die. But since we cannot in our hearts find one single spot of rebellion or trea-son, or that we have in any manner aimed at the subverting the set-tled government or attempting of the person of any either magistrate or private man, notwithstanding the several reproaches and threats of some who for sinister ends were disaffected to us and censured our innocent and honest designs, and since all people in all places where we have yet been can attest our civil, quiet, peaceable behaviour far different from that of rebellion and tumultuous persons, let truth be bold and all the world know the real foundations of pretended guilt.

We appeal to the country itself what and of what nature their oppressions have been, or by what cabal and mystery the designs of many of those whom we call great men have been transacted and carried on; but let us trace these men in authority and favour to whose hands the dispensation of the country's wealth has been commit-ted. Let us observe the sudden rise of their estates [compared] with the quality in which they first entered this country, or the reputa-tion they have held here amongst wise and discerning men. And let us see whether their extractions and education have not been vile, and by what pretence of learning and virtue they could so soon [come] into employments of so great trust and consequence. Let us consider their sudden advancement and let us also consider whether any public work for our safety and defence or for the advancement and propagation of trade, liberal arts, or sciences is here extant in any way adequate to our vast charge. Now let us compare these things together and see what sponges have sucked up the public treasure, and whether it has not been privately contrived away by unworthy favourites and juggling parasites whose tottering fortunes have been repaired and supported at the public charge. Now if it be so, judge what greater guilt can be than to offer to pry into these and to unriddle the mysterious wiles of a powerful cabal; let all people judge what can be of more dangerous import than to suspect the so long safe proceedings of some of our grandees, and whether people may with safety open their eyes in so nice a concern.

Another main article of our guilt is our open and manifest aversion of all, not only the foreign but the protected and darling Indians. This, we are informed, is rebellion of a deep dye for that both the governor and council are ... bound to defend the queen and the Appamatocks with their blood. Now, whereas we do declare and can prove that they have been for these many years enemies to the king and country, robbers and thieves and invaders of his Majesty's right and our interest and estates, but yet have by persons in authority been defended and protected even against his Majesty's loyal subjects, and that in so high a nature that even the complaints and oaths of his Majesty's most loyal subjects in a lawful manner proffered by them against those barbarous outlaws, have been by the right honourable governor rejected and the delinquents from his presence dismissed, not only with pardon and indemnity, but with all encouragement and favour; their firearms so destructful to us and by our laws prohibited, commanded to be restored them, and open declaration before witness made that they must have ammunition, although directly contrary to our law. Now what greater guilt can be than to oppose and endeavour the destruction of these honest, quiet neighbours of ours?

Another main article of our guilt is our design not only to ruin and extirpate all Indians in general, but all manner of trade and

commerce with them. Judge who can be innocent that strike at
this tender eye of interest: since the right honourable the governor
hath been pleased by his commission to warrant this trade, who
dare oppose it, or opposing it can be innocent? Although plantations be deserted, the blood of our dear brethren spilled; on all
sides our complaints; continually murder upon murder renewed
upon us; who may or dare think of the general subversion of all
manner of trade and commerce with our enemies who can or dare
impeach any of . . . traders at the heads of the rivers, if contrary to
the wholesome provision made by laws for the country's safety;
they dare continue their illegal practises and dare asperse the
right honourable governor's wisdom and justice so highly to pre-
tend to have his warrant to break that law which himself made;
who dare say that these men at the heads of the rivers buy and
sell our blood, and do still, notwithstanding the late act made to
the contrary, admit Indians painted and continue to commerce;
although these things can be proved, yet who dare be so guilty as
to do it? . . .

• • •

The Declaration of the People

For having upon specious pretences of public works, raised unjust
taxes upon the commonalty for the advancement of private favourites and other sinister ends, but no visible effects in any measure
adequate.

For not having during the long time of his government in any measure advanced this hopeful colony, either by fortification, towns or
trade.

For having abused and rendered contemptible the majesty of justice, of advancing to places of judicature scandalous and ignorant
favourites.

For having wronged his Majesty's prerogative and interest by
assuming the monopoly of the beaver trade.

By having in that unjust gain bartered and sold his Majesty's country and the lives of his loyal subjects to the barbarous heathen.

For having protected, favoured and emboldened the Indians against his Majesty's most loyal subjects, never contriving, requiring, or appointing any due or proper means of satisfaction for their many invasions, murders, and robberies committed upon us.

• • •

For having the second time attempted the same thereby calling down our forces from the defence of the frontiers, and most weak exposed places, for the prevention of civil mischief and ruin amongst ourselves, whilst the barbarous enemy in all places did invade, murder, and spoil us, his Majesty's most faithful subjects.

Of these, the aforesaid articles, we accuse Sir William Berkeley, as guilty of each and every one of the same, and as one who has traitorously attempted, violated and injured his Majesty's interest here, by the loss of a great part of his colony, and many of his faithful and loyal subjects by him betrayed, and in a barbarous and shameful manner exposed to the incursions and murders of the heathen.

And we do further demand, that the said Sir William Berkeley ... be forthwith delivered up ... within four days after the notice hereof, or otherwise we declare as followeth: that in whatsoever house, place, or ship [he] shall reside, be hid, or protected, we do declare that the owners, masters, or inhabitants of the said places, to be confederates and traitors to the people, and the estates of them, as also of all the aforesaid persons, to be confiscated. This we, the commons of Virginia, do declare desiring a prime union amongst ourselves, that we may jointly, and with one accord defend ourselves against the common enemy.

NATH BACON, Gen'l.
By the Consent of the People.

Questions

1. What are the rebels' main complaints against the government of Virginia?

2. Do Bacon and his followers envision any place for Indians in Virginia society?

16. Letter by an Immigrant to Pennsylvania (1769)

Source: Johannes Hänner: "Letter by an Immigrant to Pennsylvania, 1769," Unpublished Documents on Emigration from the Archives of Switzerland, *Albert B. Faust,* Deutsch-Amerikanische Geschichtsblätter, *Vols. 18–19, pp. 37–39. Translation by Volker Berghahn. Reprinted by permission of Volker Berghahn.*

Germans, 110,000 in all, formed the largest group of newcomers to the British colonies in the eighteenth century. The desire for religious freedom inspired many migrants, but the primary motivation for emigration was economic. German areas of Europe were plagued by persistent agricultural crises. Families found it increasingly difficult to acquire land.

Most German newcomers settled in frontier areas—rural New York, western Pennsylvania, and the southern backcountry—where they formed tightly knit farming communities in which German for many years remained the dominant language. The letter below, by a German-speaking emigrant from Switzerland to Pennsylvania, illustrates the response of many immigrants to life in America. "We have a free country," he wrote to his relatives at home, singling out ample employment opportunities, low taxes, plentiful food, and abundant land as reasons for coming to America.

Dearest Father, Brother, and Sister and Brother-in-law, ...

To begin with, we are all, thank God, fresh and healthy as long as the Lord wills, and if at last you are also in good health, this would delight my heart. What I must tell you first of all is that I have been dreaming one day after Johannis and that it seemed to me that my beloved brother-in-law in Bubendorff had died. This would pain me a lot, and the Lord will protect him of this.

I have told you quite fully about the trip, and I will tell you what will not surprise you—that we have a free country. Of the sundry craftsmen, one may do whatever one wants. Nor does the land require payment of tithes [taxes requiring payment of a portion of a farmer's produce to a local landlord, typical in Europe].... By the way, wheat is grown most frequently, rye, oats, ... apples are plentiful.... The land is very big from Canada to the east of us to Carolina in the south and to the Spanish border in the west.... Except for Carolina [there are] many large and small rivers. One can settle wherever one wants without asking anyone when he buys or leases something....

I have always enough to do and we have no shortage of food. Bread is plentiful. If I work for two days I earn more bread than in eight days [at home].... Also I can buy many things so reasonably [for example] a pair of shoes for [roughly] seven Pennsylvania shillings.... I think that with God's help I will obtain land. I am not pushing for it until I am in a better position. I would like for my brother to come ... and it will then be even nicer in the country.... I assume that the land has been described to you sufficiently by various people and it is not surprising that the immigrant agents [demand payment]. For the journey is long and it costs much to stay away for one year.... And at this point I finally greet you all with all good friends and acquaintances very cordially, and I command all of you to the care of the Lord so that you may be well in soul and body.

JOHANNES HÄNNER

Questions

1. What does Johannes Hänner seem to mean when he calls America a "free country"?

2. How does it appear that people in Europe learn about conditions in America?

---

17. An Apprentice's Indenture Contract (1718)

Source: Kenneth T. Jackson and David S. Dunbar, ed., Empire City: New York through the Centuries *(New York, 2000), pp. 54–55.*

In colonial America, young men learned a trade by apprenticing themselves to work for a skilled craftsman. This indenture from New York City, for seven years of labor and training, is typical of such agreements. Each party to the contract takes on a set of responsibilities. A cordwainer is a craftsman who makes fine leather goods such as luxury boots and shoes.

THIS INDENTURE WITNESSES that I, William Mathews, son of Marrat of the city of New York, a widow . . . does voluntarily and of his own free will and accord and by the consent of his said mother put himself as an apprentice cordwainer to Thomas Windover of the city aforesaid.

He will live and (after the manner of an apprentice) serve from August 15, 1718, until the full term of seven years be completed and ended. During all of this term, the said apprentice shall faithfully serve his said master, shall faithfully keep his secrets, and gladly obey his lawful commands everywhere. He shall do no damage to his said master, nor see any done by others without giving notice to his said master. He shall not waste his said master's goods nor lend them unlawfully to any. He shall not commit fornication nor contract matrimony within the said term.

At cards, dice, or any other unlawful game, he shall not play (whereby his said master may have damage) with his own goods or the goods of others. Without a license from his master he shall neither buy nor sell during the said term. He shall not absent himself day or night from his master's service without his leave, nor haunt alehouses, but in all things he shall behave himself as a faithful apprentice toward his master all during his said term.

The said master, during the said term, shall, by the best means or methods, teach or cause the said apprentice to be taught the art or mystery of a cordwainer. He shall find and provide unto the said apprentice sufficient meat, drink, apparel, lodging, and washing fit for an apprentice. During the said term, every night in winter he shall give the apprentice one quarter of schooling. At the expiration of the said term he shall provide him with a sufficient new suit of apparel, four shirts, and two necklets [scarves].

Questions

1. What obligations does each party assume in this document?

2. How is the liberty of the apprentice limited by the indenture?

---

18. Memorial against Non-English Immigration (1727)

Source: Historical Society of Pennsylvania. Based on typescript by Rachel Moloshok.

Only a minority of emigrants from Europe to British North America in the eighteenth century came from the British Isles. Some English settlers, such as the authors of this petition from Pennsylvania to the authorities in London, found the growing diversity of the colonial population quite disturbing.

HOW CAREFUL EVERY EUROPEAN STATE, that has colonies in America, has been of preserving the advantages arising from them wholly to their own nation and people, is obvious to all who will consider the policy & conduct of the Spanish, French & others in relation to theirs respectively and the several English Acts of Parliament provided in the like cases as fully on their part evince the same. By these not only no foreign vessel is allowed to trade or come into their ports, but it is absolutely required, that the master & at least three fourths of the mariners of all British ships shall be of his Majesties natural born subjects and the owners or some of them must swear that no foreigner directly nor indirectly hath any part share of interest in them.

Yet at the same time these acts subsist in force, methods are taking that may not only endanger the trade of these colonies, but even their obedience & subjection to the British Crown, which is humbly represented as follows.

About the year 1710 a Company of religious people called Menists from the Palatinate of the Rhine, transported themselves into the Province of Pensylvania from Holland in British shipping, and purchased lands at low rates towards the River Susquehanna. The terms & reception they met with proved so encouraging, that they invited diverse of their relations and friends to follow them. In the succeeding years the numbers of those, who from the account they heard of the country, had the same inclination to remove so considerably increased that one Shipload after another of all professions were transported, till several thousands were settled in that Province. Last winter it was reported there, that a thousand more were to go over thither this past summer, and accordingly five ships arrived there in the space of one month loaded with these people first from Rottersdam and then clear'd in England....

All these men young & old who arrived since the first, come generally very well armed many of them are Papists, & most of them appear inured to war & other hardships. They retire commonly back into the woods amongst or behind the remoter Inhabitants, sometimes purchase land, but often sit down on any piece they find vacant that they Judge convenient for them without asking questions, menacing those afterwards who offer to disturb them in their possessions.

Few of them apply now to be naturalized, . . . nor do those who have been longer in the place commonly prove the wills of their deceased in the public offices, but as they appear to affect neither the English nor their laws or rules, they generally even in these points adhere to their own customs. The part of the country they principally settle in is that towards the French of Canada, whose interest, it may be apprehended, diverse of the late comers (since several of them speak their language) would as willingly favour as the English, and it is not doubted, but at this time there are as many of these people in Pennsylvania, as on any quarrel with his Majesties natural subjects, could on a sudden rising with the arms they now have subdue that whole Province. It is hoped therefore that nothing need be added to shew the present necessity of putting a stop to that augmentation of their strength which if not prevented, may even in one year more be depended upon. . . .

That such a general provision against all foreigners may be necessary will further appear from this particular consideration. There are now, & have been, ever since the Reign of Christina, a considerable number of Swedes settled on both sides of the River Delaware, who have four churches & ministers for them duly sent over every eight or ten years by the Government of Sweden, the former ministers on the arrival of the new being recalled. These preach to & instruct their people & perform all their worship in the Swedish tongue. Few of them intermarry with any others than amongst themselves, but carefully keep up a national Distinction. In the Swedish maps geography & State of Sweden that country is called Succia Nova.

Questions

1. What do the petitioners find objectionable about non-English migrants to Pennsylvania?

2. What does the petition suggest about who should be entitled to the benefits of freedom in the American colonies?

19. Gottlieb Mittelberger on the Trade in Indentured Servants (1750)

Source: Gottlieb Mittelberger, **Gottlieb Mittelberger's Journey to Pennsylvania in the Year 1750 and Return to Germany in the Year 1754,** *trans. Carl Theo Eben (Philadelphia: John Jos. McVey, 1898), pp. 28–38.*

During the eighteenth century, most emigrants to British North America arrived either as slaves or indentured servants. Gottlieb Mittelberger, a German schoolteacher and organ player, traveled to Pennsylvania in 1750 and returned to Germany four years later. The passage below is taken from his diary, in which he vividly described conditions on the ship carrying indentured servants, and the trying situation many of them faced when they landed in Philadelphia. The German men and women he describes had borrowed money to pay for their passage and had no choice but to sign long-term labor contracts in America to pay off their debt. Although indentured servants were not held for life, as slaves were, they were bought and sold and their families could easily be broken up. Mittelberger's account offers a different perspective on immigration to the American colonies from document 16 above.

DURING THE VOYAGE there is on board these ships terrible misery, stench, fumes, horror, vomiting, many kinds of sea-sickness, fever, dysentery, headache, heat, constipation, boils, scurvy, cancer, mouthrot, and the like, all of which come from old and sharply salted food and meat, also from very bad and foul water, so that many die miserably.

Add to this want of provisions, hunger, thirst, frost, heat, dampness, anxiety, want, afflictions and lamentations, together with other trouble, as ... the lice abound so frightfully, especially on sick people, that they can be scraped off the body. The misery reaches the climax when a gale rages for 2 or 3 nights and days, so that every one believes that the ship will go to the bottom with all human beings on board. In such a visitation the people cry and pray most piteously....

No one can have an idea of the sufferings which women in confinement have to bear with their innocent children on board these ships. Few of this class escape with their lives; many a mother is cast into the water with her child as soon as she is dead. One day, just as we had a heavy gale, a woman in our ship, who was to give birth and could not give birth under the circumstances, was pushed through a loop-hole [port-hole] in the ship and dropped into the sea, because she was far in the rear of the ship and could not be brought forward.

Children from 1 to 7 years rarely survive the voyage. I witnessed misery in no less than 32 children in our ship, all of whom were thrown into the sea. The parents grieve all the more since their children find no resting-place in the earth, but are devoured by the monsters of the sea....

When the ships have landed at Philadelphia after their long voyage, no one is permitted to leave them except those who pay for their passage or can give good security; the others, who cannot pay, must remain on board the ships till they are purchased, and are released from the ships by their purchasers. The sick always fare the worst, for the healthy are naturally preferred and purchased first; and so the sick and wretched must often remain on board in front of the city for 2 or 3 weeks, and frequently die, whereas many a one, if he could pay his debt and were permitted to leave the ship immediately, might recover and remain alive.

The sale of human beings in the market on board the ship is carried on thus: Every day Englishmen, Dutchmen and High-German people come from the city of Philadelphia and other places, in part from a great distance, say 20, 30, or 40 hours away, and go on board the newly arrived ship that has brought and offers for sale passengers from Europe, and select among the healthy persons such as they deem suitable for their business, and bargain with them how long they will serve for their passage money, which most of them are still in debt for. When they have come to an agreement, it happens that adult persons bind themselves in writing to serve 3, 4, 5 or 6 years for the amount due by them, according to their age and strength. But very young people, from 10 to 15 years, must serve till they are 21 years old.

Many parents must sell and trade away their children like so many head of cattle; for if their children take the debt upon themselves, the parents can leave the ship free and unrestrained; but as the parents often do not know where and to what people their children are going, it often happens that such parents and children, after leaving the ship, do not see each other again for many years, perhaps no more in all their lives.

It often happens that whole families, husband, wife, and children, are separated by being sold to different purchasers, especially when they have not paid any part of their passage money.

When a husband or wife has died at sea, when the ship has made more than half of her trip, the survivor must pay or serve not only for himself or herself, but also for the deceased. When both parents have died over half-way at sea, their children, especially when they are young and have nothing to pawn or to pay, must stand for their own and their parents' passage, and serve till they are 21 years old. When one has served his or her term, he or she is entitled to a new suit of clothes at parting; and if it has been so stipulated, a man gets in addition a horse, a woman, a cow.

Questions

1. Which aspects of the situation of the German immigrants seems most offensive to Mittelberger?

2. How public and regular does the trade in indentured servants appear to be from his account?

20. Women in the Household Economy (1709)

Source: John Lawson, A New Voyage to Carolina *(London, 1709), pp. 84–85.*

In the household economy of eighteenth-century America, the family was the center of economic life. Most work revolved around the home, and all members—men, women, and children—contributed to the family's livelihood. John Lawson, an English naturalist, came to Carolina in 1700 and traveled over a thousand miles, studying the natural environment and trading with Indians. His *A New Voyage to Carolina* offered a very favorable description of life in the colony. Lawson's account vividly described the lives of free Carolina women and the numerous kinds of labor they performed. The work of farmers' wives and daughters often spelled the difference between a family's self-sufficiency and poverty. Lawson was captured and killed during an Indian uprising in 1711.

THE WOMEN ARE the most industrious sex in that place, and, by their good houswifery, make a great deal of cloth of their own cotton, wool and flax; some of them keeping their families (though large) very decently appareled, both with linens and woolens, so that they have no occasion to run into the merchant's debt, or lay their money out on stores for clothing. . . .

They marry very young; some at thirteen or fourteen; and she that stays till twenty, is reckoned a stale maid; which is a very indifferent character in that warm country. The women are very fruitful; most houses being full of little ones. It has been observed, that women long married, and without children, in other places, have removed to Carolina, and become joyful mothers. They have very easy travail in their child-bearing, in which they are so happy, as seldom to miscarry. . . .

Many of the women are very handy in canoes, and will manage them with great dexterity and skill, which they become accustomed to in this watery country. They are ready to help their husbands in any servile work, as planting, when the season of the weather requires expedition; pride seldom banishing good houswifery. The girls are not bred up to the [spinning] wheel and sewing only; but the dairy and affairs of the house they are very well acquainted withal; so that you shall see them, whilst very young, manage their business with a great deal of conduct and alacrity. The children of both sexes are very docile, and learn any thing with a great deal of Ease and Method; and those that have the advantages of education, write good hands, and prove good accountants, which is most coveted, and indeed most necessary in these parts.

Questions

1. What are the most important kinds of work done by Carolina women, according to Lawson?

2. How strict do gender roles appear to have been in early Carolina?

CHAPTER 4

Slavery, Freedom, and the Struggle for Empire to 1763

21. Olaudah Equiano on Slavery (1789)

Source: The Interesting Narrative of the Life of Olaudah Equiano, or Gustavas Vassa, the African, Written by Himself *(London, 1789), Vol. 1, pp. 46–49, 69–72, 83–88.*

Of the estimated 7.7 million Africans transported to the New World between 1492 and 1820, over half arrived between 1700 and 1800. Every European empire utilized slave labor and battled for control of this profitable trade. A series of triangular trading routes crisscrossed the Atlantic, carrying British goods to Africa and the colonies, colonial slave-grown products like tobacco, sugar, and rice to Europe, and slaves from Africa to the New World.

The era's most popular account of the slave experience was written by Olaudah Equiano, the son of a West African village chief, kidnapped by slave traders in the 1750s. In the passages that follow, Equiano describes his capture, encounter with other African peoples with whom he had no previous contact, passage to the New World, and sale in the West Indies. Equiano went on the purchase his freedom. His life underscored the greatest contradiction in the history of the eighteenth century—the simultaneous expansion of freedom and slavery.

MY FATHER, BESIDES many slaves, had a numerous family, of which seven lived to grow up, including myself and a sister, who was the only daughter. As I was the youngest of the sons, I became, of course, the greatest favourite with my mother, and was always with her; and she used to take particular pains to form my mind. I was trained up from my earliest years in the arts of agriculture and war: my daily exercise was shooting and throwing javelins; and my mother adorned me with emblems, after the manner of our greatest warriors. In this way I grew up till I was turned the age of eleven, when an end was put to my happiness in the following manner:— Generally, when the grown people in the neighbourhood were gone far in the fields to labour, the children assembled together in some of the neighbours' premises to play; and commonly some of us used to get up a tree to look out for any assailant, or kidnapper, that might come upon us; for they sometimes took those opportunities of our parents' absence, to attack and carry off as many as they could seize. One day, as I was watching at the top of a tree in our yard, I saw one of those people come into the yard of our next neighbour but one, to kidnap, there being many stout young people in it. Immediately, on this, I gave the alarm of the rogue, and he was surrounded by the stoutest of them, who entangled him with cords, so that he could not escape till some of the grown people came and secured him. But, alas! ere long it was my fate to be thus attacked, and to be carried off, when none of the grown people were nigh. One day, when all our people were gone out to their works as usual, and only I and my dear sister were left to mind the house, two men and a woman got over our walls, and in a moment seized us both; and, without giving us time to cry out, or make resistance, they stopped our mouths, tied our hands, and ran off with us into the nearest wood: and continued to carry us as far as they could, till night came on, when we reached a small house, where the robbers halted for refreshment, and spent the night. We were then unbound, but were unable to take any food; and, being quite overpowered by fatigue and grief, our only relief was some sleep, which allayed our misfortune for a short time.

The next morning we left the house, and continued travelling all the day....

• • •

I continued to travel, sometimes by land, sometimes by water, through different countries, and various nations, till, at the end of six or seven months after I had been kidnapped, I arrived at the sea coast. It would be tedious and uninteresting to relate all the incidents which befel me during this journey, and which I have not yet forgotten, of the various hands I passed through, and the manners and customs of all the different people among whom I lived: I shall therefore only observe, that, in all the places where I was, the soil was exceedingly rich; the pomkins, eadas, plantains, yams, &c. &c. were in great abundance, and of incredible size. There were also vast quantities of different gums, though not used for any purpose; and every where a great deal of tobacco. The cotton even grew quite wild; and there was plenty of red wood. I saw no mechanics whatever in all the way, except such as I have mentioned. The chief employment in all these countries was agriculture, and both the males and females, as with us, were brought up to it, and trained in the arts of war.

The first object which saluted my eyes when I arrived on the coast was the sea, and a slave-ship, which was then riding at anchor, and waiting for its cargo. These filled me with astonishment, which was soon converted into terror, which I am yet at a loss to describe, nor the then feelings of my mind. When I was carried on board I was immediately handled, and tossed up, to see if I were sound, by some of the crew; and I was now persuaded that I had gotten into a world of bad spirits, and that they were going to kill me. Their complexions too differing so much from ours, their long hair, and the language they spoke, which was very different from any I had ever heard, united to confirm me in this belief. Indeed, such were the horrors of my views and fears at the moment, that, if ten thousand worlds had been my own, I would have freely parted with them all to have exchanged my condition with that of the meanest slave in my own country. When I looked round the ship too, and saw a large furnace

of copper boiling, and a multitude of black people of every description chained together, every one of their countenances expressing
dejection and sorrow, I no longer doubted of my fate, and, quite overpowered with horror and anguish, I fell motionless on the deck and
fainted. When I recovered a little, I found some black people about
me, who I believed were some of those who brought me on board,
and had been receiving their pay; they talked to me in order to cheer
me, but all in vain. I asked them if we were not to be eaten by those
white men with horrible looks, red faces, and long hair? They told
me I was not; and one of the crew brought me a small portion of
spirituous liquor in a wine glass; but, being afraid of him, I would
not take it out of his hand. . . .

• • •

At last we came in sight of the island of Barbadoes, at which the
whites on board gave a great shout, and made many signs of joy to
us. We did not know what to think of this; but as the vessel drew
nearer we plainly saw the harbour, and other ships of different kinds
and sizes: and we soon anchored amongst them off Bridge Town.
Many merchants and planters now came on board, though it was in
the evening. They put us in separate parcels, and examined us attentively. They also made us jump, and pointed to the land, signifying
we were to go there. We thought by this we should be eaten by these
ugly men, as they appeared to us; and, when soon after we were all
put down under the deck again, there was much dread and trembling among us, and nothing but bitter cries to be heard all the night
from these apprehensions, insomuch that at last the white people
got some old slaves from the land to pacify us. They told us we were not
to be eaten, but to work, and were soon to go on land, where we should
see many of our country people. This report eased us much; and
sure enough, soon after we were landed, there came to us Africans
of all languages. We were conducted immediately to the merchant's
yard, where we were all pent up together like so many sheep in a fold,
without regard to sex or age. As every object was new to me, every
thing I saw filled me with surprise. What struck me first was, that

the houses were built with bricks, in stories, and in every other respect different from those I have seen in Africa: but I was still more astonished on seeing people on horseback. I did not know what this could mean; and indeed I thought these people were full of nothing but magical arts....

• • •

We were not many days in the merchant's custody before we were sold after their usual manner, which is this:—On a signal given, (as the beat of a drum), the buyers rush at once into the yard where the slaves are confined, and make choice of that parcel they like best. The noise and clamour with which this is attended, and the eagerness visible in the countenances of the buyers, serve not a little to increase the apprehensions of the terrified Africans, who may well be supposed to consider them as the ministers of that destruction to which they think themselves devoted. In this manner, without scruple, are relations and friends separated, most of them never to see each other again. I remember in the vessel in which I was brought over, in the men's apartment, there were several brothers, who, in the sale, were sold in different lots; and it was very moving on this occasion to see and hear their cries at parting. O, ye nominal Christians! might not an African ask you, learned you this from your God? who says unto you, Do unto all men as you would men should do unto you? Is it not enough that we are torn from our country and friends to toil for your luxury and lust of gain? Must every tender feeling be likewise sacrificed to your avarice? Are the dearest friends and relations, now rendered more dear by their separation from their kindred, still to be parted from each other, and thus prevented from cheering the gloom of slavery with the small comfort of being together and mingling their sufferings and sorrows? Why are parents to lose their children, brothers their sisters, or husbands their wives? Surely this is a new refinement in cruelty, which, while it has no advantage to atone for it, thus aggravates distress, and adds fresh horrors even to the wretchedness of slavery.

Questions

1. What picture of life in Africa does Equiano present?

2. What elements of slavery does he seem to think will most outrage his readers?

---

22. Advertisements for Runaway Slaves and Servants (1738)

Source: **Pennsylvania Gazette,** *July 1738.*

As advertisements in colonial newspapers demonstrated, slaves and indentured servants frequently expressed their desire for freedom by running away. Sometimes they escaped together, despite racial differences between them and the fact that slaves served for life while servants would gain their liberty after a number of years. Pennsylvania was a frequent refuge for fugitives from neighboring Maryland, where slavery and servitude were more deeply entrenched.

RUN AWAY ON the 23d of March last, from the Subscribers, in St. Mary's County, Maryland, the following Servants, and a Negroe, viz.

George Humphrey, an Englishman, aged about 19 Years, fair complexion'd, talks slow, with light brown Hair: Had on a light Cotton Jacket lined with yellow Linnen, a homespun Jacket and Breeches, coarse Shirt and an old Felt Hat.

Barnaby Higgins, an Irishman, aged about 25 Years, Low of Stature, much pockfretten, by Trade a Joyner or Carpenter: Had on a yellow Jacket and Breeches.

Michael Mara, an Irishman, aged about 25 Years, Low of Stature, swarthy Complexion, by Trade a Turner: Had on a yellow Kersey Jacket and grey Breeches. Both the Irishmen had the two first Letters of their Name marked on the Arm.

John Maine, an Englishman, bred to the Sea, middle aged, well set, much disfigured on the Face and Throat from the King's Evil.

John More, an Irishman, had a Blemish on one Eye, middle aged, high Stature, well set, a Labourer and very dextrous at the Spade: Had on a Cinnamon colored Cloth Coat, a good Jacket and Breeches.

And a Negroe Man named Peter, about 25 Years old, Country born, of a middle Stature, well set, talks notably: Had on a brownish Cloth Coat, a Country Cloth Jacket and Breeches, and a Felt Hat pretty much worn.

They all made off in a Boat on Potomack River, 15 Feet in the Keel, with two Masts and rigged after the Bermudian Manner.

Whoever secures the said Servants and Negroe, so that their Masters may have them again, shall have Thirty Pounds Reward. Maryland Currency; and a proportionable Sum for any one or more of them, and all necessary Charges paid by

Philad. July John Heard, Abraham Barns.

10. 1738 Thomas Brook, Robert Ford.

Run away this Morning from Edward Farmer of Whitemarsh, a stout lusty Mollatto, known in Philadelphia by the Name of Mollatto Memm alias James Earl, has a Scar on his Temple, a wide Mouth and thick Lips, speaks good English. He was Cloathed when he went away, with a new Duroy Jacket of a dirty colour, lined with a dark blue-grey clour'd Shalloon, trim'd with dark collour'd Mohair and Buttons, a fine Shirt, a new fine Hat, a Silk Handkerchief, a speckled Pair of Trowsers, worsted Stockings, and new Shoes and Buckles in them.

Whoever takes up and secures the said Mollatto, or brings him home to his Master, or puts him in the Workhouse of Philadelphia, shall have Five Pounds Reward, paid by

Edward Farmer

Run away on Sunday last, from Henry Sparks, of Glocester Township, West-New-Jersey, an Irish Servant Man, named James Mordox, about 60 Years of Age, of a dark Complexion, grey Hair but cut off, by Trade a Smith. Had on a Suit of brown Cloaths, new Shoes and new Stockings.

Whoever secures the said Servant so that his Master may have him again shall have Forty Shillings Reward, and reasonable Charges paid by Henry Sparks. Philad. July 6. 1738.

Run away on the 20th Inst, from Joseph James of Cohensey, a Servant Man named Lazarus Kenny, is a swarthy Fellow, his Father being a Molatto and his Mother a white Woman, he is pretty tall and well set, his Hair cut off: Had on a Felt Hat, grey Kersey Coat and Vest, old Leather Breeches, an old homespun Shirt, yarn Stockings, round toe'd Shoes and brass Buckles. He took a large white Stallion that trots altogether, with an old black Saddle and good Snaffel Bridle.

Whoever secures the said Servant and Horse so that they are had again, shall have Forty Shillings Reward and reasonable Charges, paid by Joseph James.

Philad. June 29. 1738.

Questions

1. How do owners hope their fugitives will be identified?

2. What do these advertisements tell us about relations between slaves and servants?

---

23. *The Independent Reflector* on Limited Monarchy and Liberty (1752)

Source: **The Independent Reflector** *(New York), December 21, 1752.*

During the eighteenth century, the idea of the "freeborn Englishman" became powerfully entrenched in the outlook of both colonists and Britons. More than any other principle, liberty was seen as what made the British empire distinct. The passage that follows, from the New York

monthly magazine *The Independent Reflector*, founded in 1752, offers an
example of the era's many paeans to the "inexpressible charm" of liberty
and England's role as liberty's "defender." The author, probably the magazine's editor, Edward Livingston, contrasts the national prosperity and
personal happiness enjoyed by citizens of a "free state" (defined as a limited
monarchy in which freedom of speech and religion were protected) with
the sorry condition of subjects of absolute monarchies. Until the 1770s,
most colonists believed themselves to be part of the freest political system
humankind had ever known.

WHEN ONE CONSIDERS the Difference between an absolute, and a
limited Monarchy, it seems unaccountable, that any Person in his
Senses, should prefer the former to the later....

In *limited* Monarchies, the Pride and Ambition of Princes, and
their natural Lust for Dominion, are check'd and restrained....

Liberty gives an inexpressible Charm to all our Enjoyments.
It imparts a Relish to the most indifferent Pleasure, and renders
the highest Gratification the more consummately delightful. It is the
Refinement of Life; it sooths and alleviates our Toils; smooths the
rugged Brow of Adversity, and endears and enhances every Acquisition. The Subjects of a free State, have something open and generous
in their Carriage; something of Grandeur and Sublimity in their
Appearance, resulting from their Freedom and Independence, that
is never to be met with in those dreary Abodes, where the embitter-
ing Circumstance of a precarious Property, mars the Relish of every
Gratification, and damps the most magnanimous Spirits. They can
think for themselves; publish their Sentiments, and animadvert on
Religion and Government, secure and unmolested.

• • •

But in *absolute* Monarchies, the whole Country is overspread with
a dismal Gloom. *Slavery* is stamp'd on the Looks of the Inhabitants;
and *Penury* engraved on their Visages, in strong and legible Characters. To prevent Complaints, the PRESS is prohibited; and a Vindication

of the natural Rights of Mankind, is Treason. Every generous Spirit is broke and depressed: Human Nature is degraded, insulted, spurn'd, and outrag'd: The lovely Image of GOD, is defaced and disfigur'd, and the Lord of the Creation treated like the bestial Herd. The liberal Sciences languish: The politer Arts droop their Heads: Merit is banished to Cells and Deserts; and Virtue frowned into Dungeons, or dispatched to the Gallies: Iniquity is exalted: Goodness trod under Foot: Truth perverted; and the barbarous Outrages of Tyranny, sanctified and adored. The Fields lie waste and uncultivated: Commerce is incumbered with supernumerary Duties: The Tyrant riots in the Spoils of his People; and drains their Purses, to replenish his insatiate Treasury. He wages War against his own Subjects. . . .

Does any one think the above Representation, the Result of a roving Fancy, or figur'd beyond the Life; let him take a Survey of *Rome*; e'er-while the Nurse of Heroes, and the Terror of the World; but now the obscene Haunt of sequestred Bigots, and effeminate Slaves. Where are now her *Scipios*, and *Tullys*, her *Brutuses*, and her *Catos*, with other Names of equal Lustre, who plann'd her Laws, and fought her Battles, during her Freedom and Independence? Alas! they are succeeded by cloistered Monks and castrated Musicians, in Subjection to a filthy old Harlot, that pretends to a Power of devouring her Mediator, and claims a Right to eat up her People. Let him survey all *Italy*, once the Seat of Arts and Arms, and every Thing great and valuable; now the joyless Theatre of Oppression and Tyranny, Superstition and Ignorance. Let him behold all this; and when he has finished his Survey, then let him *believe and tremble.*

But far otherwise, is the Condition of a free People. Under the mild and gentle Administration of a *limited* Prince, every Thing looks cheerful and happy, smiling and serene. Agriculture is encouraged, and proves the annual Source of immense Riches to the Kingdom: The Earth opens her fertile Bosom to the Plough-share, and luxuriant Harvests diffuse Wealth and Plenty thro' the Land: The Fields stand thick with Corn: The Pastures smile with Herbage: The Hills and Vallies are cover'd with Flocks and Herds: Manufacturies flourish; and unprecarious Plenty recompenses the Artificer's Toil: In a Word, Nothing is seen but universal Joy and Festivity. Such is the Happiness of the People, under the blissful Reign of a good King. But do they get a Prince, whose Heart is poison'd with Regard to regal Authority, and who vainly imagines; that the Grandeur of Princes consists in making themselves feared; and accordingly plays the Devil in the Name of the Lord: They boldly assert their Rights, and call aloud for Justice; They cannot, they will not be enslaved. Sooner shall the royal Sinner have the Honour of Martyrdom, and the *Lord's Anointed* perish for his Iniquity, than the whole Frame of the Government be unhinged and dissolved. . . .

• • •

How signal is our Happiness, in being blessed with a Prince, form'd for the Friend of the Nation, and the Defender of the Liberties of *Europe!* A Prince, who despises the Thought of placing his Grandeur in the Violation of the Laws; but is nobly ambitious of reigning in the Hearts of his People: A Prince, who invariably exerts his native Greatness of Soul, and all his inherent and hereditary Virtues, in the Support of Truth, Religion and Liberty: A Prince, in fine, unemulous of arbitrary Sway; but ardently aspiring after those brighter Trophies, that are earn'd in the Paths of Virtue and heroic Deeds; in relieving the Injured, protecting the Oppressed, and by a diffusive Benevolence, promoting the Happiness of Mankind. Long, oh long may he still adorn the Throne of his Ancestors! and when the Sovereign Disposer of Events, shall at last, to the keen and universal Affliction of his People, translate him to the Possession of a Crown, eternal and incorruptible; we may presage, (which will be the only Consideration capable of alleviating our Sorrow,) the greatest Glory, and the brightest Triumphs, from his Royal Highness's eminent Virtues; whose future Reign promises the most distinguished Prosperity to the Nation; and will exhibit to *Britain,* a Monarch, from his benevolent Disposition, and princely Education, the Father of his People, as well as a shining Ornament to that illustrious Family, of which we have already seen two Heroes on the *British Throne;* the Scourges of Tyrants, and the Assertors of Liberty.

Questions

1. What does the author mean by a "free state"?

2. Does the author think that the institution of monarchy is incompatible with freedom?

24. The Trial of John Peter Zenger (1735)

Source: The Trial of John Peter Zenger *(London, 1765), pp. 19–46.*

Under British and colonial law, the government could not censor newspapers, books, and pamphlets before they appeared in print, but authors and publishers could be prosecuted for "seditious libel"—a crime that included defaming government officials—or punished for contempt of public authority. In colonial America, dozens of publishers were hauled before assemblies and forced to apologize for comments regarding one or another member. If they refused, they were jailed.

The most famous colonial court case involving freedom of the press occurred in 1735. This was the trial of John Peter Zenger, a German-born printer, whose newspaper, the *Weekly Journal,* lambasted New York's governor for corruption and "tyranny." Zenger was arrested and put on trial for seditious libel. The judge instructed the jurors to consider only whether Zenger had in fact published the offending words. But Zenger's attorney, Andrew Hamilton, told the jury that the "cause of liberty" itself was at stake. If Zenger's charges were correct, he went on, they should acquit him and "every man who prefers freedom to a life of slavery will bless you." Zenger was found not guilty. The outcome demonstrated that the idea of free expression was becoming ingrained in the popular imagination.

MR. ATTORNEY. The case before the court is whether Mr. Zenger is guilty of libeling His Excellency the Governor of New York, and indeed the whole administration of the government. Mr. Hamilton has confessed the printing and publishing, and I think nothing is plainer than that the words in the information [indictment] are scandalous, and tend to sedition, and to disquiet the minds of the people of this province. And if such papers are not libels, I think it may be said there can be no such thing as a libel.

MR. HAMILTON. May it please Your Honor, I cannot agree with Mr. Attorney. For though I freely acknowledge that there are such things as libels, yet I must insist, at the same time, that what my client is charged with is not a libel. And I observed just now that Mr. Attorney, in defining a libel, made use of the words "scandalous, seditious, and tend to disquiet the people." But (whether with design or not I will not say) he omitted the word "false."

MR. ATTORNEY. I think I did not omit the word "false." But it has been said already that it may be a libel, notwithstanding it may be true.

MR. HAMILTON. In this I must still differ with Mr. Attorney; for I depend upon it, we are to be tried upon this information now before the court and jury, and to which we have pleaded not guilty, and by it we are charged with printing and publishing a certain false, malicious, seditious, and scandalous libel. This word "false" must have some meaning, or else how came it there? . . .

• • •

MR. CHIEF JUSTICE. You cannot be admitted, Mr. Hamilton, to give the truth of a libel in evidence. A libel is not to be justified; for it is nevertheless a libel that it is true. . . .

MR. HAMILTON. I thank Your Honor. Then, gentlemen of the jury, it is to you we must now appeal, for witnesses, to the truth of the facts we have offered, and are denied the liberty to prove. And let it not seem strange that I apply myself to you in this manner. I am warranted so to do both by law and reason.

The law supposes you to be summoned out of the neighborhood where the fact [crime] is alleged to be committed; and the reason of

your being taken out of the neighborhood is because you are supposed to have the best knowledge of the fact that is to be tried. And
were you to find a verdict against my client, you must take upon
you to say the papers referred to in the information, and which we
acknowledge we printed and published, are false, scandalous, and
seditious. But of this I can have no apprehension. You are citizens of
New York; you are really what the law supposes you to be, honest and
lawful men. And, according to my brief, the facts which we offer to
prove were not committed in a corner; they are notoriously known
to be true; and therefore in your justice lies our safety. And as we are
denied the liberty of giving evidence to prove the truth of what we
have published, I will beg leave to lay it down, as a standing rule in
such cases, that the suppressing of evidence ought always to be taken
for the strongest evidence; and I hope it will have weight with you. . . .

• • •

I hope to be pardoned, sir, for my zeal upon this occasion. It is an old
and wise caution that when our neighbor's house is on fire, we ought
to take care of our own. For though, blessed be God, I live in a government [Pennsylvania] where liberty is well understood, and freely
enjoyed, yet experience has shown us all (I'm sure it has to me) that a
bad precedent in one government is soon set up for an authority in
another. And therefore I cannot but think it mine, and every honest
man's duty; that (while we pay all due obedience to men in authority)
we ought at the same time to be upon our guard against power, wherever we apprehend that it may affect ourselves or our fellow subjects.

I am truly very unequal to such an undertaking on many accounts.
And you see I labor under the weight of many years, and am borne
down with great infirmities of body. Yet old and weak as I am, I
should think it my duty, if required, to go to the utmost part of the
land, where my service could be of any use, in assist—to quench the
flame of prosecutions upon informations, set on foot by the government, to deprive a people of the right of remonstrating (and com-
plaining too) of the arbitrary attempts of men in power. Men who
injure and oppress the people under their administration provoke
them to cry out and complain; and then make that very complaint

the foundation for new oppressions and prosecutions. I wish I could say there were no instances of this kind.

But to conclude. The question before the court and you, gentlemen of the jury, is not of small nor private concern. It is not the cause of a poor printer, nor of New York alone, which you are now trying. No! It may, in its consequence, affect every freeman that lives under a British government on the main [land] of America. It is the best cause. It is the cause of liberty. And I make no doubt but your upright conduct, this day, will not only entitle you to the love and esteem of your fellow citizens; but every man who prefers freedom to a life of slavery will bless and honor you, as men who have baffled the attempt of tyranny, and, by an impartial and uncorrupt verdict, have laid a noble foundation for securing to ourselves, our posterity, and our neighbors, that to which nature and the laws of our country have given us a right—the liberty both of exposing and opposing arbitrary power (in these parts of the world, at least) by speaking and writing truth.

• • •

Questions

1. Why does Hamilton equate Zenger's defense with "the cause of liberty"?

2. What does Hamilton seem to think is the greatest threat to liberty?

---

25. The Great Awakening Comes to Connecticut (1740)

Source: George Leon Walker, Some Aspects of the Religious Life of New England *(New York, 1897), pp. 89–92.*

A series of religious revivals known as the Great Awakening swept through the colonies beginning in the 1730s. The revivals were united by a commitment to a "religion of the heart," a more emotional and personal Christianity than that offered by existing churches. The Awakening was a transatlantic movement. More than any other individual, the English minister George Whitefield, who declared "the whole world his parish," sparked the Great Awakening. For two years after his arrival in America in 1739, Whitefield brought his highly emotional brand of preaching to colonies from Georgia to New England.

A Connecticut farmer, Nathan Cole, in a 200-page autobiographical manuscript, offered a vivid account of the impact of Whitefield's preaching and how ordinary colonists responded to its spiritual message. People, Cole wrote, traveled from far and wide to hear Whitefield because of "a concern for their soul." When he heard that Whitefield was nearby, Cole stopped his work, ran to get his wife, and immediately took off on horseback. Cole would later go on to form his own church, illustrating how the Great Awakening inspired ordinary people to think for themselves in religious matters.

Now IT PLEASED GOD to send Mr. Whitefield into this land; and my hearing of his preaching at Philadelphia, like one of the Old apostles, and many thousands flocking to hear him preach the Gospel, and great numbers were converted to Christ; I felt the Spirit of God drawing me by conviction, longed to see and hear him, and wished he would come this way. And I soon heard he was come to New York and the Jerseys and great multitudes flocking after him under great concern for their Souls and many converted which brought on my concern more and more hoping soon to see him but next I heard he was at Long Island, then at Boston, and next at Northampton.

Then one morning all on a Sudden, about 8 or 9 o'clock there came a messenger and said Mr. Whitefield preached at Hartford and Weathersfield yesterday and is to preach at Middletown this morning [October 23, 1740] at ten of the Clock. I was in my field at work. I dropped my tool that I had in my hand and ran home and run through my house and bade my wife get ready quick to go and hear Mr. Whitefield preach at Middletown, and run to my pasture for my horse with all my might fearing that I should be too late to hear him. I brought my horse home and soon mounted and took my wife up and went forward as fast as I thought the horse could bear, and when my horse began to be out of breath, I would get down and put my wife on the saddle and bid her ride as fast as she could and not stop or slack for me except I bade her, and so I would run until I was much out of breath, and then mount my horse again, and so I did several times to favor my horse, we improved every moment to get along as if we were fleeing for our lives, all the while fearing we should be too late to hear the Sermon, for we had twelve miles to ride double in little more than an hour. . . .

And when we came within about half a mile of the road that comes down from Hartford, Weathersfield, and Stepney to Middletown; on high land I saw before me a cloud or fog rising. I first thought it came from the great river [Connecticut River], but as I came nearer the road, I heard a noise something like a low rumbling thunder and presently found it was the noise of horses' feet coming down the road and this cloud was a cloud of dust made by the horses' feet. . . . As I drew nearer it seemed like a steady stream of horses and their riders, scarcely a horse more than his length behind another, all of a lather and foam with sweat, their breath rolling out of their nostrils in the cloud of dust every jump; every horse seemed to go with all his might to carry his rider to hear news from heaven for the saving of Souls. It made me tremble to see the sight, how the world was in a struggle, I found a [space] between two horses to slip in my horse; and my wife said . . . our clothes will be all spoiled see how they look, for they were so covered with dust, that they looked almost all of a color coats, hats, and shirts and horses.

We went down in the stream; I heard no man speak a word all the way three miles but every one pressing forward in great haste and when we got to the old meeting house there was a great multitude; it was said to be 3 or 4,000 of people assembled together, we got off from our horses and shook off the dust, and the ministers were then coming to the meeting house. I turned and looked towards the great river and saw the ferry boats running swift forward . . . bringing over loads of people; the oars rowed nimble and quick, every thing men horses and boats seemed to be struggling for life; the land and banks over the river looked black with people and horses all along the 12 miles. I saw no man at work in his field, but all seemed to be gone.

When I saw Mr. Whitefield come upon the scaffold he looked almost angelical, a young, slim slender youth before some thousands of people with a bold undaunted countenance, and my hearing how God was with him everywhere as he came along it solemnized my mind, and put me into a trembling fear before he began to preach; for he looked as if he was clothed with authority from the Great God, and a sweet solemn solemnity sat upon his brow. And my hearing him preach gave me a heart wound; by God's blessing my old foundation was broken up, and I saw that my righteousness would not save me; then I was convinced of the doctrine of Election and went right to quarreling with God about it, because all that I could do would not save me; and he had decreed from Eternity who should be saved and who not.

Questions

1. What religious doctrine does Whitefield preach?

2. How does Cole's account help us to understand why many established religious leaders were alarmed by Whitefield's appearance in the American colonies?

━━━━━━

26. Pontiac, Two Speeches (1762 and 1763)

Source: Alexander Henry, Travels and Adventures in Canada and the Indian Territories between the Years 1760 and 1776 *[1809], (Toronto, 1901), p. 44; and Francis Parkman,* The Conspiracy of Pontiac and the Indian Wars after the Conquest of Canada *(6th ed., Boston, 1874), Vol. 1, pp. 204–07.*

Victory in the Seven Years' War, confirmed in the Treaty of Paris of 1763, established British preeminence in North America east of the Mississippi River. To Indians, it was clear that the abrupt departure of the French from Canada and the Mississippi and Ohio valleys, and the continued expansion of the British settler population, posed a dire threat.

In 1763, Indians of the Ohio Valley and Great Lakes launched a revolt against British rule. Although known as Pontiac's Rebellion, after an Ottawa war leader, the rebellion owed much to the teachings of Neolin, a Delaware religious prophet. Neolin and Pontiac promoted a pan-Indian identity among members of different tribes, urging all Indians to fight to regain their lost independence. In 1763, Indians seized several British forts and killed hundreds of white settlers who had intruded onto Indian lands. British forces soon launched a counterattack, and one by one the tribes made peace. But the uprising laid the groundwork for future resistance.

———

ENGLISHMAN, ALTHOUGH YOU have conquered the French, you have not yet conquered us! We are not your slaves. These lakes, these woods and mountains, were left to us by our ancestors. They are our inheritance; and we will part with them to none. Your nation supposes that we, like the white people, cannot live without bread—and pork—and beef! But, you ought to know, that He, the Great Spirit and Master of Life, has provided food for us, in these spacious lakes, and on these woody mountains...

• • •

"A Delaware Indian [Neolin]," said Pontiac, "conceived an eager desire to learn wisdom from the Master of Life; but, being ignorant where to find him, he had recourse to fasting, dreaming, and magical incantations. By these means it was revealed to him, that, by moving forward in a straight, undeviating course, he would reach the abode of the Great Spirit. He told his purpose to no one, and having provided the equipments of a hunter,—gun, powder-horn, ammunition, and a kettle for preparing his food,—he set out on his errand. For some time he journeyed on in high hope and confidence. On the evening of the eighth day, he stopped by the side of a brook at the edge of a meadow, where he began to make ready his evening meal, when, looking up, he saw three large openings in the woods before him, and three well-beaten paths which entered them. He was much surprised; but his wonder increased, when, after it had grown dark, the three paths were more clearly visible than ever. Remembering the important object of his journey, he could neither rest nor sleep; and, leaving his fire, he crossed the meadow, and entered the largest of the three openings. He had advanced but a short distance into the forest, when a bright flame sprang out of the ground before him, and arrested his steps. In great amazement, he turned back, and entered the second path, where the same wonderful phenomenon again encountered him; and now, in terror and bewilderment, yet still resolved to persevere, he took the last of the three paths. On this he journeyed a whole day without interruption, when at length, emerging from the forest, he saw before him a vast mountain, of dazzling whiteness. So precipitous was the ascent, that the Indian thought it hopeless to go farther, and looked around him in despair: at that moment, he saw, seated at some distance above, the figure of a beautiful woman arrayed in white, who arose as he looked upon her, and thus accosted him: 'How can you hope, encumbered as you are, to succeed in your design? Go down to the foot of the mountain, throw away your gun, your ammunition, your provisions, and your clothing; wash yourself in the stream which flows there, and you will then be prepared to stand before the Master of Life.' The Indian obeyed, and again began to ascend among the rocks, while the woman, seeing him still discouraged, laughed at his faintness of heart, and told him that, if he wished for success, he must climb by the aid of one hand and one foot only. After great toil and suffering, he at length found himself at the summit. The woman had disappeared, and he was left alone. A rich and beautiful plain lay before him, and at a little distance he saw three great villages, far superior to the squalid wigwams of the Delawares. As he approached the largest, and stood hesitating whether he should enter, a man gorgeously attired stepped forth, and, taking him by the hand, welcomed him to the celestial abode. He then conducted him into the presence of the Great Spirit, where the Indian stood confounded at the unspeakable splendor which surrounded him. The Great Spirit bade him be seated, and thus addressed him:—

"'I am the Maker of heaven and earth, the trees, lakes, rivers, and all things else. I am the Maker of mankind; and because I love you, you must do my will. The land on which you live I have made for you, and not for others. Why do you suffer the white men to dwell among you? My children, you have forgotten the customs and traditions of your forefathers. Why do you not clothe yourselves in skins, as they did, and use the bows and arrows, and the stonepointed lances, which they used? You have bought guns, knives, kettles, and blankets, from the white men, until you can no longer do without them; and, what is worse, you have drunk the poison fire-water, which turns you into fools. Fling all these things away; live as your wise forefathers lived before you. And as for these English,—these dogs dressed in red, who have come to rob you of your hunting-grounds, and drive away the game,—you must lift the hatchet against them. Wipe them from the face of the earth, and then you will win my favor back again, and once more be happy and prosperous.'"

Questions

1. How does Pontiac understand the meaning of freedom?

2. What elements of Indian life does Neolin criticize most strongly?

CHAPTER 5

The American Revolution, 1763–1783

27. Virginia Resolutions on the Stamp Act (1765)

Source: John Pendleton Kennedy, ed., Journals of the House of Burgesses of Virginia 1761–1765 *(Richmond, 1907), pp. lxvi–lxvii, 360.*

The passage of the Stamp Act by Parliament in 1765 inspired the first major split between colonists and Great Britain. Pressed for funds because of the enormous expense it had incurred in fighting the Seven Years' War, Parliament for the first time attempted to raise money from direct taxes in the colonies rather than through the regulation of trade. The act required that all sorts of printed material produced in the colonies carry a stamp purchased from authorities.

By imposing the stamp tax without colonial consent, Parliament directly challenged the authority of local elites who, through the assemblies they controlled, had established their power over the raising and spending of money. They were ready to defend this authority in the name of liberty. Virginia's House of Burgesses approved four resolutions offered by the fiery orator Patrick Henry. The Burgesses rejected as too radical the last three resolutions that follow, including one calling for outright resistance to unlawful taxation.

WHEREAS, THE HONOURABLE House of Commons in England, have of late draw[n] into question how far the General Assembly of this colony hath power to enact laws for laying of taxes and imposing duties payable by the people of this, his Majesty's most ancient colony; for settling and ascertaining the same to all future times, the House of Burgesses of this present General Assembly have come to the following resolves.

Resolved, that the first adventurers, settlers of this his Majesty's colony and dominion of Virginia, brought with them and transmitted to their posterity, and all other his Majesty's subjects since inhabiting in this his Majesty's colony, all the privileges and immunities that have at any time been held, enjoyed, and possessed by the people of Great Britain.

Resolved, that by two royal charters granted by King James the first, the colonists aforesaid are declared and entitled to all privileges and immunities of natural born subjects, to all intents and purposes as if they had been abiding and born within the realm of England.

Resolved, that the taxation of the people by themselves, or by persons chosen by themselves to represent them, who can only know what taxes the people are able to bear, or the easiest method of raising them, and must themselves be affected by every tax laid on the people, is the only security against a burdensome taxation, and the distinguishing characteristic of British freedom, without which the ancient constitution cannot exist.

Resolved, that his Majesty's liege people of this ancient colony have enjoyed the right of being thus governed by their own Assembly in the article of taxes and internal police, and that the same have never been forfeited, or any other way yielded up, but have been constantly recognized by the king and people of Great Britain.

Resolved, therefore, that the General Assembly of this colony, together with his Majesty or his substitutes, have in their representatives capacity, the only exclusive right and power to lay taxes and imposts upon the inhabitants of this colony; and that every attempt to vest such power in any other person or persons whatever than the General Assembly aforesaid, is illegal, unconstitutional, and unjust, and has a manifest tendency to destroy British as well as American liberty.

Resolved, that his Majesty's liege people, the inhabitants of this colony, are not bound to yield obedience to any law or ordinance whatever, designed to impose any taxation whatsoever upon them, other than the laws or ordinances of the General Assembly aforesaid.

Resolved, that any person who shall, by speaking or writing, assert or maintain that any person or persons other than the General Assembly of this colony, have any right or power to impose or lay any taxation on the people here, shall be deemed an enemy to his Majesty's colony.

Questions

1. Why do you think the Virginia House of Burgesses adopted the first four resolutions but rejected the final three?

2. What would be the difference between resting the resolutions' arguments on "British freedom" and appealing to a more universal concept of liberty?

---

28. New York Workingmen Demand a Voice in the Revolutionary Struggle (1770)

Source: Brutus, *To the Free and Loyal Inhabitants of the City and Colony of New-York . . . (New York, 1774).*

The struggle against British taxation measures of the 1760s greatly expanded the boundaries of colonial politics. The following document illustrates how ordinary workingmen in New York City claimed the right to challenge the city's prominent merchants in determining how far resistance should go. In the aftermath of the Townshend Acts, a series of taxes imposed by Parliament on the American colonies, leaders in several colonies announced a boycott of British goods. They hoped to pressure British merchants to persuade their government to repeal the measures. By 1770, however, colonial merchants, as well as many Americans who did not want to do without British goods, decided to resume trade. In response, a New Yorker calling himself Brutus published a call for a continuation of the policy of nonimportation. He castigated the merchants as "mercantile Dons" ("Don" being a Spanish word derived from "lord" and suggesting gentry status). Mechanics (craftsmen), he insisted, had a right to a voice in public policy. The letter illustrates how the struggle for colonial rights led to a democratization of politics.

FRIENDS, FELLOW CITIZENS, fellow Countrymen, and fellow Freeman,

Nothing can be more flagrantly wrong than the assertion of some of our mercantile Dons, that the mechanics have no right to give their sentiments about the importation of British commodities. For who, I would ask, is the member of community, that is absolutely independent of the rest? Or what particular class among us, has an exclusive right to decide a question of general concern? When the Non-Importation Agreement took place, what end was it designed to answer? Not surely the private emolument of merchants, but the universal weal of the continent. It was to redeem from perdition, from total perdition, that stock of English Liberty, to which every subject, whatever may be his rank, is equally entitled. Amidst all the disparity of fortune and honors, there is one lot as common to all Englishmen, as death. It is, that we are all equally free. Sufficient is it therefore, to show the matchless absurdity of the exclusive claim, of which a few interested merchants have lately attempted, in a most assuming manner, to avail themselves, in determining on the question, whether the Non-Importation Agreement shall be rescinded, to observe, that it was not solemnly entered into for the good of the merchants alone, but for the salvation of the Liberties of us all.

Of this the trading interest of this City were convinced, when, after forming themselves into a Society for executing that Agreement, they not only requested a similar Association of the Mechanics, but by frequent meetings, conspired with them in support of the important Company. When the parties engaged in it, none doubted the necessity of so salutary a measure: every man saw, that between an importation of goods, which stern virtue ought ever to despise as a means to encourage luxury, and the sacrifice of our inestimable Rights as Englishmen, there was no medium. This view of the subject begat and brought to perfection, the important resolution, which has inspired the enemies of our Liberty on the other side of the Atlantic, with fear and astonishment. . . . Has not our Mother Country, by solemn Act of Legislation, declared that she has a right to impose internal Taxes on us? And is not such an imposition incompatible with our Liberty? But this law is a mere dead letter, unless it be carried into exercise by some future Act. For this Purpose was the Law devised, imposing a Duty upon Tea, Paper, Glass, Painters Colors, etc. the very articles which our Egyptian task-masters thought were most essential to us, as being not hitherto the produce of this country. And shall we not, for our own sakes, show that we can live without them? What are all the riches, the luxuries, and even the conveniences of life, compared with that liberty wherewith God and Nature have set us free, with that inestimable jewel which is the basis of all other enjoyments? . . . Rouse then my fellow citizen, fellow countrymen, and fellow Freemen, of all ranks, from the man of wealth, to the man whose only portion is Liberty.

Questions

1. What social divisions in the colonies are apparent in this broadside?

2. In what respect does the author believe that all colonists are equal?

29. Association of the New York Sons of Liberty (1773)

Source: Hezekiah Niles, **Principles and Acts of the Revolution in America** *(Baltimore, 1822), pp. 169–70.*

The Sons of Liberty of New York City was one of many such groups that sprang up during the Stamp Act crisis of 1765. It was led by talented and ambitious lesser merchants who enjoyed no standing among the colony's wealthy but commanded a broad following among the city's craftsmen, laborers, and sailors. The Sons took the lead in enforcing the boycott of British imports that led to Parliament's repeal of the act and a second boycott directed against the Townshend Duties of 1767.

In 1773, when Parliament passed the Tea Act, another taxation measure, the Sons again organized resistance. On December 15, the Sons of Liberty announced an agreement or association to resist the Tea Act. Signed by "a great number of the principal gentlemen of the city, merchants, lawyers, and other inhabitants of all ranks," the agreement forthrightly accused Britain of trampling on the freedom of the colonists and threatening to reduce them to "slavery."

───────

THE FOLLOWING ASSOCIATION is signed by a great number of the principal gentlemen of the city, merchants, lawyers, and other inhabitants of all ranks, and it is still carried about the city to give an opportunity to those who have not yet signed, to unite with their fellow citizens, to testify their abhorrence to the diabolical project of enslaving America.

THE ASSOCIATION OF THE SONS OF LIBERTY OF NEW YORK

It is essential to the freedom and security of a free people, that no taxes be imposed upon them but by their own consent, or their representatives. For "What property have they in that which another may, by right, take when he pleases to himself?" The former is the undoubted right of Englishmen, to secure which they expended millions and sacrificed the lives of thousands. And yet, to the astonishment of all the world, and the grief of America, the Commons of Great Britain, after the repeal of the memorable and detestable Stamp Act, reassumed the power of imposing taxes on the American colonies; and insisting on it as a necessary badge of parliamentary supremacy, passed a bill, in the seventh year of his present Majesty's reign, imposing duties on all glass, painters' colours, paper, and teas, that should, after the 20th of November, 1767, be "imported from Great Britain into any colony or plantation in America". This bill, after the concurrence of the Lords, obtained the royal assent. And thus they who, from time immemorial, have exercised the right of giving to, or withholding from the crown, their aids and subsidies, according to their *own free will and pleasure*, signified by their representatives in Parliament, do, by the Act in question, deny us, their brethren in America, the enjoyment of the same right. As this denial, and the execution of that Act, involves our slavery, and would sap the foundation of our freedom, whereby we should become slaves to our brethren and fellow subjects, born to no greater stock of freedom than the Americans—the merchants and inhabitants of this city, in conjunction with the merchants and inhabitants of the ancient American colonies, entered into an agreement to decline a part of their commerce with Great Britain, until the above mentioned Act should be totally repealed.

This agreement operated so powerfully to the disadvantage of the manufacturers of England that many of them were unemployed. To appease their clamours, and to provide the subsistence for them, which the non-importation had deprived them of, the Parliament, in 1770, repealed so much of the Revenue Act as imposed a duty on glass, painters' colours, and paper, and left the duty on tea, as *a test of the parliamentary right to tax us*. The merchants of the cities of New York and Philadelphia, having strictly adhered to the agreement, so far as it is related to the importation of articles subject to an American duty, have convinced the ministry, that some other measures must be adopted to execute parliamentary supremacy over this country, and to remove the distress brought on the East India Company, by the ill policy of that Act. Accordingly, to increase the temptation to the shippers of tea from England, an Act of Parliament passed the last session, which gives the whole duty on tea, the company were subject to pay, upon the importation of it into England, to the purchasers and exporters; and when the company have ten millions of pounds of tea in their warehouses exclusive of the quantity they may want to ship, they are allowed to export tea, discharged from the payment of that duty with which they were before chargeable.

In hopes of aid in the execution of this project, by the influence of the owners of the American ships, application was made by the company to the captains of those ships to take the tea on freight; but they virtuously rejected it. Still determined on the scheme, they have chartered ships to bring the tea to this country, which may be hourly expected, to make an important trial of our virtue. If they succeed in the sale of that tea, we shall have no property that we can call our own, and then we may bid adieu to American liberty. Therefore, to prevent a calamity which, of all others, is the most to be dreaded—slavery and its terrible concomitants—we, the subscribers, being influenced from a regard to liberty, and disposed to use all lawful endeavours in our power, to defeat the pernicious project, and to transmit to our posterity those blessings of freedom which our ancestors have handed down to us; and to contribute to the support of the common liberties of America, which are in danger to be subverted, *do*, for those important purposes, agree to associate together, under the name and style of the *sons of New York*, and engage our honour to, and with each other faithfully to observe and perform the following resolutions, viz.

1st. Resolved, that whoever shall aid or abet, or in any manner assist, in the introduction of tea from any place whatsoever, into this colony, while it is subject, by a British Act of Parliament, to the payment of a duty, for the purpose of raising a revenue in America, he shall be deemed an enemy to the liberties of America.

2d. Resolved, that whoever shall be aiding, or assisting, in the landing, or carting of such tea, from any ship, or vessel, or shall hire any house, storehouse, or cellar or any place whatsoever, to deposit the tea, subject to a duty as aforesaid, he shall be deemed an enemy to the liberties of America.

3d. Resolved, that whoever shall sell, or buy, or in any manner contribute to the sale, or purchase of tea, subject to a duty as aforesaid, or shall aid, or abet, in transporting such tea, by land or water, from this city, until the 7th George III, chap. 46, commonly called the Revenue Act, shall be totally and clearly repealed, he shall be deemed an enemy to the liberties of America.

4th. Resolved, that whether the duties on tea, imposed by this Act, be paid in Great Britain or in America, our liberties are equally affected.

5th. Resolved, that whoever shall transgress any of these resolutions, we will not deal with, or employ, or have any connection with him.

Questions

1. How do the Sons of Liberty explain Britain's motivations for passing the Tea Act?

2. What do they consider the relationship between property and liberty?

---

30. Farmington, Connecticut, Resolutions on the Intolerable Acts (1774)

Source: Peter Force, **American Archives** *(Washington, D.C., 1837–1853), Series 4, Vol. I, p. 336.*

Parliament responded to the Boston Tea Party by passing a series of coercive laws. These closed the port of Boston to all trade until the tea had been paid for, radically altered the Massachusetts Charter of 1691 by curtailing town meetings and authorizing the governor to appoint previously elected members of the council, and empowered military commanders to lodge soldiers in private homes. These measures, which Americans called the Intolerable Acts, destroyed the legitimacy of the imperial government in the eyes of many colonists. Opposition now spread to small towns and rural areas that had not participated actively in previous resistance. A gathering of 1,000 residents of Farmington, Connecticut, in May 1774 erected a liberty pole and adopted resolutions proclaiming that they were "the sons of freedom" who "scorn the chains of slavery" Britain had fashioned for America. The Farmington resolutions accused the British ministry of being "instigated by the devil." Especially in New England, the cause of liberty had become the cause of God.

PROCEEDINGS OF FARMINGTON, Connecticut, on the Boston Port Act, May 19, 1774.

Early in the morning was found the following handbill, posted up in various parts of the town, viz:

> To pass through the fire at six o'clock this evening, in honour to the immortal goddess of Liberty, the late infamous Act of the British Parliament for farther distressing the American Colonies; the place of execution will be the public parade, where all Sons of Liberty are desired to attend.

Accordingly, a very numerous and respectable body were assembled of near one thousand people, when a huge pole, just forty-five feet high, was erected and consecrated to the shrine of liberty; after which the Act of Parliament for blocking up the Boston harbour was read aloud, sentenced to the flames and executed by the hands of the common hangman; then the following resolves were passed, *nem.con.*:

1st. That it is the greatest dignity, interest and happiness of every American to be united with our parent State, while our liberties are duly secured, maintained and supported by our rightful Sovereign, whose person we greatly revere; whose government, while duly administered, we are ready with our lives and properties to support.

2d. That the present ministry, being instigated by the devil and led on by their wicked and corrupt hearts, have a design to take away our liberties and properties and to enslave us *forever.*

3d. That the late Act which their malice hath caused to be passed in Parliament, for blocking up the port of Boston, is unjust, illegal and oppressive; and that we and every American are sharers in the insults offered to the town of Boston.

4th. That those pimps and parasites who dared to advise their master to such detestable measures be held in utter abhorrence by us and every American, and their names loaded with the curses of all succeeding generations.

5th. That we scorn the chains of slavery; we despise every attempt to rivet them upon us; we are the sons of freedom and resolved that, till time shall be no more, godlike virtue shall blazon our hemisphere.

Questions

1. How does the language of the resolutions suggest that feelings toward Great Britain have hardened in the colonies?

2. How do the resolutions qualify or limit Americans' sense of loyalty to the British government?

---

31. Thomas Paine, *Common Sense* (1776)

Source: Thomas Paine, Common Sense *(2nd ed.: Philadelphia, 1776), pp. 1, 6–12, 15–30.*

Ironically, a recent emigrant from England offered the most persuasive argument for American independence. Thomas Paine arrived in Philadelphia late in 1774 and quickly became associated with a group of advocates of the American cause. His pamphlet, *Common Sense,* appeared in January

1776. It began not with a recital of colonial grievances but with an attack on the principles of hereditary rule and monarchial government. Paine then drew on the colonists' experiences to make his case for independence. Within the British empire, America's prospects were limited; trading freely with the entire world, its future prosperity was certain. With independence, moreover, the colonies could for the first time insulate themselves from involvement in the endless imperial wars of Europe. But more than such practical considerations, Paine outlined a stirring vision of the historical importance of the American Revolution. The new nation would become the home of freedom, "an asylum for mankind."

Previous political writings had generally been directed toward the educated elite. Paine pioneered a new style of political writing, one designed to expand dramatically the public sphere where political discussion took place. *Common Sense* quickly became one of the most successful and influential pamphlets in the history of political writing.

INTRODUCTION

Perhaps the sentiments contained in the following pages, are not *yet* sufficiently fashionable to procure them general Favor; a long Habit of not thinking a Thing *wrong*, gives it a superficial appearance of being *right*, and raises at first a formidable outcry in defence of Custom. But the Tumult soon subsides. Time makes more Converts than Reason.

As a long and violent abuse of power is generally the means of calling the right of it in question, (and in matters too which might never have been thought of, had not the sufferers been aggravated into the inquiry,) and as the King of England hath undertaken in his *own right*, to support the Parliament in what he calls *Theirs*, and as the good People of this Country are grievously oppressed by the Combination, they have an undoubted privilege to enquire into the Pretensions of both, and equally to reject the Usurpation of *either*.

In the following Sheets, the Author hath studiously avoided every thing which is personal among ourselves. Compliments as well as censure to individuals make no part thereof. The wise and the

worthy need not the triumph of a Pamphlet; and those whose sentiments are injudicious or unfriendly will cease of themselves, unless
too much pain is bestowed upon their conversions.

The cause of America is in a great measure the cause of all mankind. Many circumstances have, and will arise, which are not local,
but universal, and through which the principles of all lovers of mankind are affected, and in the event of which their affections are interested. The laying a country desolate with fire and sword, declaring
war against the natural rights of all mankind, and extirpating the
defenders thereof from the face of the earth, is the concern of every
man to whom nature hath given the power of feeling.

• • •

OF MONARCHY AND HEREDITARY SUCCESSION

Mankind being originally equals in the order of creation, the equality could only be destroyed by some subsequent circumstance; the
distinctions of rich, and poor, may in a great measure be accounted
for, and that without having recourse to the harsh ill sounding names
of oppression and avarice. Oppression is often the *consequence*, but
seldom or never the *means* of riches; and though avarice will preserve
a man from being necessitously poor, it generally makes him too
timorous to be wealthy.

But there is another and greater distinction for which no truly
natural or religious reason can be assigned, and that is, the distinction of men into KINGS and SUBJECTS. Male and female are the distinctions of nature, good and bad the distinctions of heaven; but how a
race of men came into the world so exalted above the rest, and distinguished like some new species, is worth enquiring into, and
whether they are the means of happiness or of misery to mankind.

• • •

All men being originally equals, no *one* by *birth* could have a right
to set up his own family in perpetual preference to all others for ever,
and though himself might deserve *some* decent degree of honors of

his contemporaries, yet his descendants might be far too unworthy to inherit them. One of the strongest *natural* proofs of the folly of hereditary right in kings, is, that nature disapproves it, otherwise she would not so frequently turn it into ridicule by giving mankind an *ass for a lion*.

As to usurpation, no man will be so hardy as to defend it; and that William the Conqueror was an usurper is a fact not to be contradicted. The plain truth is, that the antiquity of English monarchy will not bear looking into.

• • •

Thoughts on the Present State of American Affairs

In the following pages I offer nothing more than simple facts, plain arguments, and common sense: and have no other preliminaries to settle with the reader, than that he will divest himself of prejudice and prepossession, and suffer his reason and his feelings to determine for themselves: that he will put on, or rather that he will not put off, the true character of a man, and generously enlarge his views beyond the present day.

Volumes have been written on the subject of the struggle between England and America. Men of all ranks have embarked in the controversy, from different motives, and with various designs; but all have been ineffectual, and the period of debate is closed. Arms as the last resource decide the contest; the appeal was the choice of the King, and the Continent has accepted the challenge.

• • •

The Sun never shined on a cause of greater worth. 'Tis not the affair of a City, a County, a Province, or a Kingdom; but of a Continent—of at least one eighth part of the habitable Globe. 'Tis not the concern of a day, a year, or an age; posterity are virtually involved in the contest, and will be more or less affected even to the end of time, by the proceedings now. Now is the seed-time of Continental union, faith and honour. The least fracture now will be like a name engraved with the point of a pin on the tender rind of a young oak; the wound would enlarge with the tree, and posterity read it in full grown character.

• • •

As much hath been said of the advantages of reconciliation, which, like an agreeable dream, hath passed away and left us as we were, it is but right that we should examine the contrary side of the argument, and enquire into some of the many material injuries which these Colonies sustain, and always will sustain, by being connected with and dependent on Great-Britain. To examine that connection and dependence, on the principles of nature and common sense, to see what we have to trust to, if separated, and what we are to expect, if dependant.

I have heard it asserted by some, that as America has flourished under her former connection with Great-Britain, the same connection is necessary towards her future happiness, and will always have the same effect. Nothing can be more fallacious than this kind of argument. We may as well assert that because a child has thrived upon milk, that it is never to have meat, or that the first twenty years of our lives is to become a precedent for the next twenty. But even this is admitting more than is true; for I answer roundly, that America would have flourished as much, and probably much more, had no European power taken any notice of her. The commerce by which she hath enriched herself are the necessaries of life, and will always have a market while eating is the custom of Europe.

But she has protected us, say some. That she hath engrossed us is true, and defended the Continent at our expense as well as her own, is admitted; and she would have defended Turkey from the same motive, *viz.* for the sake of trade and dominion.

Alas! we have been long led away by ancient prejudices and made large sacrifices to superstition. We have boasted the protection of Great Britain, without considering, that her motive was *interest* not *attachment*; and that she did not protect us from *our enemies* on *our account*; but from *her enemies* on *her own account*, from those who had no quarrel with us on any *other account*, and who will always be our enemies on the *same account*. Let Britain waive her pretensions to the

Continent, or the Continent throw off the dependence, and we should
be at peace with France and Spain, were they at war with Britain.

• • •

But Britain is the parent country, say some. Then the more shame
upon her conduct. Even brutes do not devour their young, nor savages
make war upon their families; Wherefore, the assertion, if true, turns
to her reproach; but it happens not to be true, or only partly so, and
the phrase *parent* or *mother country* hath been jesuitically adopted by
the King and his parasites, with a low papistical design of gaining
an unfair bias on the credulous weakness of our minds. Europe, and
not England, is the parent country of America. This new World hath
been the asylum for the persecuted lovers of civil and religious liberty from *every part* of Europe. Hither have they fled, not from the
tender embraces of the mother, but from the cruelty of the monster;
and it is so far true of England, that the same tyranny which drove
the first emigrants from home, pursues their descendants still.

• • •

Our plan is commerce, and that, well attended to, will secure us the
peace and friendship of all Europe; because it is the interest of all
Europe to have America a free port. Her trade will always be a protection, and her barrenness of gold and silver secure her from invaders.

I challenge the warmest advocate for reconciliation to show a
single advantage that this continent can reap by being connected
with Great Britain. I repeat the challenge; not a single advantage is
derived. Our corn will fetch its price in any market in Europe, and
our imported goods must be paid for by them where we will.

But the injuries and disadvantages which we sustain by that connection, are without number; and our duty to mankind at large, as
well as to ourselves, instruct us to renounce the alliance: because,
any submission to, or dependence on, Great Britain, tends directly
to involve this Continent in European wars and quarrels, and set us
at variance with nations who would otherwise seek our friendship,
and against whom we have neither anger nor complaint. As Europe is
our market for trade, we ought to form no partial connection with any
part of it. It is the true interest of America to steer clear of European

contentions, which she never can do, while, by her dependence on Britain, she is made the makeweight in the scale of British politics.

• • •

'Tis repugnant to reason, to the universal order of things, to all examples from former ages, to suppose that this Continent can long remain subject to any external power. The most sanguine in Britain doth not think so. The utmost stretch of human wisdom cannot, at this time, compass a plan, short of separation, which can promise the continent even a year's security. Reconciliation is *now* a fallacious dream. Nature hath deserted the connection, and art cannot supply her place. For, as Milton wisely expresses, "never can true reconcilement grow where wounds of deadly hate have pierced so deep."

A government of our own is our natural right: and when a man seriously reflects on the precariousness of human affairs, he will become convinced, that it is infinitely wiser and safer, to form a constitution of our own in a cool deliberate manner, while we have it in our power, than to trust such an interesting event to time and chance.

• • •

O! ye that love mankind! Ye that dare oppose not only the tyranny but the tyrant, stand forth! Every spot of the old world is overrun with oppression. Freedom hath been hunted round the Globe. Asia and Africa have long expelled her. Europe regards her like a stranger, and England hath given her warning to depart. O! receive the fugitive, and prepare in time an asylum for mankind.

Questions

1. Why does Paine begin his argument for independence with an attack on the principle of monarchy and hereditary succession?

2. What passages illustrate Paine's effort to write in language ordinary readers can understand?

32. Samuel Seabury's Argument against Independence (1775)

Source: Samuel Seabury, **An Alarm to the Legislature of the Province of New York** *(New York, 1775), pp. 2–5.*

A native of Connecticut, graduate of Yale College, and Anglican minister, Samuel Seabury was a devoted Loyalist who in 1774 and 1775 published several pamphlets opposing the revolutionary movement. After being briefly jailed for his views, he took refuge in New York City when it was under British occupation during the War of Independence. Unlike many Loyalists, Seabury remained in the United States after the war and became the new nation's first Episcopal bishop.

———

WHEN YOU REFLECT upon the present confused and distressed state of this, and the other colonies, I am persuaded, that you will think no apology necessary for the liberty I have taken, of addressing you on that subject. The unhappy contention we have entered into with our parent state, would inevitably be attended with many disagreeable circumstances, with many and great inconveniences to us, even were it conducted on our part, with propriety and moderation. What then must be the case, when all proper and moderate measures are rejected? When not even the appearance of decency is regarded? When nothing seems to be consulted, but how to perplex, irritate, and affront, the British Ministry, Parliament, Nation and King? When every scheme that tends to peace, is branded with ignominy; as being the machination of slavery! When nothing is called FREEDOM but SEDITION! Nothing LIBERTY but REBELLION!

I will not presume to encroach so far upon your time, as to attempt to point out the causes of our unnatural contention with Great Britain. You are well acquainted with them.—Nor will I attempt to trace out the progress of that infatuation, which hath so deeply, so miserably, infected the Colonies. You must have observed its rise, and noted its rapid growth. But I intreat your patience and candour, while I make some observations on the conduct of the Colonies in general, and of this Colony in particular, in the present dispute with our mother country: By which it will appear, that most, if not all the measures that have been adopted, have been illegal in their beginning, tyrannical in their operation,—and that they must be ineffectual in the event.

It is the happiness of the British Government, and of all the British Colonies, that the people have a right to share in the legislature. This right they exercise by choosing representatives; and thereby constituting one branch of the legislative authority. But when they have chosen their representatives, that right, which was before diffused through the whole people, centers in their Representatives alone; and can legally be exercised by none but them. They become the guardians of the lives, the liberties, the rights and properties, of the people: And as they are under the most sacred obligations to discharge their trust with prudence and fidelity, so the people are under the strongest obligations to treat them with honour and respect; and to look to them for redress of all those grievances that they can justly complain of.

But in the present dispute with Great Britain, the representatives of the people have not only been utterly disregarded, but their dignity has been trampled upon, and their authority contravened. A Committee, chosen in a tumultuous, illegal manner, usurped the most despotic authority over the province. They entered into contracts, compacts, combinations, treaties of alliance, with the other colonies, without any power from the legislature of the province. They agreed with the other Colonies to send Delegates to meet in convention at Philadelphia, to determine upon the rights and liberties of the good people of this province, unsupported by any Law....

The state to which the Grand Congress, and the subordinate Committees, have reduced the colonies, is really deplorable. They have introduced a system of the most oppressive tyranny that can possibly be imagined;—a tyranny, not only over the actions, but over the words, thoughts, and minds, of the good people of this province.

People have been threatened with the vengeance of a mob, for speaking in support of order and good government. Every method has been used to intimidate the printers from publishing any thing, which tended to peace, or seemed in favour of government; while the most detestable libels against the King, the British parliament, and Ministry, have been eagerly read, and extravagantly commended, as the matchless productions of some heaven-born genius, glowing with the pure flame of civil liberty....

Behold, Gentlemen, behold the wretched state to which we are reduced! A foreign power is brought in to govern this province. Laws made at Philadelphia, by factious men from New-England, New-Jersey, Pennsylvania, Maryland, Virginia, and the Carolinas, are imposed upon us by the most imperious menaces. Money is levied upon us without the consent of our representatives: which very money, under color of relieving the poor people of Boston, it is too probable will be employed to raise an army against the King. Mobs and riots are encouraged, in order to force submission to the tyranny of the Congress.

Questions

1. Why does Seabury believe the Continental Congress and local committees are undermining Americans' liberties?

2. How does Seabury differ from advocates of independence in his understanding of freedom?

CHAPTER 6

The Revolution Within

33. Abigail and John Adams on Women and the American Revolution (1776)

Source: *Charles F. Adams, ed.,* Familiar Letters of John Adams and His Wife Abigail Adams during the Revolution *(New York: Hurd and Houghton, 1876), pp. 148–50, 155.*

Abigail Adams was one of the revolutionary era's most important women. During the War of Independence, she peppered her husband, John Adams, with questions about the progress of the struggle, kept him informed of events in Massachusetts, and offered opinions on political matters. When Adams served as president during the 1790s he relied on her advice more than on members of his cabinet. In March 1776, Abigail Adams wrote her best-known letter to her husband. She urged Congress, when it drew up a new "Code of Laws," to "remember the ladies." All men, she warned, "would be tyrants if they could."

At a time when many Americans—slaves, servants, women, Indians, apprentices, propertyless men—were denied full freedom, the struggle against Britain inspired challenges to all sorts of inequalities. As John Adams's reply demonstrates, not all American leaders welcomed this upheaval. To him, it was an affront to the natural order of things. To others, it formed the essence of the American Revolution.

Abigail Adams to John Adams

BRAINTREE [MASS.], MARCH 31, 1776

I wish you would ever write me a letter half as long as I write you, and tell me if you may where your fleet are gone? What sort of defense Virginia can make against our common enemy? Whether it is so situated as to make an able defense? Are not the gentry lords and the common people vassals, are they not like the uncivilized natives Britain represents us to be? I hope their riflemen who have shown themselves very savage and even blood-thirsty, are not a specimen of the generality of the people....

I have sometimes been ready to think that the passion for Liberty cannot be equally strong in the breasts of those who have been accustomed to deprive their fellow creatures of theirs. Of this I am certain, that it is not founded upon that generous and Christian principle of doing to others as we would that others should do unto us....

I feel very differently at the approach of spring to what I did a month ago. We knew not then whether we could plant or sow with safety, whether when we had toiled we could reap the fruits of our own industry, whether we could rest in our own cottages, or whether we should not be driven from the sea coasts to seek shelter in the wilderness. But now we feel as if we might sit under own vine and eat the good of the land.... I think the sun looks brighter, the birds sing more melodiously, and nature puts on a more cheerful countenance. We feel a temporary peace, and the poor fugitives are returning to their deserted habitations.

Though we felicitate ourselves, we sympathize with those who are trembling lest the lot of Boston should be theirs. But they cannot be in similar circumstances unless ... cowardice should take possession of them. They have time and warning given them to see the evil and shun it.

I long to hear that you have declared an independency, and by the way in the new Code of Laws which I suppose it will be necessary for you to make I desire you would Remember the Ladies, and be

more generous and favorable to them than your ancestors. Do not
put such unlimited power into the hands of the husbands. Remember all men would be tyrants if they could. If particular care and
attention is not paid to the Ladies we are determined to foment a
Rebellion, and will not hold ourselves bound by any laws in which
we have no voice, or representation.

That your sex are naturally tyrannical is a truth so thoroughly
established as to admit of no dispute, but such of you as wish to be
happy willingly give up the harsh title of Master for the more tender
and endearing one of Friend. Why then, not put it out of the power of
the vicious and the lawless to use us with cruelty and indignity with
impunity? Men of sense in all ages abhor those customs which treat
us only as the vassals of your sex. Regard us then as beings placed
by providence under your protection and in imitation of the
Supreme Being make use of that power only for our happiness.

John Adams to Abigail Adams

PHILADELPHIA, April 14, 1776

As to Declarations of Independency, be patient.... As to your
extraordinary Code of Laws, I cannot but laugh. We have been told
that our struggle has loosened the bands of government everywhere.
That children and apprentices were disobedient, that schools and colleges were grown turbulent, that Indians slighted their guardians
and Negroes grew insolent to their masters. But your letter was the
first intimation that another tribe more numerous and powerful
than all the rest were grown discontented. This is rather too coarse
a compliment but you are so saucy, I won't blot it out.

Depend on it. We know better than to repeal our masculine
systems. Although they are in full force, you know they are little
more than theory. We dare not exert our power in its full latitude.
We are obligated to go fair, and softly, and in practice you knew
we are the subjects. We have only the names of Masters, and rather
than give this up, which would completely subject us to the despotism of the petticoat, I hope General Washington, and all our brave

heroes, would fight. I am sure every good politician would plot, as long as he would against despotism, empire, monarchy, aristocracy, oligarchy, or ochlocracy [mob rule]. A fine story indeed.

Questions:

1. What do you think Abigail Adams has in mind when she writes of the "unlimited power" husbands exercise over their wives?

2. Why did the struggle for independence "loosen the bands of government everywhere," as John Adams remarks?

34. Jefferson's Bill for Establishing Religious Freedom (1779)

Source: Paul L. Ford, ed., The Works of Thomas Jefferson *(12 vols.: New York, 1904–05), Vol. 2, pp. 438–41.*

A strong advocate of the separation of church and state, Thomas Jefferson drafted a bill to that end in 1779. In Virginia before independence, all persons, regardless of religious persuasion, were taxed to support the Anglican church. The struggle for independence led Baptists, Methodists, and members of nonestablished churches to demand that each religion support itself, without governmental assistance. Jefferson's bill was opposed by a group including Patrick Henry, who favored offering governmental support to a variety of churches. It took until 1786 for Jefferson's measure to become law; at the time he was in Paris, serving as American ambassador to France, and James Madison shepherded it through the legislature.

SECTION I.   Well aware that the opinions and belief of men depend not on their own will, but follow involuntarily the evidence proposed to their minds; that Almighty God hath created the mind free, and manifested his supreme will that free it shall remain by making it altogether insusceptible of restraint; that all attempts to influence it by temporal punishments, or burthens, or by civil incapacitations, tend only to beget habits of hypocrisy and meanness, and are a departure from the plan of the holy author of our religion, who being lord both of body and mind, yet choose not to propagate it by coercions on either, as was in his Almighty power to do, but to exalt it by its influence on reason alone; that the impious presumption of legislature and ruler, civil as well as ecclesiastical, who, being themselves but fallible and uninspired men, have assumed dominion over the faith of others, setting up their own opinions and modes of thinking as the only true and infallible, and as such endeavoring to impose them on others, hath established and maintained false religions over the greatest part of the world and through all time: That to compel a man to furnish contributions of money for the propagation of opinions which he disbelieves and abhors, is sinful and tyrannical; that even the forcing him to support this or that teacher of his own religious persuasion, is depriving him of the comfortable liberty of giving his contributions to the particular pastor whose morals he would make his pattern, and whose powers he feels most persuasive to righteousness; and is withdrawing from the ministry those temporary rewards, which proceeding from an approbation of their personal conduct, are an additional incitement to earnest and unremitting labours for the instruction of mankind; that our civil rights have no dependance on our religious opinions, any more than our opinions in physics or geometry; and therefore the proscribing any citizen as unworthy the public confidence by laying upon him an incapacity of being called to offices of trust or emolument, unless he profess or renounce this or that religious opinion, is depriving him injudiciously of those privileges and advantages to which, in common with his fellow-citizens, he has a natural right; that it tends also to corrupt the principles of that very religion it is meant to encourage, by bribing with a monoploy of worldly honours and emoluments, those who will externally profess and conform to it; that though indeed these are criminals who do not withstand such temptation, yet neither are those innocent who lay the bait in their way; that the opinions of men are not the object of civil government, nor under its jurisdiction; that to suffer the civil magistrate to intrude his powers into the field of opinion and to restrain the profession or propagation of principles on supposition of their ill tendency is a dangerous falacy, which at once destroys all religious liberty, because he being of course judge of that tendency will make his opinions the rule of judgment, and approve or condemn the sentiments of others only as they shall square with or suffer from his own; that it is time enough for the rightful purposes of civil government for its officers to interfere when principles break out into overt acts against peace and good order; and finally, that truth is great and will prevail if left to herself; that she is the proper and sufficient antagonist to error, and has nothing to fear from the conflict unless by human interposition disarmed of her natural weapons, free argument and debate; errors ceasing to be dangerous when it is permitted freely to contradict them.

SECT. II.   We the General Assembly of Virginia do enact that no man shall be compelled to frequent or support any religious worship, place, or ministry whatsoever, nor shall be enforced, restrained, molested, or burthened in his body or goods, or shall otherwise suffer, on account of his religious opinions or belief; but that all men shall be free to profess, and by argument to maintain, their opinions in matters of religion, and that the same shall in no wise diminish, enlarge, or affect their civil capacities.

SECT. III.   And though we well know that this Assembly, elected by the people for their ordinary purposes of legislation only, have no power to restrain the acts of succeeding Assemblies, constituted with powers equal to our own, and that therefore to declare this act to be irrevocable would be of no effect in law; yet we are free to declare, and do declare, that the rights hereby asserted are of the natural rights of mankind, and that if any act shall be hereafter passed to repeal the present or to narrow its operations, such act will be an infringement of natural right.

Questions

1. Why does Jefferson declare that religious freedom is a "natural right"?

2. Does Jefferson seek to weaken or strengthen religion by prohibiting governmental enforcement of religious belief?

━━━━━━━

35. The Right of "Free Suffrage" (1776)

Source: Letter by "Watchman," Maryland Gazette (Annapolis), August 15, 1776.

Among the dramatic changes in American life inspired by the War of Independence was the expansion of the right to vote. As ordinary Americans engaged in public debates, enlisted in state militias, and took part in legal and extralegal committees that enforced the orders of Congress, they demanded an end to property qualifications for voting.

The essay that follows, which appeared in a Maryland newspaper in 1776, illustrates the democratic upsurge that accompanied independence. The writer challenged the decision of the colony's leaders to restrict voting to those with property. The essay also shows how equality—"an equal claim to all the privileges, liberties, and immunities" of citizens, including the right to vote—had become linked to many Americans' understanding of freedom. By the 1780s, with the exceptions of Virginia, Maryland, and New York, a large majority of the adult white male population could meet voting requirements.

━━━━━━━

WHEN DESPOTISM REARED her head, and regal power was straining every nerve to ruin and enslave this country, opposition became expedient, opposition became absolutely necessary. The old government, ever treacherous and oppressive, could not be trusted, [and] the mode of government by convention was therefore instituted. But such mode of government proving extremely imperfect, attended with many inconveniences, and not competent to the exigencies of affairs, and the honorable Congress having recommended that a government be formed, in each colony, under the "authority of the people," of such colony only,... the last convention resolved, that a convention be elected for the express purpose of forming a new government, by the authority of the people only, and enacting and ordering all things for the preservation, safety, and general weal of this colony.

Unfortunately, in the same sitting, they passed a resolve restricting the right of voting, thereby excluding nearly half of the members of this state [from] the enjoyment of their inherent right of free suffrage.... Is it not an insult to common sense to say that a government can be formed by the authority of the people only, when near half of them are excluded from any share in the election of the convention which is to form the government? This inequality of representation, contained in the resolve, cannot be justified on any principle. Every freeman must stand amazed at it. It struck at the grandest right of a freeman.... The ultimate end of all freedom is the enjoyment of a free suffrage. A constitution formed without this important right of free voting being preserved to the people, would be despotic.... For a people governed contrary to their inclination, or by persons to whom they have given no commission for that purpose, are, in the properest sense of the phrase, an *enslaved people*, if ever there was an enslaved people. That a *part* of the people should engross the power of electing legislators for the *whole* community is the grossest injustice that can be imagined....

• • •

Every poor man has a life, a personal liberty, and a right to his earnings, and is in danger of being injured by government in a variety of ways; therefore it is necessary that these people should enjoy the right of voting for representatives, to be protectors of their lives, personal liberty, and their little property which, though small, is yet, upon the whole, a very great object to them. It would be unjust and oppressive in the extreme to shut out the poor in having a share in declaring who shall be the lawmakers of their country, and yet bear a very heavy share in the support of government. Would not the rich complain grievously if they had no power of electing representatives?... Every member of this state, who lends his aid to the support of it, has an equal claim to all the privileges, liberties, and immunities with every [one] of his fellow countrymen; circumstances which are essential to the existence of a free state, and inseparable from the exercise and operation of a free people.... No power in the state can legally diminish this *equal right*, either by reducing the number of those privileges to which the whole community is justly entitled, or by imparting to men, or particular societies of men, such degrees of power and privilege that shall, in fact, render the other members less free or more subservient to the purposes of others, than the equal right of freedom can allow. If these be not the innate rights and privileges of the people, they are *not* free....

Let, therefore, all hateful distinctions cease, and elections [be] made open and by the free suffrage of the people stand good and valid.... And let a government be established, where equal liberty can be enjoyed, the interest of the people promoted, and the cause of America maintained.

Questions

1. How does the writer define freedom and slavery?

2. What are his arguments for allowing men without property to vote?

———

36. Noah Webster on Equality (1787)

Source: Noah Webster, An Examination into the Leading Principles of the Federal Constitution *(Philadelphia, 1787), pp. 46–47.*

Americans of the revolutionary generation were preoccupied with the social conditions of freedom. Could a republic survive with a sizable dependent class of citizens? In the excerpt that follows, from a pamphlet published in 1787, the educator and political writer Noah Webster identified equality as essential for the stability of republican government. Citing and amending the teachings of the French political theorist Montesquieu, Webster proclaimed, "A general and tolerably equal distribution of landed property is the whole basis of national freedom." "Equality," he added, was "the very soul of a republic."

To most free Americans, "equality" meant equal opportunity, rather than equality of condition. Many leaders of the Revolution nevertheless assumed that in the exceptional circumstances of the New World, with its vast areas of available land and large population of independent farmers and artisans, the natural workings of society would enable all free Americans to acquire land and achieve, if not complete equality, at least the economic independence necessary for political "virtue."

IN AMERICA, WE begin our empire with more popular privileges than the Romans ever enjoyed. We have not to struggle against a monarch or an aristocracy—power is lodged in the mass of the people.

On reviewing the English history, we observe a progress similar to that in Rome—an incessant struggle for liberty from the date of Magna Charta, in John's reign, to the revolution. The struggle has been successful, by abridging the enormous power of the nobility. But we observe that the power of the people has increased in an exact proportion to their acquisitions of property. Wherever the right of primogeniture is established, property must accumulate and remain in families. Thus the landed property in England will never be sufficiently distributed, to give the powers of government wholly into the hands of the people. But to assist the struggle for liberty, commerce has interposed, and in conjunction with manufacturers, thrown a vast weight of property into the democratic scale. Wherever we cast our eyes, we see this truth, that *property* is the basis of *power;* and this, being established as a cardinal point, directs us to the means of preserving our freedom. Make laws, irrevocable laws in every state, destroying and barring entailments; leave real estates to revolve from hand to hand, as time and accident may direct; and no family influence can be acquired and established for a series of generations—no man can obtain dominion over a large territory— the laborious and saving, who are generally the best citizens, will possess each his share of property and power, and thus the balance of wealth and power will continue where it is, in the *body of the people.*

A general and tolerably equal distribution of landed property is the whole basis of national freedom: The system of the great Montesquieu will ever be erroneous, till the words *property or lands in fee simple* are substituted for *virtue,* throughout his *Spirit of Laws.*

Virtue, patriotism, or love of country, never was and never will be, till mens' natures are changed, a fixed, permanent principle and support of government. But in an agricultural country, a general possession of land in fee simple, may be rendered perpetual, and the inequalities introduced by commerce, are too fluctuating to endanger government. An equality of property, with a necessity of alienation, constantly operating to destroy combinations of powerful families, is the very *soul of a republic*—While this continues, the people will inevitably possess both *power* and *freedom;* when this is lost, power departs, liberty expires, and a commonwealth will inevitably assume some other form.

The liberty of the press, trial by jury, the Habeas Corpus writ, even Magna Charta itself, although justly deemed the palladia of freedom, are all inferior considerations, when compared with a general distribution of real property among every class of people. The power of entailing estates is more dangerous to liberty and republican government, than all the constitutions that can be written on paper, or even than a standing army. Let the people have property, and they *will* have power—a power that will for ever be exerted to prevent a restriction of the press, and abolition of trial by jury, or the abridgement of any other privilege. The liberties of America, therefore, and her forms of government, stand on the broadest basis. Removed from the fears of a foreign invasion and conquest, they are not exposed to the convulsions that shake other governments;

and the principles of freedom are so general and energetic, as to exclude the possibility of a change in our republican constitutions.

Questions

1. Why does Webster consider an equal distribution of landed property more important to freedom than liberty of the press, trial by jury, and other rights?

2. Why does Webster believe the republican institutions of the United States will survive indefinitely?

---

37. Liberating Indentured Servants (1784)

Source: New York Independent Journal, *January 24, 1784.*

The upsurge of demands for equality during the Revolution brought into question many forms of inequality. In 1784, a group of "respectable" New Yorkers proposed to "liberate" a newly arrived shipload of indentured servants on the grounds that their status was "contrary to ... the idea of liberty this country has so happily established." The incident was one small contribution to the rapid decline of indentured servitude, which by 1800 had all but disappeared from the United States. This development sharpened the distinction between freedom and slavery, and between a northern economy relying on what would come to be called "free labor" (that is, working for wages or owning a farm or shop) and a South ever more heavily dependent on the labor of slaves.

WHEREAS THE TRAFFIC of *White people*, heretofore countenanced by this State while under the arbitrary control of the British Government, is contrary to the feelings of a number of respectable Citizens, and to the idea of *liberty* this country has so happily established.

And whereas it is necessary to encourage emigration to this country, upon the most liberal plan, and for that purpose, a number of Citizens of this State, have proposed to *liberate* a cargo of Servants just arrived, by paying their passage, and repaying themselves by a small rateable deduction out of the wages of such Servants, Such of the Citizens of this State as wish to encourage so laudable an undertaking, and if necessary, to petition the Legislature for a completion of their humane intentions, are requested to meet at the Hyderally Tavern, the lower end of King Street, *this Evening*, at Six of the Clock.

Questions

1. What practical reason does the notice give for eliminating indentured servitude?

2. Why do you think the notice singles out the sale of "White people" as contrary to liberty?

38. Letter of Phillis Wheatley (1774)

Source: **Connecticut Gazette; and the Universal Intelligencer,** *March 11, 1774*

The revolutionary generation's emphasis on liberty inevitably raised questions about the future of slavery in the new republic. Many slaves saw the struggle for independence as an opportunity to assert their own claims to freedom. This letter to the Rev. Samson Occom, a Native American poet and Presbyterian minister, from the celebrated black poet Phillis Wheatley of Massachusetts, who would not gain her own freedom until 1778, is an early antislavery statement pointing to the contradiction between the revolutionary language of liberty and the continued reality of slavery. But the stark fact is that slavery survived the Revolution and continued to grow. The first national census, in 1790, revealed that despite the many who had become free through state laws, voluntary manumission, and escape, there were 700,000 slaves in the United states—200,000 more than in 1776.

Rev'd and honor'd Sir,

I have this Day received your obliging kind epistle, and am greatly satisfied with your reasons respecting the Negroes, and think highly reasonable what you offer in vindication of their natural rights: Those that invade them cannot be insensible that the divine light is chasing away the thick darkness which broods over the land of Africa; and the chaos which has reign'd so long, is converting into beautiful order, and reveals more and more clearly, the glorious dispensation of civil and religious Liberty, which are so inseparably limited, that there is little or no enjoyment of one without the other.

Otherwise, perhaps, the Israelites had been less solicitous for their freedom from Egyptian slavery; I do not say they would have been contented without it, by no means, for in every human breast, God has implanted a principle, which we call love of freedom; it is impatient of oppression, and pants for deliverance; and by the leave of our modern Egyptians I will assert, that the same principle lives in us. God grant deliverance in his own way and time, and get him honour upon all those whose avarice impels them to countenance and help forward the calamities of their fellow creatures.

This I desire not for their hurt, but to convince them of the strange absurdity of their conduct whose words and actions are so diametrically, opposite. How well the cry for liberty, and the reverse disposition for the exercise of oppressive power over others agree,—I humbly think it does not require the penetration of a philosopher to determine.

Questions

1. What does Wheatley mean by the "absurdity" of Americans' conduct?

2. How does she use the language of the white revolutionaries to argue for an end to slavery?

39. Benjamin Rush, Thoughts upon Female Education (1787)

Source: The Universal Asylum *and* The Columbian Magazine, *April, 1790, pp. 209–13, May, 1790, 288–92.*

A leader of the struggle for independence in Pennsylvania and a signer of the Declaration of Independence, Benjamin Rush was also a physician and a leading reformer, an advocate of the abolition of slavery and capital punishment, and a proponent of public education. In 1787, in a speech to the Board of Visitors of the Young Ladies Academy of Philadelphia, Rush explained why conditions of life in the United States and the republican form of government established by the Revolution made it imperative to extend educational opportunities to American women. Rush was hardly a believer in full equality for women. Their political role, he believed, was to train their sons in "the principles of liberty" so that they could act as virtuous citizens. But he also noted that many economic opportunities were open to American women that did not exist in Europe and that to take advantage of them, women needed greater access to education than they had enjoyed in the past. Rush's lecture illustrates how the struggle for independence threw into question many long-standing assumptions about how society should be organized.

THE EDUCATION OF young ladies, in this country, should be conducted upon principles very different from what it is in Great Britain, and in some respects different from what it was when we were part of a monarchical empire.

There are several circumstances in the situation, employments, and duties of women, in America, which require a peculiar mode of education.

I. The early marriages of our women, by contracting the time allowed for education, render it necessary to contract its plan, and to confine it chiefly to the more useful branches of literature.

II. The state of property, in America, renders it necessary for the greatest part of our citizens to employ themselves, in different occupations, for the advancement of their fortunes. This cannot be done without the assistance of the female members of the community. They must be the stewards, and guardians of their husbands' property. That education, therefore, will be most proper for our women, which teaches them to discharge the duties of those offices with the most success and reputation.

III. ... A principal share of the instruction of children naturally devolves upon the women. It becomes us therefore to prepare them by a suitable education, for the discharge of this most important duty of mothers.

IV. The equal share that every citizen has in the liberty, and the possible share he may have in the government, of our country, make it necessary that our ladies should be qualified to a certain degree by a peculiar and suitable education, to concur in instructing their sons in the principles of liberty and government....

The branches of literature most essential for a young lady, in this country, appear to be,

I. A knowledge of the English language. She should not only read, but speak and spell it correctly. The usual mode of teaching English syntax by means of rules committed to memory, appears to be as absurd as to teach a child to walk, by instructing it in the names and powers of the muscles which move the lower extremities.... Familiar conversations are alone proper for this purpose....

II. Pleasure and interest conspire to make the writing of a fair and legible hand, a necessary branch of female education....

III. Some knowledge of figures and book-keeping is absolutely necessary to qualify a young lady for the duties which await her in this country....

IV. An acquaintance with geography and some instruction in chronology will enable a young lady to read history, biography, and travels, with advantage; and thereby qualify her not only for a general intercourse with the world, but, to be an agreeable companion for a sensible man. To these branches of knowledge may be added, in some instances, a general acquaintance with the ... principles of chemistry, and natural philosophy, particularly with such parts of them as are applicable to domestic and culinary purposes.

V. Vocal music should never be neglected, in the education of a young lady, in this country. Besides preparing her to join in that part of public worship which consists in psalmody, it will enable her to soothe the cares of domestic life.

VI. Dancing is by no means an improper branch of education for an American lady. It promotes health and renders the figure and motions of the body easy and agreeable. I anticipate the time when the resources of conversation shall be so far multiplied, that the amusement of dancing shall be wholly confined to children. But in our present state of society and knowledge, I conceive it to be an agreeable substitute for the ignoble pleasures of drinking, and gaming, in our assemblies of grown people.

VII. The attention of our young ladies should be directed, as soon as they are prepared for it, to the reading of history-travels-poetry and moral essays ... they subdue that passion for reading novels, which so generally prevails among the fair sex.... They (novels) hold up life, it is true, but it is not as yet life, in America. Our passions have not as yet 'overstepped the modesty of nature.' ...

Let, therefore, all the branches of education which have been mentioned be connected with regular instruction in the Christian religion.... The female breast is the natural soil of Christianity....

Questions

1. What role does Rush foresee for women in the new American republic?

2. What benefits does he anticipate for society and the family from extending educational opportunities to women?

CHAPTER 7

Founding a Nation, 1783–1791

40. Petition of Inhabitants West of the Ohio River (1785)

Source: Petition, signed by sixty persons, April 11, 1785, in Archer B. Hulbert, ed., Ohio in the Time of the Confederation *(Marietta, 1918), pp. 103–06.*

After independence, American leaders believed that the republic's economic health required that farmers have access to land in the West. But they also saw land sales as a potential source of revenue and worried that unregulated settlement would produce endless conflicts with the Indians. Land companies, which lobbied Congress vigorously, hoped to profit by purchasing real estate and reselling it to settlers. The government, they insisted, should step aside and allow private groups to take control of the West's economic development.

The arrival of peace triggered a large population movement from settled parts of the original states into frontier areas like upstate New York and across the Appalachians into Kentucky, Tennessee, and Ohio. In 1785, a group of Ohioans who had suffered severely during the War of Independence petitioned Congress, assailing landlords and speculators who monopolized available acreage and asking that preference in access to "vacant lands" be given to "actual settlements." They proclaimed, "Grant us liberty."

———

To the honorable the President of the Honorable Congress of the United States of America.

The petition, of us the subscribers now residing on the western side of the Ohio, humbly show our grateful acknowledgments to those patriots of our country who under Divine Providence so wisely directed and steered the helm of government in that great and unparalleled conflict for liberty, bringing to a happy period the troubles of the states, laying the foundation . . . of the most glorious form of government any people on earth could ever yet boast of.

• • •

Notwithstanding when the joyful sound of peace had reached our ears, we had scarce enough left us to support the crying distresses of our families occasioned wholly by being exposed to the ravages of a cruel and savage enemy, on an open frontier where the most of us had the misfortune to reside through the whole continuance of the war, where the only recourse was to sit confined in forts for the preservation of our lives, by which we were reduced almost to the lowest ebb of poverty, the greatest part of us having no property in lands, our stocks reduced almost to nothing, our case seemed desperate.

But viewing as it appeared to us an advantage offering of vacant lands which the alarming necessities we were under joined with the future prospect of bettering our circumstances, invited us to enter on those lands fully determined to comply with every requisition of the legislature. . . . With hopes of future happiness we sat content in the enjoyment of our scanty morsel, thinking ourself safe under the protection of government, when on the fifth of this instant we were visited by a command of men sent by the commandant at Fort McIntosh, with orders from government . . . to dispossess us and to destroy our dwellings . . . by which order it now appears our conduct in settling here is considered by the legislature to be prejudicial to the common good, of which we had not the least conception until now. We are greatly distressed in our present circumstances, and humbly pray if you in your wisdom think proper to grant us liberty, to rest where we are and to grant us the preference to our actual settlements when the land is to be settled by order of the government.

• • •

Questions

1. Who do the authors of the petition consider to be the greatest enemies of their liberty?

2. Who do the authors claim ought to have preference when western land is distributed?

---

41. David Ramsey, American Innovations in Government (1789)

Source: David Ramsey, **The History of the American Revolution** *(2 vols.: Philadelphia, 1789), pp. 355–57.*

A member of the Continental Congress from South Carolina, David Ramsey published his history of the Revolution in the year the Constitution was ratified. In this excerpt, he lauds the principles of representative government, and the right of future amendment, embodied in the state constitutions and adopted in the national one, as unique American political principles and the best ways of securing liberty. Like many Americans of his era, Ramsey insisted that the political system of the United States was fundamentally different from that of Europe, and offered an opportunity to demonstrate to the rest of the world humankind's capacity for self-government.

THE FAMED SOCIAL compact between the people and their rulers, did not apply to the United States. The sovereignty was in the people. In their sovereign capacity by their representatives, they agreed on forms of government for their own security, and deputed certain individuals as their agents to serve them in public stations agreeably to constitutions, which prescribed their conduct.

The world has not hitherto exhibited so fair an opportunity for promoting social happiness. It is hoped for the honor of human nature, that the result will prove the fallacy of those theories that mankind are incapable of self government. The ancients, not knowing the doctrine of representation, were apt in their public meetings to run into confusion, but in America this mode of taking the sense of the people, is so well understood, and so completely reduced to system, that its most populous states are often peaceably convened in an assembly of deputies, not too large for orderly deliberation, and yet representing the whole in equal proportion. These popular branches of legislature are miniature pictures of the community, and from their mode of election are likely to be influenced by the same interests and feelings with the people whom they represent.... These circumstances give us as great a security that laws will be made, and government administered for the good of the people, as can be expected from the imperfection of human institutions.

In this view of the formation and establishment of the American constitutions, we behold our species in a new situation. In no age before, and in no other country, did man ever possess an election of the kind of government, under which he would choose to live. The constituent parts of the ancient free governments were thrown together by accident. The freedom of modern European governments was, for the most part, obtained by concessions, or liberality of monarchs, or military leaders. In America alone, reason and liberty concurred in the formation of constitutions.... In one thing they were all perfect. They left the people in the power of altering and amending them, whenever they pleased. In this happy peculiarity they placed the science of politics on a footing with the other sciences, by opening it to improvements from experience, and the discoveries of future ages. By means of this power of amending American constitutions, the friends of mankind have fondly hoped that oppression will one day be no more.

Questions

1. In what ways, according to Ramsey, does the formation of governments in the United States differ from precedents in other times and places?

2. Why does Ramsey feel that the power to amend the Constitution is so important a political innovation?

42. Patrick Henry's Anti-Federalist Argument (1788)

Source: Patrick Henry: "Anti-Federalist Argument" from The Complete Anti-Federalist, *Volume 1, pp. 285–90, edited by Herbert J. Storing. Copyright © The University of Chicago Press. Reprinted by permission of The University of Chicago Press.*

Opponents of the ratification of the Constitution, called Anti-Federalists, insisted that the document shifted the balance between liberty and power too far in the direction of the latter. They predicted that the new government would fall under the sway of wealthy Americans hostile to the liberties of ordinary folk. Popular self-government, they claimed, flourished best in small communities, where rulers and ruled interacted daily.

Among the leaders of the movement for independence who opposed ratification of the Constitution, few were as eloquent as Patrick Henry. In June 1788 he unsuccessfully implored the Virginia convention called to consider ratification to reject the document, arguing that it would create a "consolidated" national government that would suppress Americans' liberties and completely overshadow the governments of the states.

An OPINION HAS gone forth, we find, that we are a contemptible people: The time has been when we were thought otherwise: Under this same despised Government, we commanded the respect of all Europe: Wherefore are we now reckoned otherwise? The American spirit has fled from hence: It has gone to regions, where it has never been expected: It has gone to the people of France in search of a splendid Government—a strong energetic Government. Shall we imitate the example of those nations who have gone from a simple to a splendid Government? Are those nations more worthy of our imitation? What can make an adequate satisfaction to them for the loss they suffered in attaining such a Government for the loss of their liberty? If we admit this Consolidated Government it will be because we like a great splendid one. Some way or other we must be a great and mighty empire; we must have an army, and a navy, and a number of things: When the American spirit was in its youth, the language of America was different: Liberty, Sir, was then the primary object. We are descended from a people whose Government was founded on liberty: Our glorious forefathers of Great-Britain, made liberty the foundation of every thing. That country is become a great, mighty, and splendid nation; not because their Government is strong and energetic; but, Sir, because liberty is its direct end and foundation: We drew the spirit of liberty from our British ancestors; by that spirit we have triumphed over every difficulty.

But now, Sir, the American spirit, assisted by the ropes and chains of consolidation, is about to convert this country to a powerful and mighty empire: If you make the citizens of this country agree to become the subjects of one great consolidated empire of America, your Government will not have sufficient energy to keep them together: Such a Government is incompatible with the genius of republicanism: There will be no checks, no real balances, in this Government: What can avail your specious imaginary balances, your rope-dancing, chain-rattling, ridiculous ideal checks and contrivances? But, Sir, we are not feared by foreigners: we do not make nations tremble: Would this, Sir, constitute happiness, or secure liberty? I trust, Sir, our political hemisphere will ever direct their operations to the security of those objects. Consider our situation, Sir: Go to the poor man, ask him what he does; he will inform you, that he enjoys the fruits of his labour, under his own fig-tree, with his wife and children around him, in peace and security. Go to every other member of the society, you will find the same tranquil ease and content; you will find no alarms or disturbances: Why then tell us of dangers to terrify us into an adoption of this new Government? and yet who knows the dangers that this new system may produce; they are out of the sight of the common people: They cannot foresee latent consequences: I dread the operation of it on the middling and lower class of people: It is for them I fear the adoption of this system.

We are told that this Government collectively taken, is without an example—That it is national in this part, and federal in that part, &c. We may be amused if we please, by a treatise of political anatomy. In the brain it is national: The stamina are federal—some limbs are federal—others national. The Senators are voted for by the State Legislatures, so far it is federal.—Individuals choose the members of the first branch; here it is national. It is federal in conferring general powers; but national in retaining them. It is not to be supported by the States—The pockets of individuals are to be searched for its maintenance. What signifies it to me, that you have the most curious anatomical description of it in its creation? To all the common purposes of Legislation it is a great consolidation of Government. You are not to have a right to legislate in any but trivial cases: You are not to touch private contracts: You are not to have the right of having arms in your own defence: You cannot be trusted with dealing out justice between man and man. What shall the States have to do? Take care of the poor—repair and make highways—erect bridges, and so on, and so on. Abolish the State Legislatures at once. What purposes should they be continued for? Our Legislature will indeed be a ludicrous spectacle—180 men marching in solemn farcical procession, exhibiting a mournful proof of the lost liberty of their country—without the power of restoring it. But, Sir, we have the consolation that it is a mixed Government: That is, it may work sorely on your neck; but you will have some comfort by saying, that it was a Federal Government in its origin.

I beg Gentlemen to consider—lay aside your prejudices—Is this a Federal Government? Is it not a Consolidated Government for every purpose almost? Is the Government of Virginia a State Government after this Government is adopted? I grant that it is a Republican

Government—but for what purposes? For such trivial domestic considerations, as render it unworthy the name of a Legislature.

The State Governments, says he, will possess greater advantages than the General Government, and will consequently prevail. His opinion and mine are diametrically opposite. Bring forth the Federal allurements, and compare them with the poor contemptible things that the State Legislatures can bring forth. On the part of the State Legislatures, there are Justices of Peace and militia officers—And even these Justices and officers, are bound by oath in favour of the Constitution. A constable is the only man who is not obliged to swear paramount allegiance to this beloved Congress. On the other hand, there are rich, fat Federal emoluments—your rich, snug, fine, fat Federal offices—The number of collectors of taxes and excises will outnumber any thing from the States. Who can cope with the excisemen and taxmen? There are none in this country, that can cope with this class of men alone. But, Sir, is this the only danger? Would to Heaven that it were. If we are to ask which will last the longest—the State or the General Government, you must take an army and a navy into the account. Lay these things together, and add to the enumeration the superior abilities of those who manage the General Government. Can then the State Governments look it in the face? You dare not look it in the face now, when it is but an *embryo*. The influence of this Government will be such, that you never can get amendments; for if you propose alterations, you will affront them. Let the Honorable Gentleman consider all these things and say, whether the State Governments will last as long as the Federal Government.

Questions

1. What are Henry's most important objections to the new Constitution?

2. Why does Henry feel that a "consolidated" government is a danger to liberty?

43. A July Fourth Oration (1800)

Source: American Mercury *(Hartford, Conn.), July 10, 1800.*

From the earliest days of the new nation, July Fourth became a day of public commemoration. In 1800, a speaker whose name was not reported in
the press delivered an Independence Day oration at Hartford, Connecticut.
He celebrated the "universal principles" of the Declaration of Independence but chastised his fellow citizens for failing to live up to them fully.
Like many other Americans, he rejoiced in the revolutions that, beginning in France, had swept parts of Europe, predicted further progress for
the rights of man in years to come, and identified the American example
as the catalyst for the spread of freedom overseas.

On the other hand, the speaker condemned slavery as a flagrant violation of American values and a source of shame for the nation, asking point-
edly, "Declaration of Independence! Where art thou now?" He went on to
urge that "our daughters" ought to enjoy the same rights as "our sons," an
idea that had been put forth by a few writers in the 1790s but was quite
unusual for the time. Overall, the speech offered both an illustration of
American nationalism in the aftermath of the Revolution and a telling
commentary on the extent and limits of American freedom at the dawn
of the nineteenth century.

* * *

TO THE PRINCIPLES, the genuine, universal principles of the Declaration of Independence, we consecrate this day. Our festivity is
not on account of the achievements of armies, nor merely because
the seat of government is removed from London to Philadelphia, but
because the American people have calmly and deliberately declared,
that "all men are created equal," and in the presence of the supreme
God have, in support of this declaration, pledged their lives, their
fortunes, and their sacred honor.

* * *

Whatever may be the future fate of America, she has destroyed the
Bastille, she has liberated Belgium, her principles have scaled the Alps,

and inundated the plains of Italy, they have climbed the walls of
Rome.... [Before] long Ireland shall take her harp ... and shake the air
with notes of liberty. Greece shall wake from her long slumber, some
new Demosthenes shall plead the Rights of Man, while new Homers
sing the triumphs of the free.... The Spanish monarchy totters at its
base, exhausted by frequent wars, impoverished by a profligate administration. Farther degrees of colonial oppression will be the [attempted
cure].... Then will the inward burnings of colonial rage burst into a
flame, then will the Rights of Man echo from Florida to Chile, and re-
echo from Lima to St. Salvador. The principles of freedom will then be
learned from those who now wield the scourge of slavery, the benevolent system of Jesus shall resound from the ruins of the ... Inquisition.

• • •

And thou, sable Ethiop! Suffering brother, let the principles of
this day irradiate thy benighted countenance! Already has the voice
of thy tears and blood reached heaven! ... St. Domingo [has] seen thy
race revenged, and their chains broken on the tyrants' heads.

• • •

Citizens, my soul shrinks from herself, and startles at the name
of Africa! Where we have heaped crime upon crime! Where we have
excited murders, robberies, and burnings, that we might punish them
in our own land with endless, hopeless slavery.... Declaration of
Independence! Where art thou now?

• • •

It is pleasing to turn from the contemplation of our inconsisten-
cies, to the purity of our principles. The basis of the Declaration,
from which the friend of his species hopes so much, is the Equality
of Man. How the idea first got abroad, that men were not equal, is
difficult to conceive, unless we refer the claim to the arrogance of
power in the dark ages of the world.... The Equality of Man is the
bond of our union and the constituted law of the land.

• • •

Citizens, you must teach your children the principles of this day,
and by the best education in your power to bestow, teach them to

understand them. . . . But citizens, in this, as in all other things, if you do not begin well, you will never end well. Those principles of freedom, which embrace only half mankind, are only half systems, and will no more support the burden of humanity, than [a] section of an arch will support a column. Our daughters are the same relations to us as our sons, we owe them the same duties, they . . . are equally competent to their attainments. The contrary idea originated in the same abuse of power, as monarchy and slavery, and owes its little remaining support to the same sophistry.

• • •

What is liberty? Is it a something that men may keep without care and lose without injury? No citizens. Liberty is a tender plant, which wants the constant vigilance of its owner—he must weed and water, and defend it *himself*; hirelings may destroy it by carelessness, by accident, or by design, and once it withers, it is difficult to be restored.

The habits of men who have been [raised] under a monarchy ill comport with the simplicity of republicanism. It is not enough that we have a republican form of government, we must acquire a *republican mind*. We must be frugal, sober, industrious, self-dependent, privately and publicly hospitable. . . . We must eradicate national prejudices. . . . We must always remember that *men*, and not soil, constitute the state.

Questions

1. How does the speaker seek to persuade his audience of the evils of slavery?

2. What does the speaker identify as the major reasons to celebrate American independence?

44. Thomas Jefferson on Race and Slavery (1781)

Source: Thomas Jefferson, Notes on the State of Virginia *(Philadelphia, 1788), pp. 145–53, 172–73.*

No American of the revolutionary generation did more to shape prevailing views on race than Thomas Jefferson. His writings reflected a divided, even tortured mind. In *Notes on the State of Virginia*, written in 1781 and published a few years later, Jefferson ruminated on whether blacks should be considered inferior to whites. Although generally, Jefferson attributed different peoples' varying degrees of civilization to environmental factors, he concluded that what he considered blacks' inferiority was innate. Jefferson made clear that he understood that slavery violated the principles of the Declaration of Independence he had written. He looked forward to the day when slaves would be emancipated. But, he insisted, once freed, they must be removed from the United States. Blacks, in Jefferson's view, could never become equal members of the American nation.

MANY OF THE laws which were in force during the monarchy being relative merely to that form of government, or inculcating principles inconsistent with republicanism, the first assembly which met after the establishment of the commonwealth appointed a committee to revise the whole code.... The following are the most remarkable alterations proposed....

To emancipate all slaves born after passing the act. The bill reported by the revisors does not itself contain this proposition; but an amendment containing it was prepared, to be offered the legislature whenever the bill should be taken up, and further directing, that they should continue with their parents to a certain age, then be brought up, at the public expence, to tillage, arts or sciences, according to their geniusses, till the females should be eighteen, and the males twenty-one years of age, when they should be colonized to such place as the circumstances of the time should render most proper, sending them out with arms, implements of household and of the handicraft arts, seeds, pairs of the useful domestic animals, &c. to declare them a free and independant people, and extend to them our alliance and protection, till they have acquired strength; and to send vessels to the other parts of the world for an equal number of white inhabitants; to induce whom to migrate hither, proper encouragements were to be proposed. It will probably be asked, Why not retain and incorporate the blacks into the state, and thus save the expence of supplying, by importation of white settlers, the vacancies they will leave? Deep rooted prejudices entertained by the whites; ten thousand recollections, by the blacks, of the injuries they have sustained; new provocations; the real distinctions which nature has made; and many other circumstances, will divide us into parties, and produce convulsions which will probably never end but in the extermination of one or the other race.

• • •

—To these objections, which are political, may be added others, which are physical and moral. The first difference which strikes us is that of colour. Whether the black of the negro resides in the reticular membrane between the skin and scarf-skin, or in the scarf-skin itself; whether it proceeds from the colour of the blood, the colour of the bile, or from that of some other secretion, the difference is fixed in nature, and is as real as if its seat and cause were better known to us. And is this difference of no importance? Is it not the foundation of a greater or less share of beauty in the two races? Are not the fine mixtures of red and white, the expressions of every passion by greater or less suffusions of colour in the one, preferable to that eternal monotony, which reigns in the countenances, that immoveable veil of black which covers all the emotions of the other race? . . .

They seem to require less sleep. A black after hard labour through the day, will be induced by the slightest amusements to sit up till midnight, or later though knowing he must be out with the first dawn of the morning. They are at least as brave, and more adventuresome. But this may perhaps proceed from a want of forethought, which prevents their seeing a danger till it be present. When present, they do not go through it with more coolness or steadiness than the whites. They are more ardent after their female: but love seems with them to be more an eager desire, than a tender delicate mixture of sentiment and sensation. Their griefs are transient. Those numberless afflictions, which render it doubtful whether heaven has given life to us in mercy or in wrath, are less felt, and sooner forgotten with them. In general, their existence appears to participate more of sensation than reflection....

—The opinion, that they are inferior in the faculties of reason and imagination, must be hazarded with great diffidence. To justify a general conclusion, requires many observations, even where the subject may be submitted to the anatomical knife, to optical glasses, to analysis by fire, or by solvents. How much more then where it is a faculty, not a substance, we are examining; where it eludes the research of all the senses; where the conditions of its existence are various and variously combined; where the effects of those which are present or absent bid defiance to calculation; let me add too, as a circumstance of great tenderness, where our conclusion would degrade a whole race of men from the rank in the scale of beings which their Creator may perhaps have given them.... I advance it therefore as a suspicion only, that the blacks, whether originally a distinct race, or made distinct by time and circumstances, are inferior to the whites in the endowments both of body and mind....

There must doubtless be an unhappy influence on the manners of our people produced by the existence of slavery among us. The whole commerce between master and slave is a perpetual exercise of the most boisterous passions, the most unremitting despotism on the one part, and degrading submissions on the other. Our children see this, and learn to imitate it; for man is an imitative animal. This quality is the germ of all education in him. From his cradle to his grave he is learning to do what he sees others do. If a parent could find no motive either in his philanthropy or his self-love, for restraining the intemperance of passion towards his slave, it would always be a sufficient one that his child is present. But generally it is not sufficient. The parent storms, the child looks on, catches the lineaments of wrath, puts on the same airs in the circle of smaller slaves, gives a loose to his worst of passions, and thus nursed, educated, and daily exercised in tyranny, cannot but be stamped by it with odious peculiarities. The man must be a prodigy who can retain his manners and morals undepraved by such circumstances. And with what execration should the statesman be loaded, who permitting one half the citizens thus to trample on the rights of the other, transforms those into despots, and these into enemies, destroys the morals of the one part, and the amor patriae of the other. For if a slave can have a country in this world, it must be any other in preference to that in which he is born to live and labour for another: in which he must lock up the faculties of his nature, contribute as far as depends on his individual endeavours to the evanishment of the human race, or entail his own miserable condition on the endless generations proceeding from him. With the morals of the people, their industry also is destroyed. For in a warm climate, no man will labour for himself who can make another labour for him. This is so true, that of the proprietors of slaves a very small proportion indeed are ever seen to labour. And can the liberties of a nation be thought secure when we have removed their only firm basis, a conviction in the minds of the people that these liberties are of the gift of God? That they are not to be violated but with his wrath? Indeed I tremble for my country when I reflect that God is just: that his justice cannot sleep for ever.

Questions

1. What reasons does Jefferson offer for colonizing blacks outside the United States in the event of emancipation?

2. How does Jefferson describe the effect of slavery on the morals and behavior of white Virginians?

45. J. Hector St. John de Crèvecoeur, "What, Then, Is the American?" (1782)

Source: J. Hector St. John de Crèvecoeur, Letters from an American Farmer *(London, 1782), pp. 48–56.*

In the era of the Revolution, many foreigners celebrated the United States as not only an independent nation, but a new society in which individuals could enjoy opportunities unknown in the Old World and where a new nationality was being forged from the diverse populations of Europe. No one promoted this image of America more enthusiastically than J. Hector St. John de Crèvecoeur, who had settled in New York and married the daughter of a prominent landowner after serving in the French army during the Seven Years' War. He later returned to France and published a glowing account of life in the United States, entitled *Letters from an American Farmer.* As one who had lived in both Europe and the United States, he outlined the differences a newcomer was likely to note between the two societies. His description of the emergence of a "new man" from the diverse populations of Europe would later be popularized as the idea of the American melting pot.

I wish I could be acquainted with the feelings and thoughts which must agitate the heart and present themselves to the mind of an enlightened Englishman, when he first lands on this continent. He must greatly rejoice that he lived at a time to see this fair country discovered and settled; he must necessarily feel a share of national pride, when he views the chain of settlements which embellishes these extended shores. When he says to himself, this is the work of my countrymen, who, when convulsed by factions, afflicted by a variety of miseries and wants, restless and impatient, took refuge here. They brought along with them their national genius, to which they principally owe what liberty they enjoy, and what substance they possess.

Here he sees the industry of his native country displayed in a new manner, and traces in their works the embryos of all the arts, sciences, and ingenuity which flourish in Europe. Here he beholds fair cities, substantial villages, extensive fields, an immense country filled with decent houses, good roads, orchards, meadows, and bridges, where an hundred years ago all was wild, woody and uncultivated!... He is arrived on a new continent; a modern society offers itself to his contemplation, different from what he had hitherto seen. It is not composed, as in Europe, of great lords who possess every thing and of a herd of people who have nothing. Here are no aristocratical families, no courts, no kings, no bishops, no ecclesiastical dominion, no invisible power giving to a few a very visible one; no great manufacturers employing thousands, no great refinements of luxury. The rich and the poor are not so far removed from each other as they are in Europe. Some few towns excepted, we are all tillers of the earth, from Nova Scotia to West Florida. We are a people of cultivators, scattered over an immense territory communicating with each other by means of good roads and navigable rivers, united by the silken bands of mild government, all respecting the laws, without dreading their power, because they are equitable. We are all animated with the spirit of an industry which is unfettered and unrestrained, because each person works for himself. If he travels through our rural districts he views not the hostile castle, and the haughty mansion, contrasted with the clay-built hut and miserable cabin, where cattle and men help to keep each other warm, and dwell in meanness, smoke, and indigence. A pleasing uniformity of decent competence appears throughout our habitations. The meanest of our log-houses is a dry and comfortable habitation. Lawyer or merchant are the fairest titles our towns afford; that of a farmer is the only appellation of the rural inhabitants of our country.... We have no princes, for whom we toil, starve, and bleed: we are the most perfect society now existing in the world. Here man is free; as he ought to be....

The next wish of this traveler will be to know whence came all these people? they are mixture of English, Scotch, Irish, French, Dutch, Germans, and Swedes. From this promiscuous breed, that race now called Americans have arisen.... In this great American asylum, the poor of Europe have by some means met together....

Urged by a variety of motives, here they came. Every thing has tended to regenerate them; new laws, a new mode of living, a new social system; here they are become men: in Europe they were as so many useless plants, wanting vegitative mould, and refreshing showers; they withered, and were mowed down by want, hunger, and war. . . .

What then is the American, this new man? He is either an European, or the descendant of an European, hence that strange mixture of blood, which you will find in no other country. . . . He is an American, who leaving behind him all his ancient prejudices and manners, receives new ones from the new mode of life he has embraced, the new government he obeys, and the new rank he holds.

Questions

1. What characteristics of American life does Crèvecoeur emphasize as being different from European society?

2. What aspects of society, and which parts of the people living in the United States, are left out of his description?

CHAPTER 8

Securing the Republic, 1790–1815

46. Benjamin F. Bache, A Defense of the French Revolution (1792–1793)

Source: The General **Advertiser** *(Philadelphia), December 12, 1792, January 25, 1793.*

The French Revolution reverberated strongly in the United States. From its outbreak in 1789, Americans eagerly followed the course of events. Initially, nearly all Americans hailed the overthrow of the monarchy as a fulfillment of the ideals of their own revolution. But as France descended into bloodshed and war broke out between Great Britain and France, Federalists condemned the Revolution, and Republicans remained sympathetic while criticizing its excesses. In his editorials for the Philadelphia newspaper he edited, Benjamin Franklin Bache, a grandson of Benjamin Franklin and himself a leading Republican, defended the actions of the French revolutionaries, insisting that a long-established system of "despotism" could not be overthrown without turmoil. The opposition to change, he insisted, was more deeply entrenched in France than it had been in America, and hence the struggle for liberty had to be more extreme.

Later in the 1790s, Bache was arrested under the Sedition Act, which made it a crime to criticize the policies of President John Adams. His experience illustrates how early American politics was profoundly influenced by events elsewhere in the Atlantic world.

IN ADVERTING TO the present disastrous situation of France, many, perhaps may be inclined to reprobate that revolution which has produced effects so horrible. But if we survey the effects with the eye of cool deliberation, we shall find that though they certainly emanated from the revolution, yet that our reprobation ought to be turned into another channel. The change which took place in the system of government, emancipated twenty-four millions of the human species.—Prima facie, therefore, the most cautious reasoning must allow it to be an event of infinite advantage to the world.

But though it was effected with the consent and support of nine parts out of ten, yet the tenth part viewed it in a different light. A long series of years had transmitted to them hereditary rights & privileges which placed them above the great body of the nation. The King exercised a despotic power without restraint. The nobles described around them a circle equally tyrannical, though of extent less ample. To those who know how dear the possession of power to the human mind, it will not appear strange that such persons should view the revolution with the eye of anger, in as much as it wrested from them those exclusive rights which had descended to them covered with the reverend rust of antiquity; neither will it be a matter of wonder that they should attempt to impede the progress of a system to them so distasteful.... Let us recollect, that though much blood may be shed ere Liberty be firmly established; yet that when it shall be established the effusion will cease. A system of Despotism, however, cannot be supported without blood, and we have no reason to believe that as long as it continues, the sanguinary torrent will ever cease. Until we know the real cause of those ferocious acts, which no honest man can approve nor no honest man contemplate without horror, it is treason against a good cause to attribute them to the friends of the Revolution....

There is that difference between the French and American Revolutions, that the latter was not opposed by cunning priests, nor cruel aristocrats determined to overthrow every principle of honesty and humanity.... A royal puppet on this spot, did not dance on the wire of a band of courtiers; the most despicable and abandoned wretches that ever disgraced mankind. The focus of both despotism and nobility was far from this land of liberty, and its glorious adherents could not be infected with the pernicious breath of mad royalty and impudent aristocracy. The popular cause was opposed openly, sword in hand, and victoriously fought by the friends to the rights of men; had the French republicans met with such opponents, they had not done those excesses, the king, the nobles and clergy have roused them to by the most perfidious contrivances. A king did not forswear himself in America, nor had the American people more than one [Benedict] Arnold; their tempers were soured neither by misery nor by a complicated system of treachery, framed coolly and pursued with the greatest obstinacy. The American people were not loaded with enormous taxes that had reduced millions of their fellow citizens to the utmost misery to maintain haughty plunderers in sloth and profligacy. All this odds must be reckoned by impartial men; to explain the difference insidiously delineated between the two revolutions, by some desperate royalty, or a narrow minded plan.

Questions

1. Why does Bache believe that Americans should support the French Revolution despite the bloodshed taking place in France?

2. What does he see as the similarities and differences between the American and French Revolutions?

───────

47. Address of the Democratic-Republican Society of Pennsylvania (1794)

Source: Democratic-Republican Society of Pennsylvania: Excerpt from minutes of The Democratic Society of Pennsylvania, December 18, 1794. The Historical Society of Pennsylvania (HSP), Collection # Am. 315/3150. Reprinted with permission.

Another example of the spread of public involvement in politics during the 1790s was the emergence in 1793 and 1794 of the Democratic-Republic societies. The societies harshly criticized the policies of George Washington's administration, which they claimed were planting the seeds of aristocracy in the United States.

Federalists saw the societies as an example of how American freedom was getting out of hand. The government, not "self-created societies," declared the president, was the authentic voice of the American people. They also accused the societies of helping to foment the Whiskey Rebellion of 1794, in which farmers in western Pennsylvania resisted paying a new federal tax on distilled liquor. Forced to justify their existence, the societies developed a defense of the right of the people to debate political issues and organize to affect public policy. As a statement adopted by the Democratic-Republican Society of Pennsylvania insisted, "freedom of opinion" was the "bulwark of liberty," a natural right that no government could restrict.

———

THE DEMOCRATIC SOCIETY of Pennsylvania, established in Philadelphia, to their Fellow Citizens throughout the United States.

FELLOW CITIZENS,

The principles and proceedings of our Association have lately been calumniated. We should think ourselves unworthy to be ranked as Freemen, if awed by the name of any man, however he may command the public gratitude for past services, we could suffer in silence so sacred a right, so important a principle, as the freedom of opinion to be infringed, by attack on Societies which stand on that constitutional basis.

We shall not imitate our opponents, by resorting to declamation and abuse, instead of calm reasoning, and substituting assertion for proof. They have termed us anarchists; they have accused us of fomenting the unfortunate troubles in the western counties of this State:—yet not a single fact have they been able to adduce in support of the charge,—They have accused us of aiming at the overthrow of the Constitution; and this also rests upon their bare assertion. Neither shall we recriminate; though we might with at least as much plausibility assert, that endeavours to crush the freedom of opinion and of speech, denote liberticide intentions. But we shall content ourselves with a bare examination of the question, which has agitated the public mind; and refute the calumnies heaped on our Institution.

Freedom of thought, and a free communication of opinions by speech or through the medium of the press, are the safeguards of our Liberties. Apathy as to public concerns, too frequent even in Republics, is the reason for usurpation: by the communication or collision of sentiments, knowledge is increased, and truth prevails.

By the freedom of opinion, cannot be meant the right of thinking merely; for of this right the greatest Tyrant cannot deprive his meanest slave; but, it is freedom in the communication of sentiments, [by] speech or through the press. This liberty is an imprescriptable right, independent of any Constitution or social compact: it is as complete a right as that which any man has to the enjoyment of his life. These principles are eternal—they are recognized by our Constitution; and that nation is already enslaved that does not acknowledge their truth.

In the expression of sentiments, speech is the natural organ—the press an artificial one and though the latter, from the services it has rendered, has obtained the just appellation of Bulwark of Liberty; it would not be difficult to show that the former should be more prized because more secure from usurpation.

If freedom of opinion, in the sense we understand it, is the right of every Citizen, by what mode of reasoning can that right be denied to an assemblage of Citizens? A conviction that the exercise of this right collectively could not be questioned, led to the formation of our institution; and in the conduct the Society have held since their first establishment, they trust, no instance can be adduced in which they have overstepped the just bounds of the right, of which they claim the enjoyment....

• • •

The Society are free to declare that they never were more strongly impressed with a sentiment of the importance of associations, on the principles which they hold, than at the present time. The germ of an odious Aristocracy is planted among us—it has taken root,— and has indeed already produced fruit worthy of the parent stock. If it be imprudent to eradicate this baneful exotic, let us at least unite in checking its growth. Let us remain firm in attachment to principles, and with a jealous eye guard our rights against the least infringement. The enlightened state of the public mind in this country, frees us, we trust, of all apprehension from bold and open usurpation; but the gradual approaches of artful ambition, are the source of great danger. Let us especially guard, with firmness, the outposts of our Liberties: and, if we wish to baffle the efforts of the enemies of freedom, whatever garb they may assume, let us be particularly watchful to preserve inviolate the freedom of opinion, assured that it is the most effectual weapon for the protection of our liberty.

Resolved, That the said Address be signed by the President and attested by the Acting Secretary: and that it be published.

Questions

1. How do the members of the Democratic-Republican Society defend their right to form a society that comments on public affairs?

2. What do they mean by writing that "the germ of an odious Aristocracy" has been planted in the United States?

---

48. Judith Sargent Murray, "On the Equality of the Sexes" (1790)

Source: Judith Sargent Murray, "On the Equality of the Sexes," Massachusetts Magazine, *Vol. 2 (March 1790), pp. 132–35.*

The expansion of the public sphere during the era of the Revolution offered women an opportunity to take part in political discussions, read newspapers, and hear orations even though outside of New Jersey they could not vote. Judith Sargent Murray, one of the era's most accomplished American women, wrote plays, novels, and poetry. She also wrote essays on public issues for the *Massachusetts Magazine* and other journals under the pen name "The Gleaner."

Although Murray could not attend college because of her sex, she studied alongside her brother with a tutor preparing the young man for admission to Harvard. In her essay "On the Equality of the Sexes," written in 1779 and published in 1790, Murray insisted that women had as much right as men to exercise all their talents and should be allowed equal educational opportunities to enable them to do so. Murray forthrightly demanded "equality" for women and attacked the common idea that women's happiness rested on devoting themselves to their duties within the family.

━━━━━━━

• • •

IS IT UPON mature consideration we adopt the idea, that nature is thus partial in her distributions? Is it indeed a fact, that she hath yielded to one half of the human species so unquestionable a mental superiority? I know that to both sexes elevated understandings, and the reverse, are common. But, suffer me to ask, in what the minds of females are so notoriously deficient, or unequal. May not the intellectual powers be ranged under these four heads—imagination, reason, memory and judgment. The province of imagination hath long since been surrendered up to us, and we have been crowned undoubted sovereigns of the regions of fancy. Invention is perhaps the most arduous effort of the mind; this branch of imagination hath been particularly ceded to us, and we have been time out of mind invested with that creative faculty. Observe the variety of fashions (here I bar the contemptuous smile) which distinguish and adorn the female world; how continually are they changing, insomuch that they almost render the wise man's assertion problematical, and we are ready to say, *there is something new under the sun.* Now what a playfulness, what an exuberance of fancy, what strength of inventive imagination, doth this continual variation discover?

Again, it hath been observed, that if the turpitude of the conduct of our sex, hath been ever so enormous, so extremely ready are we, that the very first thought presents us with an apology, so plausible, as to produce our actions even in an amiable light. Another instance of our creative powers, is our talent for slander; how ingenious are we at inventive scandal? what a formidable story can we in a moment fabricate merely from the force of a prolifick imagination? how many reputations, in the fertile brain of a female, have been utterly despoiled? how industrious are we at improving a hint? suspicion how easily do we convert into conviction, and conviction, embellished by the power of eloquence, stalks abroad to the surprise and confusion of unsuspecting innocence. Perhaps it will be asked if I furnish these facts as instances of excellency in our sex. Certainly not; but as proofs of a creative faculty, of a lively imagination. Assuredly great activity of mind is thereby discovered, and was this activity properly directed, what beneficial effects would follow. Is the needle and kitchen sufficient to employ the operations of a soul thus organized? I should conceive not. Nay, it is a truth that those very departments leave the intelligent principle vacant, and at liberty for speculation.

Are we deficient in reason? we can only reason from what we know, and if an opportunity of acquiring knowledge hath been denied us, the inferiority of our sex cannot fairly be deduced from thence. Memory, I believe, will be allowed us in common, since every one's experience must testify, that a loquacious old woman is as frequently met with, as a communicative old man; their subjects are alike drawn from the fund of other times, and the transactions of their youth, or of maturer life, entertain, or perhaps fatigue you, in the evening of their lives. "But our judgment is not so strong—we do not distinguish so well."—Yet it may be questioned, from what doth this superiority, in this determining faculty of the soul, proceed. May we not trace its source in the difference of education, and continued advantages?

Will it be said that the judgment of a male of two years old, is more sage than that of a female's of the same age? I believe the reverse is generally observed to be true. But from that period what partiality! how is the one exalted, and the other depressed, by the contrary modes of education which are adopted! the one is taught to aspire, and the other is early confined and limited. As their years increase, the sister must be wholly domesticated, while the brother is led by the hand through all the flowery paths of science. Grant that their minds are by nature equal, yet who shall wonder at the *apparent* superiority, if indeed custom becomes *second nature*; nay if it taketh place of nature, and that it doth the experience of each day will evince. At length arrived at womanhood, the uncultivated fair one feels a void, which the employments allotted her are by no means capable of filling. What can she do? to books she may not apply; or if she doth, *to those only of the novel kind,* lest she merit the appellation of a *learned lady*; and what ideas have been affixed to this term, the observation of many can testify. Fashion, scandal, and sometimes what is still more reprehensible, are then called in to her relief; and who can say to what lengths the liberties she takes may proceed. Meantime she herself is most unhappy; she feels the want of a culti- vated mind. Is she single, she in vain seeks to fill up time from sexual employments or amusements. Is she united to a person whose soul nature made equal to her own, education hath set him so far above her, that in those entertainments which are productive of such ratio- nal felicity, she is not qualified to accompany him. She experiences a mortifying consciousness of inferiority, which embitters every enjoy- ment. Doth the person to whom her adverse fate hath consigned her, possess a mind incapable of improvement, she is equally wretched, in being so closely connected with an individual whom she cannot but despise. Now, was she permitted the same instructors as her brother, (with an eye however to their particular departments) for the employ- ment of a rational mind an ample field would be opened....

Will it be urged that those acquirements would supersede our domestic duties. I answer that every requisite in female economy is easily attained; and, with truth I can add, that when once attained, they require no further *mental attention*. Nay, while we are pursuing the needle, or the superintendency of the family, I repeat, that our minds are at full liberty for reflection; that imagination may exert itself in full vigor; and that if a just foundation is early laid, our ideas will then be worthy of rational beings. If we were industrious we might easily find time to arrange them upon paper, or should avocations press too hard for such an indulgence, the hours allotted for conversation would at least become more refined and rational. Should it still be vociferated, "Your domestic employments are sufficient"—I would calmly ask, is it reasonable, that a candidate for immortality, for the joys of heaven, an intelligent being, who is to spend an eternity in contemplating the works of Deity, should at present be so degraded, as to be allowed no other ideas, than those which are suggested by the mechanism of a pudding, or the sewing the seams of a garment? Pity that all such censurers of female improvement do not go one step further, and deny their future existence; to be consistent they surely ought.

Yes, ye lordly, ye haughty sex, our souls are by nature *equal* to yours; the same breath of God animates, enlivens, and invigorates us; and that we are not fallen lower than yourselves, let those witness who have greatly towered above the various discouragements by which they have been so heavily oppressed.... Were we to grant that animal strength proved any thing, taking into consideration the accustomed impartiality of nature, we should be induced to imagine, that she had invested the female mind with superior strength as an equivalent for the bodily powers of man. But waving this however palpable advantage, for *equality only*, we wish to contend.

• • •

Questions

1. Why does Murray refer to the "variety of fashions" among women as an argument for their intellectual capacity?

2. How does she answer the charge that offering educational opportunities to women will lead to neglect of their "domestic duties"?

---

49. Protest against the Alien and Sedition Acts (1798)

Source: Jonathan Elliott, ed., The Debates in the Several State Conventions on the Adoption of the Federal Constitution, *2nd. ed. (Philadelphia: J. B. Lippincott & Co., 1836–59), Vol. 5, pp. 528–29.*

From the adoption of the Constitution, the relative powers of the state and federal governments have remained a point of dispute. In 1798, faced with mounting opposition from opponents (among them foreign-born Jeffersonian newspaper editors), President John Adams and the Federalist party moved to silence criticism of the administration. Congress passed the Alien Act, which allowed the deportation of "dangerous" foreigners, and the Sedition Act, set to expire after the presidential election of 1800, which made it a crime to criticize the government in print or a public assembly. In response, James Madison and Thomas Jefferson wrote resolutions of protest. Virginia's legislature approved Madison's and Kentucky adopted Jefferson's. Both claimed that states could "interpose" their power to prevent the federal government from acting in a despotic manner. Southern advocates of nullification and secession later cited the resolutions to justify their position.

RESOLVED, THAT THE General Assembly of Virginia doth unequivocally express a firm resolution to maintain and defend the Constitution of the United States, and the Constitution of this state, against every aggression, either foreign or domestic; and that they will support the government of the United States in all measures warranted by the former.

That this Assembly most solemnly declares a warm attachment to the union of the states, to maintain which it pledges its powers;

and that, for this end, it is their duty to watch over and oppose every infraction of those principles which constitute the only basis of that union, because a faithful observance of them can alone secure its existence and the public happiness.

That this Assembly doth explicitly and peremptorily declare, that it views the powers of the federal government as resulting from the compact to which the states are parties, as limited by the plain sense and intention of the instrument constituting that compact, as no further valid than they are authorized by the grants enumerated in that compact; and that, in case of a deliberate, palpable, and dangerous exercise of other powers, not granted by the said compact, the states, who are parties thereto, have the right, and are in duty bound, to interpose, for arresting the progress of the evil, and for maintaining, within their respective limits, the authorities, rights, and liberties, appertaining to them.

That the General Assembly doth also express its deep regret, that a spirit has, in sundry instances, been manifested by the federal government to enlarge its powers by forced constructions of the constitutional charter which defines them; and that indications have appeared of a design to expound certain general phrases (which, having been copied from the very limited grant of powers in the former Articles of Confederation, were the less liable to be misconstrued) so as to destroy the meaning and effect of the particular enumeration which necessarily explains and limits the general phrases, and so as to consolidate the states, by degrees, into one sovereignty, the obvious tendency and inevitable result of which would be, to transform the present republican system of the United States into an absolute, or, at best, a mixed monarchy.

That the General Assembly doth particularly PROTEST against the palpable and alarming infractions of the Constitution, in the two late cases of the "Alien and Sedition Acts," passed at the last session of Congress; the first of which exercises a power nowhere delegated to the federal government, and which, by uniting legislative and judicial powers to those of executive, subverts the general principles of free government, as well as the particular organization and positive provisions of the Federal Constitution; and the other of which acts exercises, in like manner, a power not delegated by the Constitution, but, on the contrary, expressly and positively forbidden by one of the amendments thereto,—a power which, more than any other, ought to produce universal alarm, because it is levelled against the right of freely examining public characters and measures, and of free communication among the people thereon, which has ever been justly deemed the only effectual guardian of every other right.

That this state having, by its Convention, which ratified the Federal Constitution, expressly declared that, among other essential rights, "the liberty of conscience and the press cannot be cancelled, abridged, restrained, or modified, by any authority of the United States," and from its extreme anxiety to guard these rights from every possible attack of sophistry and ambition, having, with other states, recommended an amendment for that purpose, which amendment was, in due time, annexed to the Constitution,—it would mark a reproachful inconsistency, and criminal degeneracy, if an indifference were now shown to the most palpable violation of one of the rights thus declared and secured, and to the establishment of a precedent which may be fatal to the other.

That the good people of this commonwealth, having ever felt, and continuing to feel, the most sincere affection for their brethren of the other states; the truest anxiety for establishing and perpetuating the union of all; and the most scrupulous fidelity to that Constitution, which is the pledge of mutual friendship, and the instrument of mutual happiness,—the General Assembly doth solemnly appeal to the like dispositions in the other states, in confidence that they will concur with this commonwealth in declaring, as it does hereby declare, that the acts aforesaid are unconstitutional; and that the necessary and proper measures will be taken by each for cooperating with this state, in maintaining unimpaired the authorities, rights, and liberties, reserved to the states respectively, or to the people.

Questions

1. In what ways does the resolution claim that the Alien and Sedition Acts violate the principles of "free government"?

2. How does the resolution define the relationship between the federal government and the states under the Constitution?

50. George Tucker on Gabriel's Rebellion (1801)

Source: Letter to a Member of the General Assembly of Virginia on the Subject of the Late Conspiracy of the Slaves; With a Proposal for Their Colonization *(Baltimore, 1801), pp. 5–18.*

In 1800, a plot by slaves in Virginia to gain their freedom was organized by a Richmond blacksmith, Gabriel. The plot was soon discovered and the leaders arrested. Twenty-six slaves, including Gabriel, were hanged and dozens more transported out of the state. The conspiracy, commented George Tucker, a member of one of the state's most prominent families, demonstrated that slaves possessed "the love of freedom" as fully as other men. Gabriel's language, he added, reflected "the advance of knowledge" among Virginia's slaves, which would inevitably continue.

Like Thomas Jefferson, James Madison, and many others of his generation, Tucker opposed slavery but could not envision the United States as a biracial society of free citizens. He proposed that the Virginia legislature adopt a plan to emancipate the slaves and settle them outside of the state, somewhere "on the western side" of the Mississippi River (an area then under the control of Spain). The legislature, however, moved in the opposite direction. It tightened controls over the black population and severely restricted the ability of masters to free their slaves voluntarily.

———

THERE IS OFTEN a progress in human affairs which may indeed be retarded, but which nothing can arrest. Moving on with slow and silent steps, it is marked only by comparing distant periods. The causes which produce it are either so minute as to be invisible, or, if preceived, are too numerous and complicated to be subject to human controul. Of such sort is the advancement of knowledge among the negroes of this country. It is so striking, as to be obvious to a man of the most ordinary observation. Every year adds to the number of those who can read and write; and he who has made any proficiency in letters, becomes a little centre of instruction to others. This increase of knowledge is the principal agent in evolving the spirit we have to fear. The love of freedom, sir, is an inborn sentiment, which the God of nature has planted deep in the heart: long may it be kept under by the arbitrary institutions of society; but, at the first favourable moment, it springs forth, and flourishes with a vigour that defies all check. This celestial spark, which fires the breast of the savage, which glows in that of the philosopher, is not extinguished in the bosom of the slave. It may be buried in the embers; but it still lives; and the breath of knowledge kindles it into flame. Thus we find, sir, there never have been slaves in any country, who have not seized the first favorable opportunity to revolt.

• • •

In our infant country, where population and wealth increase with unexampled rapidity, the progress of liberal knowledge is proportionally great. In this vast march of the mind, the blacks, who are far behind us, may be supposed to advance at a pace equal to our own; but, sir, the fact is, they are likely to advance much faster. The growth and multiplication of our towns tend a thousand ways to enlighten and inform them. The very nature of our government, which leads us to recur perpetually to the discussion of natural rights, favors speculation and enquiry.

• • •

There is one argument to which I have not even hinted; but which some may think of more weight than any other;—I mean the ease with which they may become the tools of a foreign enemy. Granting that the danger from themselves is slight or remote, this, it must be confessed, depends upon an event that is altogether uncertain. War

is sometimes inevitable; no human prudence can guard against an
event that may be brought about by the insolence, the injustice, or
the caprice of *any* nation. Whenever we are involved in this calamity, if our enemies hold out the lure of freedom, they will have, in
every negro, a decided friend. The passage is easy from friends to aux-
iliaries: little address would be necessary to excite insurrection; to
put arms into their hands, and to convert a willing multitude into a
compact and disciplined army.

• • •

The following hints I submit to your serious and candid consideration.

That application be made to the United States, to procure from the
Spanish government, or to furnish from its own territory, such a tract
of country as shall be deemed sufficient for the colony proposed.
The consideration of future peace would recommend the western
side of the Mississipi. Present convenience and economy would
advise a purchase of some part of the Indian country, comprehended
within the limits of the state of Georgia.

That this colony be under the protection and immediate government of this state, or the United States, until it contained a number
of inhabitants sufficient to manage their own concerns: and that
it be exclusively appropriated to the colonization and residence of
people of colour.

Questions

1. Why does Tucker think that "progress in human affairs" will inevitably
lead slaves to become more discontented?

2. In what ways does Tucker believe that living in Virginia has affected the
ideas of the slaves?

51. Tecumseh on Indians and Land (1810)

Source: Samuel G. Drake, The Book of the Indians; or, Biography and History of the Indians of North America *(8th ed.: Boston, 1841), Book 5, pp. 121–22.*

By 1800, nearly 400,000 American settlers lived west of the Appalachian Mountains. They far outnumbered remaining Indians. Some Indians determined to root out European influences and resist further white encroachment on Indian lands. The most militant were two Shawnee brothers, Tecumseh, a chief who had refused to sign the Treaty of Greenville in 1795, and Tenskwatawa, a religious prophet who called for complete separation from whites, the revival of traditional Indian culture, and resistance to federal policies.

In 1810, Tecumseh met with William Henry Harrison, the territorial governor of Indiana. He predicted war if white incursions on Indian land continued and condemned chiefs who had sold land to the federal government. Indians, he proclaimed, should "unite in claiming a common and equal right in the land, as it was at first." During the War of 1812, Tecumseh was commissioned an officer in the British army. He died at the Battle of the Thames, near Detroit.

▬▬▬

• • •

IT IS TRUE I am a Shawanee. My forefathers were warriors. Their son is a warrior. From them I only take my existence; from my tribe I take nothing. I am the maker of my own fortune; and oh! that I could make that of my red people, and of my country, as great as the conceptions of my mind, when I think of the Spirit that rules the universe. I would not then come to Governor *Harrison*, to ask him to tear the treaty, and to obliterate the landmark; but I would say to him, Sir, you have liberty to return to your own country. The being within, communing with past ages, tells me, that once, nor until lately, there was no white man on this continent. That it then all belonged to red men, children of the same parents, placed on it by the Great Spirit that made them, to keep it, to traverse it, to enjoy its productions, and to fill it with the same race. Once a happy race. Since made miserable by the white people, who are never contented, but always encroaching. The way, and the only way to check and to stop this evil, is, for all the red men to unite in claiming a common and equal right in the land, as it was at first, and should be yet; for it never was divided, but belongs to all, for the use of each. That no part has a right to sell, even to each other, much less to strangers; those who want all, and will not do with less. The white people have no right to take the land from the Indians, because they had it first; it is theirs. They may sell, but all must join. Any sale not made by all is not valid. The late sale is bad. It was made by a part only. Part do not know how to sell. It requires all to make a bargain for all. All red men have equal rights to the unoccupied land. The right of occupancy is as good in one place as in another. There cannot be two occupations in the same place. The first excludes all others. It is not so in hunting or travelling; for there the same ground will serve many, as they may follow each other all day; but the camp is stationary, and that is occupancy. It belongs to the first who sits down on his blanket or skins, which he has thrown upon the ground, and till he leaves it no other has a right.

• • •

Questions

1. How does Tecumseh's speech illustrate differences between Indian and American views of land as private property?

2. What evidence does he offer that whites cannot be trusted by the Indians?

52. Felix Grundy, Battle Cry of the War Hawks (1811)

Source: Annals of Congress, *12th Congress, 1st Session, pp. 425–27 (December 10, 1811).*

In the months leading up to the War of 1812, a group of younger congressmen, mostly from the West, called for war with Britain. Known as the War Hawks, this new generation of political leaders had come of age after the winning of independence and were ardent nationalists. Their leaders included Henry Clay of Kentucky, elected Speaker of the House of Representatives in 1810, and John C. Calhoun of South Carolina. The War Hawks spoke passionately of defending the national honor against British insults, but also had more practical goals in mind, notably the annexation of Canada. Their views were expressed in a speech in the House of Representatives by Felix Grundy of Tennessee. To British interference with American shipping, the main concern of the Madison administration, Grundy added the aim of acquiring Canada (British territory) and Florida (owned by Spain) to the United States, thereby expanding the Union and undermining the remaining power of Indian tribes.

WHAT, MR. SPEAKER, are we now called on to decide? It is, whether we will resist by force the attempt, made by [the British] Government, to subject our maritime rights to the arbitrary and capricious rule of her will; for my part I am not prepared to say that this country shall submit to have her commerce interdicted or regulated, by any foreign nation. Sir, I prefer war to submission.

Over and above these unjust pretensions of the British Government, for many years past they have been in the practice of impressing our seamen, from merchant vessels; this unjust and lawless invasion of personal liberty, calls loudly for the interposition of this Government. To those better acquainted with the facts in relation to it, I leave it to fill up the picture. My mind is irresistibly drawn to the West. . . .

It cannot be believed by any man who will reflect, that the savage tribes, uninfluenced by other Powers, would think of making war on the United States. They understand too well their own weakness, and our strength. They have already felt the weight of our arms; they know they hold the very soil on which they live as tenants at sufferance. How, then, sir, are we to account for their late conduct? In one way only; some powerful nation must have intrigued with them, and turned their peaceful disposition towards us into hostilities. Great Britain alone has intercourse with those Northern tribes; I therefore infer, that if British gold has not been employed, their baubles and trinkets, and the promise of support and a place of refuge if necessary, have had their effect....

This war, if carried on successfully, will have its advantages. We shall drive the British from our Continent—they will no longer have an opportunity of intriguing with our Indian neighbors, and setting on the ruthless savage to tomahawk our women and children. That nation will lose her Canadian trade, and, by having no resting place in this country, her means of annoying us will be diminished.... I am willing to receive the Canadians as adopted brethren; it will have beneficial political effects; it will preserve the equilibrium of the Government. When Louisiana shall be fully peopled, the Northern States will lose their power; they will be at the discretion of others; they can be depressed at pleasure, and then this Union might be endangered—I therefore feel anxious not only to add the Floridas to the South, but the Canadas to the North of this empire....

Questions

1. Why does Grundy think that acquiring Canada will strengthen the American Union?

2. Whom does Grundy hold responsible for Tecumseh's uprising (the "late conduct" of the Indian tribes he mentions)?

53. Mercy Otis Warren on Religion and Virtue (1805)

Source: Mercy Otis Warren, History of the Rise, Progress and Termination of the American Revolution *(3 vols.: Boston, 1805), Vol. 3, pp. 412–18.*

A sister of the Massachusetts patriot leader James Otis and wife of James Warren, who was paymaster for George Washington's army, Mercy Otis Warren emerged as one of the leading women writers of her generation and an insightful commentator on political events. She promoted the revolutionary cause in poetry and dramas, and advocated the addition of a Bill of Rights to the Constitution. In 1805 she published a three-volume history of the American Revolution. In one section, she worried about what she considered the spread of religious infidelity and declining virtue in Europe, and wondered if the United States would eventually go down this road. But she remained confident that Americans would not soon emulate Europe in the loss of liberty.

———

IT IS NEITHER a preference to republican systems, nor an attachment to monarchic or aristocratic forms of government that disseminates the wild opinions of infidelity. It is the licentious manners of courts of every description, the unbridled luxury of wealth, and the worst passions of men let loose on the multitude by the example of their superiors. Bent on gratification, at the expense of every moral tie, they have broken down the barriers of religion, and the spirit of infidelity is nourished at the fount; thence the poisonous streams run through every grade that constitutes the mass of nations.

It may be further observed, that there is a variety of additional causes which have led to a disposition among some part of mankind, to reject the obligations of religion, and even to deny their God. This propensity in some may easily be elucidated, without casting any part of the odium on the spirit of free inquiry relative to civil and political liberty, which had been widely disseminated, and had produced two such remarkable revolutions as those of America and France. It may be imputed to the love of novelty, the pride of opinion, and an extravagant propensity to speculate and theorize on subjects beyond the comprehension of mortals, united with a desire of being released from the restraints on their appetites and passions: restraints dictated both by reason and revelation; and which, under the influence of sober reflection, forbid the indulgence of all gratifications that are injurious to man. Further elucidations, or more abstruse causes, which contribute to lead the vain inquirer, who steps over the line prescribed by the Author of nature, to deviations from, and forgetfulness of its Creator, and to involve him in a labyrinth of darkness, from which his weak reasonings can never disentangle him, may be left to those who delight in metaphysical disquisitions.

The world might reasonably have expected, from the circumstances connected with the first settlement of the American colonies, which was in consequence of their attachment to the religion of their fathers, united with a spirit of independence relative to civil government, that there would have been no observable dereliction of those honorable principles, for many ages to come. From the sobriety of their manners, their simple habits, their attention to the education and moral conduct of their children, they had the highest reason to hope, that it might have been long, very long, before the faith of their religion was shaken, or their principles corrupted, either by the manners, opinions, or habits of foreigners, bred in the courts of despotism, or the schools of licentiousness.

This hope shall not yet be relinquished. There has indeed been some relaxation of manners, and the appearance of a change in public opinion not contemplated when revolutionary scenes first shook the western world. But it must be acknowledged, that the religious and moral character of Americans yet stands on a higher grade of excellence and purity, than that of most other nations. It has been observed, that "a violation of manners has destroyed more states than the infraction of laws." It is necessary for every *American*, with becoming energy to endeavour to stop the dissemination of principles evidently destructive of the cause for which they have bled. It must be the combined virtue of the rulers and of the people to do this, and to rescue and save their civil and religious rights from the outstretched arm of tyranny, which may appear under any mode or form of government.

Let not the frivolity of the domestic taste of the children of Columbia, nor the examples of strangers of high or low degree, that may intermix among them, or the imposing attitude of distant nations, or the machinations of the bloody tyrants of Europe, who have united themselves, and to the utmost are exerting their strength to extirpate the very name of *republicanism*, rob them of their character, their morals, their religion, or their liberty....

It is to be regretted that Americans are so much divided on this point as well as on many other questions: we hope the spirit of division will never be wrought up to such a height as to terminate in a disseveration of the states, or any internal hostilities. Any civil convulsions would shake the fabric of government, and perhaps entirely subvert the present excellent constitution; a strict adherence to which, it may be affirmed, is the best security of the rights and liberties of a country that has bled at every vein, to purchase and transmit them to posterity. The sword now resheathed, the army dismissed, a wise, energetic government established and organized, it is to be hoped many generations will pass away in the lapse of time, before America again becomes a theatre of war.

Indeed the United States of America embrace too large a portion of the globe, to expect their isolated situation will forever secure them from the encroachments of foreign nations, and the attempts of potent Europeans to interrupt their peace. But if the education of youth, both public and private, is attended to, their industrious and economical habits maintained, their moral character and that assemblage of virtues supported, which is necessary for the happiness of individuals and of nations, there is not much danger that they will for a long time be subjugated by the arms of foreigners, or that their republican system will be subverted by the arts of domestic enemies. Yet, probably some distant day will exhibit the extensive continent of America, a portrait analogous to the other quarters of the globe, which have been laid waste by ambition, until misery has spread her sable veil over the inhabitants. But this will not be done, until ignorance, servility and vice, have led them to renounce their ideas of freedom, and reduced them to that grade of baseness which renders them unfit for the enjoyment of that rational liberty which is the natural inheritance of man. The expense of blood and treasure, lavished for the purchase of freedom, should teach Americans to estimate its real worth, nor ever suffer it to be depreciated by the vices of the human mind, which are seldom single. The sons of America ought ever to bear in grateful remembrance the worthy band of patriots, who first supported an opposition to the tyrannic measures of Great Britain. Though some of them have long since been consigned to the tomb, a tribute of gratitude is ever due to their memory, while the advantages of freedom and independence are felt by their latest posterity.

Questions

1. What does Warren consider the greatest threats to freedom?

2. What does she consider the most significant legacy of the American Revolution?

CHAPTER 9

The Market Revolution, 1800–1840

54. Complaint of a Lowell Factory Worker (1845)

Source: Factory Tracts Number One. **Factory Life As It Is** *(Lowell, 1845).*

The early industrial revolution centered on factories producing cotton textiles with water-powered spinning and weaving machinery. In the 1820s, a group of merchants created a new factory town near Boston, incorporated as the city of Lowell in 1836. Here, they built a group of modern textile factories that brought together all phases of production from the spinning of thread to the weaving and finishing of cloth. By 1850, Lowell's fifty-two mills employed more than 10,000 workers.

At Lowell, young unmarried women from Yankee farm families dominated the workforce that tended the spinning machines. Competition among the mills led to a deterioration in working conditions and, beginning in the 1830s, protests among the workers. They engaged in strikes or "turn outs," and petitioned the legislature to limit their hours of labor. Founded in 1845, the Lowell Female Labor Reform Association published a series of Factory Tracts to expose conditions in the mills. Frequently, as in this account by an unnamed worker, they drew an analogy between their conditions and those of southern slaves.

PHILANTHROPISTS OF THE nineteenth century!—shall not the operatives of our country be permitted to speak for themselves? Shall they be compelled to listen in silence to [those] who speak for gain, and are the mere echo of the will of the corporations? Shall the worthy laborer be awed into silence by wealth and power, and for fear of being deprived of the means of procuring his daily bread? Shall tyranny and cruel oppression be allowed to rivet the chains of physical and mental slavery on the millions of our country who are the real producers of all its improvements and wealth, and they fear to speak out in noble self-defense? Shall they fear to appeal to the sympathies of the people, or the justice of this far-famed republican nation? God forbid!

Much has been written and spoken in woman's behalf, especially in America; and yet a large class of females are, and have been, destined to a state of servitude as degrading as unceasing toil can make it. I refer to the female operatives of New England—the free states of our union—the states where no colored slave can breathe the balmy air, and exist as such;—but yet there are those, a host of them, too, who are in fact nothing more nor less than slaves in every sense of the word! Slaves to a system of labor which requires them to toil from five until seven o'clock, with one hour only to attend to the wants of nature, allowed—slaves to the will and requirements of the "powers that be," however they may infringe on the rights or conflict with the feelings of the operative—slaves to ignorance—and how can it be otherwise? What time has the operative to bestow on moral, religious or intellectual culture? How can our country look for aught but ignorance and vice, under the existing state of things? When the whole system is exhausted by unremitting labor during twelve and thirteen hours per day, can any reasonable being expect that the mind will retain its vigor and energy? Impossible! Common sense will teach every one the utter impossibility of improving the mind under these circumstances, however great the desire may be for knowledge.

Again, we hear much said on the subject of benevolence among the wealthy and so called, Christian part of community. Have we not cause to question the sincerity of those who, while they talk benevolence in the parlor, compel their help to labor for a mean, paltry pittance in the kitchen? And while they manifest great concern for the souls of the heathen in distant lands, care nothing for the bodies and intellects of those within their own precincts? Shall we esteem men honest in their pretensions to piety and benevolence, who compel their help to labor on the Sabbath day or lose their situation? . . .

In the strength of our united influence we will soon show these driveling cotton lords, this mushroom aristocracy of New England, who so arrogantly aspire to lord it over God's heritage, that our rights cannot be trampled upon with impunity; that we WILL not longer submit to that arbitrary power which has for the last ten years been so abundantly exercised over us.

Questions

1. Why does the female factory worker compare her conditions with those of slaves?

2. Why does she doubt the sincerity of the Christian beliefs of the factory owners?

---

55. Joseph Smith, The Wentworth Letter (1842)

Source: Times and Seasons *(March–May 1842).*

Among the most successful of the religions that sprang up in pre–Civil War America was the Church of Jesus Christ of Latter-day Saints, or Mormons. The Mormons were founded in the 1820s by Joseph Smith, a farmer in upstate New York who as a youth began to experience religious visions. He claimed to have been led by an angel to a set of golden plates covered with strange writing. Smith translated and published them as *The Book of*

Mormon, after a fourth-century prophet. In 1842, at the request of John Wentworth, a Chicago editor, Smith wrote an account of his life to that point and his religious beliefs, which Wentworth republished in a magazine Smith edited. Not long afterward, Smith was arrested in Nauvoo, Illinois, where the Mormons had settled after being driven out of New York, Ohio, and Missouri because of popular outrage at Smith's insistence that *The Book of Mormon* was as much the word of God as the Bible, and his doctrine of polygamy (that one man may have several wives). While in jail, Smith was murdered by a group of intruders. In 1847, his successor as Mormon leader, Brigham Young, led more than 2,000 followers across the Great Plains and Rocky Mountains to the shores of the Great Salt Lake in present-day Utah.

MY FATHER WAS a farmer and taught me the art of husbandry. When about fourteen years of age I began to reflect upon the importance of being prepared for a future state, and upon enquiring [of] the plan of salvation I found that there was a great clash in religious sentiment; if I went to one society they referred me to one plan, and another to another, each one pointing to his own particular creed as the summum bonum of perfection: considering that all could not be right, and that God could not be the author of so much confusion I determined to investigate the subject more fully, believing that if God had a church it would not be split up into factions, and that if he taught one society to worship one way, and administer in one set of ordinances, He would not teach another, principles which were diametrically opposed. Believing the word of God I had confidence in the declaration of James; "If any man lack wisdom let him ask of God who giveth to all men liberally and upbraideth not and it shall be given him." I retired to a secret place in a grove and began to call upon the Lord, while fervently engaged in supplication my mind was taken away from the objects with which I was surrounded, and I was enwrapped in a heavenly vision and saw two glorious personages who exactly resembled each other in features and likeness, surrounded with a brilliant light which eclipsed the sun at noon-day. They told me that all religious denominations were believing in incorrect doctrines and that none of them was acknowledged of God as His Church and kingdom. And I was expressly commanded to "go not after them," at the same time receiving a promise that the fullness of the gospel should at some future time be made known unto me....

I was informed that I was chosen to be an instrument in the hands of God to bring about some of His purposes in this glorious dispensation.

I was also informed concerning the aboriginal inhabitants of this country [America], and shown who they were, and from whence they came; a brief sketch of their origin, progress, civilization, laws, governments, of their righteousness and iniquity, and the blessings of God being finally withdrawn from them as a people was made known unto me: I was also told where there was deposited some plates on which were engraven an abridgment of the records of the ancient prophets that had existed on this continent. The angel appeared to me three times the same night and unfolded the same things. After having received many visits from the angels of God unfolding the majesty and glory of the events that should transpire in the last days, on the morning of the 22d of September, A.D. 1827, the angel of the Lord delivered the records into my hands.

These records were engraven on plates which had the appearance of gold, each plate was six inches wide and eight inches long and not quite so thick as common tin. They were filled with engravings, in Egyptian characters and bound together in a volume, as the leaves of a book with three rings running through the whole. The volume was something near six inches in thickness, a part of which was sealed. The characters on the unsealed part were small, and beautifully engraved. The whole book exhibited many marks of antiquity in its construction and much skill in the art of engraving. With the records was found a curious instrument which the ancients called

"Urim and Thummim," which consisted of two transparent stones set in the rim of a bow fastened to a breastplate....

As soon as the news of this discovery was made known, false reports, misrepresentation, and slander flew as on the wings of the wind in every direction, the house was frequently beset by mobs, and evil designing people, several times I was shot at, and very narrowly escaped, and every device was made use of to get the plates away from me, but the power and blessing of God attended me, and several began to believe my testimony....

In the situation before alluded to we arrived in the state of Illinois in 1839, where we found a hospitable people and a friendly home; a people who were willing to be governed by the principles of law and humanity. We have commenced to build a city called "Nauvoo" in Hancock co., we number from six to eight thousand here besides vast numbers in the county around and in almost every county of the state. We have a city charter granted us and a charter for a legion the troops of which now number 1500. We have also a charter for a university, for an agricultural and manufacturing society, have our own laws and administrators, and possess all the privileges that other free and enlightened citizens enjoy.

Persecution has not stopped the progress of truth, but has only added fuel to the flame, it has spread with increasing rapidity, proud of the cause which they have espoused and conscious of our innocence and of the truth of their system amidst calumny and reproach have the elders of this Church gone forth, and planted the gospel in almost every state in the Union; it has penetrated our cities, it has spread over our villages and has caused thousands of our intelligent, noble, and patriotic citizens to obey its divine mandates, and be governed by its sacred truths. It has also spread into England, Ireland, Scotland, and Wales: in the year 1839 where a few of our missionaries were sent over five thousand joined the standard of truth, there are numbers now joining in every land.

Questions

1. What does the Mormon experience suggest about the extent and limits of religious freedom in the pre–Civil War United States?

2. What in Smith's letter might offend non-Mormon Americans?

---

56. A Woman in the Westward Movement (1824)

Source: Elizabeth F. Ellet, Pioneer Women of the West (New York, 1852), pp. 388–95.

The westward migration plays a central part in American lore. The image of the hardy pioneer triumphing over the wilderness (and Indians) has been immortalized in countless works of literature and Hollywood movies. Reality on the frontier was often less appealing, especially for pioneer women.

The end of the War of 1812, which broke the power of Indian tribes in the Old Northwest and ended the British presence there, unleashed a wave of migration from eastern states. Land was cheap, but travel remained extremely difficult. In this account, written in 1824, Harriet L. Noble describes her family's migration from New York to Michigan, then a sparsely settled territory (it would not become a state until 1837). Her vivid description of the hardships her family endured places special emphasis on the burdens pioneer life placed on women. Nonetheless, she ends by reaffirming the opportunities offered by westward migration and her family's decision to move West.

MY HUSBAND WAS seized with the mania, and accordingly made preparation to start in January with his brother. They took the Ohio route, and were nearly a month in getting through; coming by way of Monroe, and thence to Ypsilanti and Ann Arbor. Mr. John Allen and Walter Rumsey with his wife and two men had been there some four or five weeks, had built a small house, moved into it the day my husband and his brother arrived, and were just preparing their first meal, which the newcomers had the pleasure of partaking. They spent a few days here, located a farm a little above the town on the river Huron, and returned through Canada. They had been so much pleased with the country, that they immediately commenced preparing to emigrate; and as near as I can recollect, we started about the 20th of September, 1824, for Michigan.

We traveled from our house in Geneva to Buffalo in wagons. The roads were bad, and we were obliged to wait in Buffalo four days for a boat, as the steamboat "Michigan" was the only one on the lake. After waiting so long we found she had put into Erie for repairs, and had no prospect of being able to run again for some time. The next step was to take passage in a schooner.... We were seven days on Lake Erie, and so entirely prostrated with seasickness, as scarcely to be able to attend to the wants of our little ones. I had a little girl of three years, and a babe some months old, and Sister Noble had six children, one an infant. It was a tedious voyage; the lake was very rough most of the time, and I thought if we were only on land again, I should be satisfied, it was a wilderness. I could not then realize what it would be to live without a comfortable house through the winter, but sad experience afterwards taught me a lesson not to be forgotten.

I think it was on the 3d of October we started from Detroit, with a pair of oxen and a wagon, a few articles for cooking, and such necessaries as we could not do without. It was necessary that they should be few as possible, for our families were a full load for this mode of traveling.... My sister and myself could assist but little, so fatigued were we with walking and carrying our infants.... We were all pretty cheerful, until we began to think of lying down for the night. The men did not seem to dread it, however, and were soon fast asleep, but sleep was not for me in such a wilderness. I could think of nothing but wild beasts, or something as bad; so that I had the pleasure of watching while the others slept. It seemed a long, long night, and never in my life did I feel more grateful for the blessing of returning day.... We met a large number of Indians; and one old squaw followed us some distance with her papoose, determined to swap babies. At last she gave it up, and for one I felt relieved.

We passed two log houses between this and Ann Arbor. About the middle of the afternoon we found ourselves at our journey's end—but what a prospect? There were some six or seven log huts occupied by as many inmates as could be crowded into them.... We cooked our meals in the open air, there being no fire in the house but a small box-stove.... We lived in this way until our husbands got a log house raised and the roof on; this took them about six weeks, at the end of which time we went into it, without door, floor, chimney, or anything but logs and roof.... We enjoyed uninterrupted health, but in the spring the ague with its accompaniments gave us a call, and by the middle of August there were but four out of fourteen who could call themselves well. We then fancied we were too near the river for health. We sold out and bought again ten miles west of Ann Arbor, a place which suited us better.... The next thing wanted was a chimney; winter was close at hand and the stone was not drawn.... My husband and myself were four days building it. I suppose most of my lady friends would think a woman quite out of "her legitimate sphere" in turning mason, but I was not at all particular what kind of labor I performed, so we were only comfortable and provided with the necessaries of life.

I am not of a desponding disposition, nor often low-spirited, and having left New York to make Michigan my home, I had no idea of going back, or being very unhappy. Yet the want of society, of church privileges, and in fact almost every thing that makes life desirable, would often make me sad in spite of all effort to the contrary. I had no ladies' society for one year ... except that of sister Noble and a Mrs. Taylor, and was more lonely than either of them, my family being so small.

When I look back upon my life, and see the ups and downs, the hardships and privations I have been called upon to endure, I feel no wish to be young again. I was in the prime of life when I came to Michigan—only twenty-one, and my husband was thirty-three. Neither of us knew the reality of hardship. Could we have known what it was to be pioneers in a new country, we should never come, but I am satisfied that with all the disadvantages of raising a family in a new country, there is a consolation in knowing that our children are prepared to brave the ills of life, I believe, far better than they would have been had we never left New York.

Questions

1. In what ways did the experience of moving West alter traditional expectations of women's roles?

2. What are Mrs. Noble's main complaints about her situation on the frontier, and why does she still not regret having moved to Michigan?

---

57. Ralph Waldo Emerson, "The American Scholar" (1837)

Source: "The American Scholar [1837]," in Ralph Waldo Emerson, Nature, Addresses, and Lectures *(Boston, 1892), pp. 79–80, 99–103.*

Ralph Waldo Emerson was perhaps the most prominent member of a group of New England intellectuals known as the Transcendentalists, who insisted on the primacy of individual judgment over existing social traditions and institutions. Emerson was a proponent of "individualism," a word that entered the language in the 1820s. The keynote of the times, he declared, was "the new importance given to the single person." In a widely reprinted 1837 address, "The American Scholar," delivered at Harvard College, he called on Americans engaged in writing and thinking to trust their own judgment and "never defer to the popular cry." In Emerson's own definition, rather than a preexisting set of rights or privileges, freedom was an open-ended process of self-realization by which individuals could remake themselves and their own lives. He particularly urged young scholars to free themselves from European literary and artistic ideas and create their own intellectual traditions based on American life.

Mr. President, and Gentlemen,

I greet you on the re-commencement of our literary year. Our anniversary is one of hope, and, perhaps, not enough of labor. We do not meet for games of strength or skill, for the recitation of histories, tragedies and odes, like the ancient Greeks; for parliaments of love and poesy, like the Troubadours; nor for the advancement of science, like our contemporaries in the British and European capitals. Thus far, our holiday has been simply a friendly sign of the survival of the love of letters amongst a people too busy to give to letters any more. As such, it is precious as the sign of an indestructible instinct. Perhaps the time is already come, when it ought to be, and will be something else; when the sluggard intellect of this continent will look from under its iron lids and fill the postponed expectation of the world with something better than the exertions of mechanical skill. Our day of dependence, our long apprenticeship to the learning of other lands, draws to a close. The millions that around us are rushing into life, cannot always be fed on the sere remains of foreign harvests. Events, actions arise, that must be sung, that will sing themselves. Who can doubt that poetry will revive and lead in a new age, as the star in the constellation Harp which now flames in our zenith, astronomers announce, shall one day be the pole-star for a thousand years.

• • •

In self-trust, all the virtues are comprehended. Free should the scholar be,—free and brave. Free even to the definition of freedom, "without any hindrance that does not arise out of his own constitution." Brave; for fear is a thing which a scholar by his very function puts behind him. Fear always springs from ignorance. It is a shame to him if his tranquility, amid dangerous times, arise from the presumption that like children and women, his is a protected class; or if he seek a temporary peace by the diversion of his thoughts from politics or vexed questions, hiding his head like an ostrich in the flowering bushes, peeping into microscopes, and turning rhymes, as a boy whistles to keep his courage up. So is the danger a danger still: so is the fear worse. Manlike let him turn and face it. Let him look into its eye and search its nature, inspect its origin—see the whelping of this lion,—which lies no great way back; he will then find in himself a perfect comprehension of its nature and extent; he will have made his hands meet on the other side, and can henceforth defy it, and pass on superior. The world is his who can see through its pretension. What deafness, what stoneblind custom, what over-grown error you behold, is there only by sufferance,—by your suffer-ance. See it to be a lie, and you have already dealt it its mortal blow.

Yes, we are the cowed,—we the trustless. It is a mischievous notion that we are come late into nature; that the world was finished a long time ago. As the world was plastic and fluid in the hands of God, so it is ever to so much of his attributes as we bring to it. To ignorance and sin, it is flint. They adapt themselves to it as they may; but in proportion as a man has anything in him divine, the firmament flows before him, and takes his signet [seal] and form. Not he is great who can alter matter, but he who can alter my state of mind. They are the kings of the world who give the color of their present thought to all nature and all art, and persuade men by the cheerful serenity of their carrying the matter, that this thing which they do, is the apple which the ages have desired to pluck, now at last ripe, and invit-ing nations to the harvest. The great man makes the great thing. . . . The day is always his, who works in it with serenity and great aims. The unstable estimates of men crowd to him whose mind is filled with a truth, as the heaped waves of the Atlantic follow the moon.

• • •

Another sign of our times, also marked by an analogous political movement is, the new importance given to the single person. Every thing that tends to insulate the individual,—to surround him with barriers of natural respect, so that each man shall feel the world is his, and man shall treat with man as a sovereign state with a sovereign state:—tends to true union as well as greatness. "I learned," said the melancholy Pestalozzi, [a Swiss educator] "that no man in God's wide earth is either willing or able to help any other man." Help must come from the bosom alone. The scholar is that man who must take up into himself all the ability of the time, all the contributions of the past, all the hopes of the future. He must be an university of knowledges. If there be one lesson more than another which should pierce his ear, it is, The world is nothing, the man is all; in yourself is the law of all nature, and you know not yet how a globule of sap ascends; in yourself slumbers the whole of Reason; it is for you to know all, it is for you to dare all. Mr. President and Gentlemen, this confidence in the unsearched might of man, belongs by all motives, by all prophecy, by all preparation, to the American Scholar. We have listened too long to the courtly muses of Europe. The spirit of the American freeman is already suspected to be timid, imitative, tame. Public and private avarice make the air we breathe thick and fat. The scholar is decent, indolent, complaisant. See already the tragic consequence. The mind of this country taught to aim at low objects, eats upon itself. There is no work for any but the decorous and the complaisant. Young men of the fairest promise, who begin life upon our shores, inflated by the mountain winds, shined upon by all the stars of God, find the earth below not in unison with these,—but are hindered from action by the disgust which the principles on which business is managed inspire, and turn drudges, or die of disgust,— some of them suicides. What is the remedy? They did not yet see, and thousands of young men as hopeful now crowding to the barriers for the career, do not yet see, that if the single man plant himself indomitably on his instincts, and there abide, the huge world will come round to him. Patience—patience;—with the shades of all the good and great for company; and for solace, the perspective of your own infinite life; and for work, the study and the communication of principles, the making those instincts prevalent, the conversion of the world. It is not the chief disgrace in the world, not to be an unit;—not to be reckoned one character;—not to yield that peculiar fruit which each man was created to bear, but to be reckoned in the gross, in the hundred, or the thousand, of the party, the section, to which we belong; and our opinion predicted geographically, as the north, or the south. Not so, brothers and friends,—please God, ours shall not be so. We will walk on our own feet; we will work with our own hands; we will speak our own minds. Then shall man be no longer a name for pity, for doubt, and for sensual indulgence. The dread of man and the love of man shall be a wall of defence and a wreath of love around all. A nation of men will for the first time exist, because each believes himself inspired by the Divine Soul which also inspires all men.

Questions

1. Why does Emerson feel that American writers and artists are "cowed" and need to develop more boldness and originality?

2. Why does Emerson describe self-reliance as a "manlike" quality?

58. Henry David Thoreau, *Walden* (1854)

Source: Henry David Thoreau, Walden *(Boston, 1854), pp. 10–17.*

Henry David Thoreau, Emerson's neighbor in Concord, Massachusetts, became persuaded that modern society stifled individual judgment by making men "tools of their tools," trapped in stultifying jobs by their obsession with acquiring wealth. Americans, he believed, were so preoccupied with material things that they had no time to contemplate the beauties of nature.

To escape this fate, Thoreau retreated from 1845 to 1847 to a cabin on Walden Pond in Concord, where he could enjoy the freedom of isolation from the misplaced values he believed ruled American society. He subsequently wrote *Walden* (1854), an account of his experiences. Unlike writers who celebrated the market revolution, Thoreau insisted that it was degrading both Americans' values and the natural environment. Americans, he believed, should adopt a pace of life more attuned to the rhythms of nature. Genuine freedom, he insisted, lay not in the accumulation of material goods, but within. One of the most influential works of American literature ever written, *Walden* would be rediscovered by later generations who criticized social conformity, materialism, and the degradation of the natural environment.

• • •

THE MASS OF men lead lives of quiet desperation. What is called resignation is confirmed desperation. From the desperate city you go into the desperate country, and have to console yourself with the bravery of minks and muskrats. A stereotyped but unconscious despair is concealed even under what are called the games and amusements of mankind. There is no play in them, for this comes after work. But it is a characteristic of wisdom not to do desperate things.

The greater part of what my neighbours call good I believe in my soul to be bad, and if I repent of anything, it is very likely to be my good behaviour. What demon possessed me that I behaved so well? You may say the wisest thing you can, old man—you who have lived seventy years, not without honour of a kind—I hear an irresistible voice which invites me away from all that. One generation abandons the enterprises of another like stranded vessels.

I think that we may safely trust a good deal more than we do. We may waive just so much care of ourselves as we honestly bestow elsewhere. Nature is as well adapted to our weakness as to our strength.... Let us consider for a moment what most of the trouble and anxiety which I have referred to is about, and how much it is necessary that we be troubled, or at least, careful. It would be some advantage to live a primitive and frontier life, though in the midst of an outwards civilisation, if only to learn what are the gross necessaries of life and what methods have been taken to obtain them; or even to look over the old day-books of the merchants, to see what it was that the men most commonly bought at the stores, what they stored, that is, what are the grossest groceries. For the improvements of ages have had but little influence on the essential laws of man's existence: as our skeletons, probably, are not to be distinguished from those of our ancestors.

By the words, *necessary of life*, I mean whatever, of all that man obtains by his own exertions, has been from the first, or from long use has become, so important to human life that few, if any, whether from savageness, or poverty, or philosophy, ever attempt to do without it.... Most of the luxuries, and many of the so-called comforts of life, are not only not indispensable, but positive hindrances to the elevation of mankind. With respect to luxuries and comforts, the wisest have ever lived a more simple and meagre life than the poor. The ancient philosophers, Chinese, Hindoo, Persian, and Greek, were a class than which none has been poorer in outward riches, none so rich in inward...

• • •

I went to the woods because I wished to live deliberately, to [confront] only the essential facts of life, and see if I could not learn what it had to teach, and not, when I came to die, discover that I had not lived. I did not wish to live what was not life, living is so dear, nor did I wish to practice resignation, unless it was quite necessary. I wanted to live deep and suck out all the marrow of life, to live so sturdily and Spartan-like as to put rout all that was not life, to cut a broad swath and shave close, to drive life into a corner, and reduce it to its lowest terms, and, if it proved to be mean, why then to get the whole and genuine meanness of it, and publish its meanness to the world; or if it were sublime, to know it by experience, and be able to give a true account of it in my next excursion. For most men, it appears to me, are in a strange uncertainty about it, whether it is of the devil or of God, and have somewhat hastily concluded that it is the chief end of man here to "glorify God and enjoy him forever."

Still we live meanly, like ants; though the fable tells us that we were long ago changed into men; like pygmies we fight with cranes; it is error upon error, and clout upon clout, and our best virtue has for its occasion a superfluous and inevitable wretchedness. Our life is frittered away by detail. An honest man has hardly need to count more than his ten fingers, or in extreme cases he may add his ten toes, and lump the rest. Simplicity, simplicity, simplicity! I say, let your affairs be as two or three, and not a hundred or a thousand; instead of a million, count half a dozen, and keep your accounts on your thumb nail.... Simplify, simplify. Instead of three meals a day, if it be necessary eat but one; instead of a hundred dishes, five; and reduce other things in proportion....

The nation itself, with all its so called internal improvements, which, by the way, are all external and superficial, is just such an unwieldy and overgrown establishment, cluttered with furniture and tripped up by its own traps, ruined by luxury and heedless expense, by want of calculation and a worthy aim, as the million households in the land; and the only cure for them is in a rigid economy, a stern and more than Spartan simplicity of life and elevation of purpose. It lives too fast. Men think that it is essential that the Nation have commerce, and export ice, and talk through a telegraph, and ride thirty miles an hour, without a doubt, whether they do or not; but whether we should live like baboons or like men, is a little uncertain.

If we do not get our sleepers, and forge rails, and devote days and nights to the work, but go tinkering upon our lives to improve them, who will build railroads? And if railroads are not built, how shall we get to heaven in season? But if we stay at home and mind our business, who will want railroads? We do not ride on the railroad; it rides upon us. Did you ever think what those sleepers are that underlie the railroad? Each one is a man, an Irishman, or a

Yankee man. The rails are laid on them, and they are covered with sand, and the cars run smoothly over them. They are sound sleepers, I assure you. And every few years a new lot is laid down and run over; so that if some have the pleasure of riding on a rail, others have the misfortune to be ridden upon.

Why should we live with such a hurry and waste of life? We are determined to be starved before we are hungry. Men say that a stitch in time saves nine, and so they take a thousand stitches today to save nine tomorrow.

• • •

Questions

1. Thoreau's statement, "The mass of men lead lives of quiet desperation," is one of the most famous lines in American literature. What does he mean, and what does he think is the cause?

2. What does Thoreau mean when he writes, "We do not ride on the railroad; it rides upon us"?

59. Charles G. Finney, "Sinners Bound to Change Their Own Hearts" (1836)

Source: "Sinners Bound to Change Their Own Hearts," in Charles G. Finney, Sermons on Important Subjects *(3rd ed.: New York, 1836), pp. 3–42.*

Beginning in the early nineteenth century, a series of religious revivals, known as the Second Great Awakening, swept over the United States. They reached a crescendo in the 1820s and early 1830s, when the Rev. Charles Grandison Finney held months-long revival meetings in upstate New York and New York City. His sermons warned of hell in vivid language while offering the promise of salvation to converts who abandoned their sinful ways. He rejected the idea that man is a sinful creature with a preordained fate, promoting instead the doctrine of free will and the possibility of salvation. Every person, Finney insisted, was a moral free agent, that is, a person free to choose between a Christian life and a life of sin.

The Second Great Awakening democratized American Christianity, making it a truly mass enterprise. At the time of independence, fewer than 2,000 Christian ministers preached in the United States. In 1845, they numbered 40,000. Americans, wrote Alexis de Tocqueville when he visited the United States in the 1830s, "combine the notions of Christianity and of liberty so intimately in their minds that it is impossible to make them conceive the one without the other."

——————

Ezek. xviii, 31: Make you a new heart and a new spirit, for why will ye die?

• • •

A CHANGE OF HEART . . . consists in changing the controlling preference of the mind in regard to the *end* of pursuit. The selfish heart is a preference of self-interest to the glory of God and the interests of his kingdom. A new heart consists in a preference of the glory of God and the interests of his kingdom to one's own happiness. In other words, it is a change from selfishness to benevolence, from having a supreme regard to one's own interest to an absorbing and controlling choice of the happiness and glory of God and his kingdom.

It is a change in the choice of a *Supreme Ruler.* The conduct of impenitent sinners demonstrates that they prefer Satan as the ruler of the world, they obey his laws, electioneer for him, and are zealous for his interests, even to martyrdom. They carry their attachment to him and his government so far as to sacrifice both body and soul to promote his interest and establish his dominion. A new heart is the choice of JEHOVAH as the supreme ruler; a deep-seated and abiding preference of his laws, and government, and character, and person, as the supreme Legislator and Governor of the universe.

Thus the world is divided into two great political parties; the difference between them is, that one party choose Satan as the god of this world, yield obedience to his laws, and are devoted to his interest.

Selfishness is the law of Satan's empire, and all impenitent sinners yield it a willing obedience. The other party choose Jehovah for their governor, and consecrate themselves, with all their interests, to his service and glory. Nor does this change imply a constitutional alteration of the powers of body or mind, any more than a change of mind in regard to the form or administration of a human government....

God has established a government, and proposed by the exhibition of his own character, to produce the greatest practicable amount of happiness in the universe. He has enacted laws wisely calculated to promote this object, to which he conforms all his own conduct, and to which he requires all his subjects perfectly and undeviatingly to conform theirs. After a season of obedience, Adam changed his heart, and set up for himself. So with every sinner, although he *does not first obey, as Adam did;* yet his wicked heart consists in setting up his own interest in opposition to the interest and government of God. In aiming to promote his own private happiness, in a way that is opposed to the general good. Self-gratification becomes the law to which he conforms his conduct. It is that minding of the flesh, which is enmity against God. A change of heart, therefore, is to prefer a different *end*. To prefer supremely the glory of God and the public good, to the promotion of his own interest; and whenever this preference is changed, we see of course a corresponding change of conduct. If a man change sides in politics, you will see him meeting with those that entertain the same views and feelings with himself; devising plans and using his influence to elect the candidate which he has now chosen. He has new political friends on the one side, and new political enemies on the other. So with a sinner; if his heart is changed, you will see that Christians become his friends—Christ his candidate. He aims at honoring him and promoting his interest in all his ways. Before, the language of his conduct was, "Let Satan govern the world." Now, the language of his heart and of his life is, "Let Christ rule King of nations, as he is King of saints." Before, his conduct said, "O Satan, let thy kingdom come, and let thy will be done." Now, his heart, his life, his lips cry out, "O

Jesus, let thy kingdom come, let thy will be done on earth as it is in heaven." . . .

• • •

As God requires men to make to themselves a new heart, on pain of eternal death, it is the strongest possible evidence that they are able to do it. To say that he has commanded them to do it, without telling them they are able, is consummate trifling. Their ability is implied as strongly as it can be, in the command itself. . . .

The strivings of the Spirit of God with men, is not a physical scuffling, but a debate; a strife not of body with body, but of mind with mind; and that in the action and reaction of vehement argumentation. From these remarks, it is easy to answer the question sometimes put by individuals who seem to be entirely in the dark upon this subject, whether in converting the soul the Spirit acts directly on the mind, or on the truth. This is the same nonsense as if you should ask, whether an earthly advocate who had gained his cause, did it by acting directly and physically on the jury, or on his argument. . . .

You see from this subject that a sinner, under the influence of the Spirit of God, is just as free as a jury under the arguments of an advocate. . . .

• • •

So if a minister goes into a desk to preach to sinners, believing that they have no power to obey the truth, and under the impression that a direct physical influence must be exerted upon them before they *can* believe, and if his audience be of the same opinion, in vain does he preach, and in vain do they hear, "for they are yet in their sins;" they sit and quietly wait for some invisible hand to be stretched down from heaven, and perform some surgical operation, infuse some new principle, or implant some constitutional taste; *after* which they suppose they shall be *able* to obey God. Ministers should labor with sinners, as a lawyer does with a jury, and upon the same principles of mental philosophy; and the sinner should weigh his arguments, and make up his mind as upon oath and for his life, and give a verdict upon the spot, according to law and evidence. . . .

Sinner! instead of waiting and praying for God to change your heart, you should at once summon up your powers, put forth the effort, and change the governing preference of your mind....

Sinner! your obligation to love God is equal to the excellence of his character, and your guilt in not obeying him is of course equal to your obligation. You cannot therefore for an hour or a moment defer obedience to the commandment in the text, without deserving eternal damnation....

And now, sinner; while the subject is before you, will you yield? To keep yourself away from under the motives of the gospel, by neglecting church, and neglecting your Bible, will prove fatal to your soul. And to be careless when you do attend, or to hear with attention and refuse to make up your mind and yield, will be equally fatal. And now, "I beseech you, by the mercies of God, that you at *this time* render your body and soul, a living sacrifice to God, which is your reasonable service." Let the truth take hold upon your conscience— throw down your rebellious weapons—give up your refuges of lies— fix your mind steadfastly upon the world of considerations that should instantly decide you to close in with the offer of reconciliation while it now lies before you. Another moment's delay, and it may be too late forever. The Spirit of God may depart from you—the offer of life may be made no more, and this one more slighted offer of mercy may close up your account, and seal you over to all the horrors of eternal death. Hear, then, O sinner, I beseech you, and obey the word of the Lord—"Make you a new heart and a new spirit, for why will ye die?"

Questions

1. What precisely does Finney mean by a "change of heart"?

2. How does the fact that he is preaching in an era of mass political democracy affect Finney's language?

CHAPTER 10

Democracy in America, 1815–1840

60. The Monroe Doctrine (1823)

Source: James D. Richardson, ed., A Compilation of the Messages and Papers of the Presidents *(10 vols.: Washington, D.C., 1896–1899), Vol. 2, pp. 778, 786–88.*

Between 1810 and 1822, Spain's Latin American colonies rose in rebellion and established a series of independent nations, including Mexico, Venezuela, Ecuador, and Peru. By 1825, Spain's once vast American empire had been reduced to the islands of Cuba and Puerto Rico. The uprisings inspired a wave of sympathy in the United States. In 1822, the Monroe administration became the first government to extend diplomatic recognition to the new Latin American republics. The following year, President James Monroe included in his annual message a passage, written by Secretary of State John Quincy Adams, that became known as the Monroe Doctrine. It outlined principles that would help to govern the country's relations with the rest of the world for nearly a century—that the Western Hemisphere was no longer open to European colonization and that the United States would remain uninvolved in the wars of Europe. In effect, Monroe declared the Americas a sphere of influence of the United States.

AT THE PROPOSAL of the Russian Imperial government, made through the minister of the Emperor residing here, a full power and instructions have been transmitted to the minister of the United States at St. Petersburg to arrange by amicable negotiation the respective rights and interests of the two nations on the northwest coast of this continent. A similar proposal has been made by His Imperial Majesty to the government of Great Britain, which has likewise been acceded to. The government of the United States has been desirous by this friendly proceeding of manifesting the great value which they have invariably attached to the friendship of the Emperor and their solicitude to cultivate the best understanding with his government.

In the discussions to which this interest has given rise and in the arrangements by which they may terminate the occasion has been judged proper for asserting, as a principle in which the rights and interests of the United States are involved, that the American continents, by the free and independent condition which they have assumed and maintain, are henceforth not to be considered as subjects for future colonization by any European powers....

It was stated at the commencement of the last session that a great effort was then making in Spain and Portugal to improve the condition of the people of those countries, and that it appeared to be conducted with extraordinary moderation. It need scarcely be remarked that the results have been so far very different from what was then anticipated. Of events in that quarter of the globe, with which we have so much intercourse and from which we derive our origin, we have always been anxious and interested spectators. The citizens of the United States cherish sentiments the most friendly in favor of the liberty and happiness of their fellow-men on that side of the Atlantic. In the wars of the European powers in matters relating to themselves we have never taken any part, nor does it comport with our policy to do so. It is only when our rights are invaded or seriously menaced that we resent injuries or make preparation for our defense. With the movements in this hemisphere we are of necessity more immediately connected, and by causes which must be obvious to all enlightened and impartial observers. The political system of the allied powers [of Europe] is essentially different in this respect from that of America. . . .

We owe it, therefore, to candor and to the amicable relations existing between the United States and those powers to declare that we should consider any attempt on their part to extend their system to any portion of this hemisphere as dangerous to our peace and safety. With the existing colonies or dependencies of any European power we have not interfered and shall not interfere. But with the Governments who have declared their independence and maintain it, and whose independence we have, on great consideration and on just principles, acknowledged, we could not view any interposition for the purpose of oppressing them, or controlling in any other manner their destiny, by any European power in any other light than as the manifestation of an unfriendly disposition toward the United States. . . .

It is impossible that the allied powers should extend their political system to any portion of [North or South America] without endangering our peace and happiness; nor can anyone believe that our southern brethren, if left to themselves, would adopt it of their own accord. It is equally impossible, therefore, that we should behold such interposition in any form with indifference. If we look to the comparative strength and resources of Spain and those new governments, and their distance from each other, it must be obvious that she can never subdue them. It is still the true policy of the United States to leave the parties to themselves, in hope that other powers will pursue the same course.

Questions

1. Why does Monroe think that the "systems" of Europe and the Western Hemisphere are fundamentally different?

2. Why does Monroe mention Russia at the beginning of his address?

61. John Quincy Adams on the Role of the National Government (1825)

Source: James D. Richardson, ed., A Compilation of the Messages and Papers of the Presidents (10 vols.: Washington, D.C., 1896–1899), Vol. 2., pp. 878–82.

Many Americans in the first half of the nineteenth century saw a powerful federal government as a threat to individual liberty. Others, however, believed that by promoting economic expansion and encouraging the development of the arts and sciences, the government would enhance Americans' freedom. Among the proponents of an activist federal government was John Quincy Adams, who served as president from 1825 to 1829.

In his first annual message to Congress, in December 1825, he set forth a comprehensive program for government action. He called for legislation promoting agriculture, commerce, and manufacturing, and "the mechanical and elegant arts." His plans included government-financed improvements in transportation, scientific expeditions, and the establishment of a national astronomical observatory. Adams astonished many listeners with his bold statement, "liberty is power." The United States, the freest nation on earth, he predicted, would also become the mightiest.

Adams's proposals alarmed all believers in strict construction of the Constitution. Few of his ambitious ideas received support in Congress. Not until the twentieth century would the kind of national economic planning and educational and scientific involvement envisioned by Adams be realized.

IN ASSUMING HER station among the civilized nations of the earth it would seem that our country had contracted the engagement to contribute her share of mind, of labor, and of expense to the improvement of those parts of knowledge which lie beyond the reach of individual acquisition, and particularly to geographical and astronomical science. Looking back to the history only of the half century since the declaration of our independence, and observing the generous emulation with which the Governments of France,

Great Britain, and Russia have devoted the genius, the intelligence, the treasures of their respective nations to the common improvement of the species in these branches of science, is it not incumbent upon us to inquire whether we are not bound by obligations of a high and honorable character to contribute our portion of energy and exertion to the common stock? The voyages of discovery prosecuted in the course of that time at the expense of those nations have not only redounded to their glory, but to the improvement of human knowledge. We have been partakers of that improvement and owe for it a sacred debt, not only of gratitude, but of equal or proportional exertion in the same common cause. Of the cost of these undertakings, if the mere expenditures of outfit, equipment, and completion of the expeditions were to be considered the only charges, it would be unworthy of a great and generous nation to take a second thought. One hundred expeditions of circumnavigation ... would not burden the exchequer of the nation fitting them out so much as the ways and means of defraying a single campaign in war. But if we take into the account the lives of those benefactors of mankind of which their services in the cause of their species were the purchase, how shall the cost of those heroic enterprises be estimated, and what compensation can be made to them or to their countries for them? Is it not by bearing them in affectionate remembrance? Is it not still more by imitating their example by enabling countrymen of our own to pursue the same career and to hazard their lives in the same cause?

• • •

In inviting the attention of Congress to the subject of internal improvements upon a view thus enlarged it is not my design to recommend the equipment of an expedition for circumnavigating the globe for purposes of scientific research and inquiry. We have objects of useful investigation nearer home, and to which our cares may be more beneficially applied. The interior of our own territories has yet been very imperfectly explored. Our coasts along many degrees of latitude upon the shores of the Pacific Ocean, though much frequented by our spirited commercial navigators, have been barely

visited by our public ships. The River of the West, first fully discovered and navigated by a countryman of our own, still bears the name
of the ship in which he ascended its waters, and claims the protection
of our armed national flag at its mouth. With the establishment of a
military post there or at some other point of that coast, recommended
by my predecessor and already matured in the deliberations of the
last Congress, I would suggest the expediency of connecting the
equipment of a public ship for the exploration of the whole northwest coast of this continent. . . .

• • •

Connected with the establishment of an university, or separate
from it, might be undertaken the erection of an astronomical observatory, with provision for the support of an astronomer, to be in
constant attendance of observation upon the phenomena of the
heavens, and for the periodical publication of his observations. It is
with no feeling of pride as an American that the remark may be
made that on the comparatively small territorial surface of Europe
there are existing upward of 130 of these light-houses of the skies,
while throughout the whole American hemisphere there is not one.
If we reflect a moment upon the discoveries which in the last four
centuries have been made in the physical constitution of the universe by the means of these buildings and of observers stationed in
them, shall we doubt of their usefulness to every nation? And while
scarcely a year passes over our heads without bringing some new
astronomical discovery to light, which we must fain receive at second hand from Europe, are we not cutting ourselves off from the
means of returning light for light while we have neither observatory nor observer upon our half of the globe and the earth revolves
in perpetual darkness to our unsearching eyes?

The Constitution under which you are assembled is a charter of
limited powers. After full and solemn deliberation upon all or any of
the objects which, urged by an irresistible sense of my own duty, I
have recommended to your attention should you come to the conclusion that, however desirable in themselves, the enactment of laws for
effecting them would transcend the powers committed to you by

that venerable instrument which we are all bound to support, let no consideration induce you to assume the exercise of powers not granted to you by the people. But if the power to exercise exclusive legislation in all cases whatsoever over the District of Columbia; if the power to lay and collect taxes, duties, imposts, and excises, to pay the debts and provide for the common defense and general welfare of the United States; if the power to regulate commerce with foreign nations and among the several States and with the Indian tribes, to fix the standard of weights and measures, to establish post-offices and post-roads, to declare war, to raise and support armies, to provide and maintain a navy, to dispose of and make all needful rules and regulations respecting the territory or other property belonging to the United States, and to make all laws which shall be necessary and proper for carrying these powers into execution—if these powers and others enumerated in the Constitution may be effectually brought into action by laws promoting the improvement of agriculture, commerce, and manufactures, the cultivation and encouragement of the mechanic and of the elegant arts, the advancement of literature, and the progress of the sciences, ornamental and profound, to refrain from exercising them for the benefit of the people themselves would be to hide in the earth the talent committed to our charge—would be treachery to the most sacred of trusts.

The spirit of improvement is abroad upon the earth. It stimulates the hearts and sharpens the faculties not of our fellow-citizens alone, but of the nations of Europe and of their rulers. While dwelling with pleasing satisfaction upon the superior excellence of our political institutions, let us not be unmindful that liberty is power; that the nation blessed with the largest portion of liberty must in proportion to its numbers be the most powerful nation upon earth, and that the tenure of power by man is, in the moral purposes of his Creator, upon condition that it shall be exercised to ends of beneficence, to improve the condition of himself and his fellowmen. While foreign nations less blessed with that freedom which is power than ourselves are advancing with gigantic strides in the career of public improvement, were we to slumber in indolence or fold up our arms and proclaim to the world that we are palsied by the will of our constituents, would it not be to cast away the bounties of Providence and doom ourselves to perpetual inferiority? In the course of the year now drawing to its close we have beheld, under the auspices and at the expense of one State of this Union, a new university unfolding its portals to the sons of science and holding up the torch of human improvement to eyes that seek the light. We have seen under the persevering and enlightened enterprise of another State the waters of our Western lakes mingle with those of the ocean. If undertakings like these have been accomplished in the compass of a few years by the authority of single members of our Confederation, can we, the representative authorities of the whole Union, fall behind our fellow-servants in the exercise of the trust committed to us for the benefit of our common sovereign by the accomplishment of works important to the whole and to which neither the authority nor the resources of any one State can be adequate?

Questions

1. Why does President Adams believe that the federal government should promote the sciences and arts?

2. What does he mean by the remark, "liberty is power"?

62. John C. Calhoun, The Concurrent Majority (ca. 1845)

Source: "A Disquisition on Government," in Richard K. Crallé, ed., The Works of John C. Calhoun *(New York, 1854–1857), Vol. 1, pp. 28–29.*

The Nullification Crisis of the early 1830s pitted South Carolina, which claimed the right to nullify a national tariff law of which it disapproved,

against President Andrew Jackson. John C. Calhoun, once a strong national-
ist, emerged as the leading theorist of nullification. The national government, he insisted, had been created by an agreement between sovereign
states, each of which retained the right to prevent the enforcement within
its borders of acts of Congress that exceeded the powers spelled out in the
Constitution.

In the aftermath of the crisis, Calhoun began thinking about other constitutional mechanisms that could preserve both the Union and the
South's rights, especially as Southerners were becoming a distinct minority.
He developed the theory of the "concurrent majority." Rather than relying
on a simple numerical majority to ascertain the popular will, Calhoun
argued, the only way to ensure the stability of a large, diverse nation was
for each major interest (including slaveowners) to have the right to veto
all measures that affected it. Calhoun began writing his *Disquisition on
Government*, from which the excerpt below is taken, during the 1840s, but
it was not published until after his death in 1850.

———

THERE ARE TWO different modes in which the sense of the community may be taken; one, simply by the right of suffrage, unaided; the
other, by the right through a proper organism. Each collects the sense
of the majority. But one regards numbers only, and considers the
whole community as a unit, having but one common interest throughout; and collects the sense of the greater number of the whole, as
that of the community. The other, on the contrary, regards interests
as well as numbers;—considering the community as made up of different and conflicting interests, as far as the action of the government is concerned; and takes the sense of each, through its majority
or appropriate organ, and the united sense of all, as the sense of the
entire community. The former of these I shall call the numerical, or
absolute majority; and the latter, the concurrent, or constitutional
majority. I call it the constitutional majority, because it is an essential element in every constitutional government,—be its form what
it may. So great is the difference, politically speaking, between the
two majorities, that they cannot be confounded, without leading to

great and fatal errors; and yet the distinction between them has been so entirely overlooked, that when the term *majority* is used in political discussions, it is applied exclusively to designate the numerical,—as if there were no other. Until this distinction is recognized, the better understood, there will continue to be great liability to error in properly constructing constitutional governments, especially of the popular form, and of preserving them when properly constructed. Until then, the latter will have a strong tendency to slide, first, into the government of the numerical majority, and finally, into absolute government of some other form. To show that such must be the case, and at the same time to mark more strongly the difference between the two, in order to guard against the danger of overlooking it, I propose to consider the subject more at length.

The first and leading error which naturally arises from overlooking the distinction referred to, is, to confound the numerical majority with the people; and this so completely as to regard them as identical. This is a consequence that necessarily results from considering the numerical as the only majority. All admit, that a popular government, or democracy, is the government of the people; for the terms imply this. A perfect government of the kind would be one which would embrace the consent of every citizen or member of the community; but as this is impracticable, in the opinion of those who regard the numerical as the only majority, and who can perceive no other way by which the sense of the people can be taken,—they are compelled to adopt this as the only true basis of popular government, in contradistinction to governments of the aristocratical or monarchical form. Being thus constrained, they are, in the next place, forced to regard the numerical majority, as, in effect, the entire people....

• • •

The necessary consequence of taking the sense of the community by the concurrent majority is, as has been explained, to give to each interest or portion of the community a negative on the others. It is this mutual negative among its various conflicting interests, which invests each with the power of protecting itself;—and places the rights and safety of each, where only they can be securely placed, under its own guardianship. Without this there can be no systematic, peaceful, or effective resistance to the natural tendency of each to come into conflict with the others: and without this there can be no constitution. It is this negative power,—the power of preventing or arresting the action of the government,—be it called by what term it may,—veto, interposition, nullification, check, or balance of power,—which, in fact, forms the constitution. They are all but different names for the negative power.

Questions

1. How does Calhoun distinguish between the "numerical" and "concurrent" majorities?

2. Which Americans would be most likely to object to Calhoun's proposed constitutional system?

---

63. Virginia Petition for the Right to Vote (1829)

Source: Proceedings and Debates of the Virginia State Convention of *1829–1830 (Richmond, 1830), pp. 25–31.*

The challenge to property qualifications for voting, which began during the American Revolution, reached its culmination in the first part of the nineteenth century. No state that entered the Union after the original thirteen required ownership of property to vote. In the older states, constitutional conventions during the 1820s and 1830s debated once again who should be able to participate in American democracy.

By the 1820s, only North Carolina, Rhode Island, and Virginia still retained property qualifications for voting. One of the first actions of Virginia's constitutional convention of 1829–1830 was to consider a memorial from "non-freeholders" of Richmond—men who did not possess enough land to enable them to vote. Those who owned property, declared their statement, did not necessarily possess "moral or intellectual endowments" superior to those of the poor. "They alone deserve to be called free," they added, "who participate in the formation of their political institutions." The large slaveholders who dominated Virginia politics successfully resisted demands for changes in voting qualifications in 1829, but a subsequent constitutional convention, in 1850, eliminated the property requirement.

YOUR MEMORIALISTS, AS their designation imports, belong to that class of citizens, who, not having the good fortune to possess a certain portion of land, are, for that cause only, debarred from the enjoyment of the right of suffrage. Experience has but too clearly evinced, what, indeed, reason had always foretold, by how frail a tenure they hold every other right, who are denied this, the highest prerogative of freemen. The want of it has afforded both the pretext and the means of excluding the entire class, to which your memorialists belong, from all participation in the recent election of the body, they now respectfully address. Comprising a very large part, probably a majority of male citizens of mature age, they have been passed by, like aliens or slaves, as if destitute of interest, or unworthy of a voice, in measures involving their future political destiny: whilst the freeholders, sole possessors, under the existing Constitution, of the elective franchise, have, upon the strength of that possession alone, asserted and maintained in themselves, the exclusive power of new-modelling the fundamental laws of the State: in other words, have seized upon the sovereign authority.

It cannot be necessary, in addressing the Convention now assembled, to expatiate on the momentous importance of the right of suffrage, or to enumerate the evils consequent upon its unjust limitation. Were there no other than that your memorialists have brought to your attention, and which has made them feel with full force their degraded condition, well might it justify their best efforts to obtain the great privilege they now seek, as the only effectual method of preventing its recurrence. To that privilege, they respectfully contend, they are entitled equally with its present possessors. Many are bold enough to deny their title. None can show a better. It rests upon no subtle or abstruse reasoning; but upon grounds simple in their character, intelligible to the plainest capacity, and such as appeal to the heart, as well as the understanding, of all who comprehend and duly appreciate the principles of free Government....

How do the principles thus proclaimed, accord with the existing regulation of suffrage? A regulation, which, instead of the equality nature ordains, creates an odious distinction between members of the same community; robs of all share, in the enactment of the laws, a large portion of the citizens, bound by them, and whose blood and treasure are pledged to maintain them, and vests in a favoured class, not in consideration of their public services, but of their private possessions, the highest of all privileges....

Surely it were much to be desired that, every citizen should be qualified for the proper exercise of all his rights, and the due performance of all his duties. But the same qualifications that entitle him to assume the management of his private affairs, and to claim all other privileges of citizenship, equally entitle him, in the judgment of your memorialists, to be entrusted with this, the dearest of all his privileges, the most important of all his concerns. But if otherwise, still they cannot discern in the possession of land any evidence of peculiar merit, or superior title. To ascribe to a landed possession, moral or intellectual endowments, would truly be regarded as ludicrous, were it not for the gravity with which the proposition is maintained, and still more for the grave consequences flowing from it. Such possession no more proves him who has it, wiser or better, than it proves him taller or stronger, than him who has it not. That cannot be a fit criterion for the exercise of any right, the possession of which does not indicate the existence, nor the want of it the absence, of any essential qualification....

Your memorialists do not design to institute a comparison; they fear none that can be fairly made between the privileged and the proscribed classes. They may be permitted, however, without disrespect, to remark, that of the latter, not a few possess land: many, though not proprietors, are yet cultivators of the soil: others are engaged in avocations of a different nature, often as useful, presupposing no less integrity, requiring as much intelligence, and as fixed a residence, as agricultural pursuits. Virtue, intelligence, are not among the products of the soil. Attachment to property, often a sordid sentiment, is not to be confounded with the sacred flame of patriotism. The love of country, like that of parents and offspring, is engrafted in our nature. It exists in all climates, among all classes, under every possible form of Government, Riches oftener impair it than poverty. Who has it not is a monster. . . .

Let us concede that the right of suffrage is a social right; that it must of necessity be regulated by society. Still the question recurs, is the existing limitation proper? For obvious reasons, by almost universal consent, women and children, aliens and slaves, are excluded. It were useless to discuss the propriety of a rule that scarcely admits of diversity of opinion. What is concurred in by those who constitute the society, the body politic, must be taken to be right. But the exclusion of these classes for reasons peculiarly applicable to them, is no argument for excluding others to whom no one of those reasons applies.

It is said to be *expedient*, however, to exclude non-freeholders also. Who shall judge of this expediency? The society: and does that embrace the proprietors of certain portions of land only? Expedient, for whom? for the freeholders. A harsh appellation would he deserve, who, on the plea of expediency, should take from another his property: what, then, should be said of him who, on that plea, takes from another his rights, upon which the security, not of his property only, but of his life and liberty depends? . . .

They alone deserve to be called free, or have a guarantee for their rights, who participate in the formation of their political institutions, and in the control of those who make and administer the laws.

Questions

1. What "obvious reasons" exclude women, children, noncitizens, and slaves from the right to vote, and why do the non-freeholders not question them?

2. How do the writers define political freedom?

---

64. Appeal of the Cherokee Nation (1830)

Source: E. C. Tracy, Memoir of the Life of Jeremiah Evarts *(Boston, 1845), pp. 149–58.*

One of the early laws of Andrew Jackson's administration, the Indian Removal Act of 1830, provided for uprooting the Cherokee and four other tribes, with a total population of around 60,000 living in the Southeast. The Cherokee had made great efforts to become citizens, establishing schools, adopting a constitution modeled on that of the United States, and becoming successful farmers, many of whom owned slaves. But in his messages to Congress, Jackson referred to them as "savages" and supported Georgia's effort to seize Cherokee land and nullify the tribe's laws.

Cherokee leaders petitioned Congress, proclaiming their desire to "remain on the land of our fathers," as guaranteed in treaties with the federal government. They also went to court to protect their rights. Chief Justice John Marshall held that Georgia's action in extending its jurisdiction over the Cherokee violated the tribe's treaties with Washington. But presidents Jackson and Van Buren refused to recognize the ruling's validity. Eventually, nearly all the Cherokee, along with the other "civilized tribes," were forced to leave their homes. More than 4,000 Indians perished during the winter of 1838–1839 on the Trail of Tears, as the removal route to present-day Oklahoma came to be called.

WE ARE AWARE that some persons suppose it will be for our advantage to remove beyond the Mississippi. We think otherwise. Our people universally think otherwise. Thinking that it would be fatal to their interests, they have almost to a man sent their memorial to Congress, deprecating the necessity of a removal. This question was distinctly before their minds when they signed their memorial. Not an adult person can be found, who has not an opinion on the subject; and if the people were to understand distinctly, that they could be protected against the laws of the neighboring States, there is probably not an adult person in the nation, who would think it best to remove; though possibly a few might emigrate individually. There are doubtless many who would flee to an unknown country, however beset with dangers, privations and sufferings, rather than be sentenced to spend six years in a Georgia prison for advising one of their neighbors not to betray his country. And there are others who could not think of living as outlaws in their native land, exposed to numberless vexations, and excluded from being parties or witnesses in a court of justice. It is incredible that Georgia should ever have enacted the oppressive laws to which reference is here made, unless she had supposed that something extremely terrific in its character was necessary, in order to make the Cherokees willing to remove. We are not willing to remove; and if we could be brought to this extremity, it would be, not by argument; not because our judgment was satisfied; not because our condition will be improved—but only because we cannot endure to be deprived of our national and individual rights, and subjected to a process of intolerable oppression.

We wish to remain on the land of our fathers. We have a perfect and original right to claim this, without interruption or molestation. The treaties with us, and laws of the United States made in pursuance of treaties, guaranty our residence, and our privileges, and secure us against intruders. Our only request is, that these treaties may be fulfilled, and these laws executed.

But if we are compelled to leave our country, we see nothing but ruin before us. The country west of the Arkansas territory is unknown to us. From what we can learn of it, we have no prepossessions in its favor. All the inviting parts of it, as we believe, are preoccupied by various Indian nations, to which it has been assigned. They would regard us as intruders, and look upon us with an evil eye. The far greater part of that region is, beyond all controversy, badly supplied with wood and water; and no Indian tribe can live as agriculturists without these articles. All our neighbors, in case of our removal, though crowded into our near vicinity, would speak a language totally different from ours, and practice different customs. The original possessors of that region are now wandering savages, lurking for prey in the neighborhood. They have always been at war, and would be easily tempted to turn their arms against peaceful emigrants. Were the country to which we are urged much better than it is represented to be, and were it free from the objections which we have made to it, still it is not the land of our birth, nor of our affections. It contains neither the scenes of our childhood, nor the graves of our fathers.

Questions

1. What reasons do the Cherokee give for rejecting the idea of moving beyond the Mississippi River?

2. How do the Cherokee understand their "national and individual rights"?

65. Appeal of Forty Thousand Citizens (1838)

Source: Appeal of Forty Thousand Citizens Threatened with Disfranchisement, to the People of Pennsylvania *(Philadelphia, 1838), pp. 3–11.*

The expansion of political democracy for white men went hand in hand with the elimination of democratic participation for blacks. Every state that entered the Union between 1800 and 1860, with the single exception of Maine, limited the right to vote to whites. And several states that had allowed black men to vote, including Connecticut, New York, and Tennessee, either eliminated the right entirely or added such high property qualifications that few could qualify. In 1837, a constitutional convention in Pennsylvania, home to the largest free black community in the North, stripped blacks of the right to vote. (Thaddeus Stevens, later a leading advocate of emancipation and black suffrage in Congress, refused to sign the document because of this provision.) In response, a large gathering in Philadelphia issued a protest to "fellow citizens" of Pennsylvania.

FELLOW CITIZENS:—We appeal to you from the decision of the "Reform Convention," which has stripped us of a right peaceably enjoyed during forty-seven years under the Constitution of this commonwealth. We honor Pennsylvania and her noble institutions too much to part with our birthright as her free citizens without a struggle. To all her citizens the right of suffrage is valuable in proportion as she is free; but surely there are none who can so ill afford to spare it as ourselves.

Was it the intention of the people of this commonwealth that the convention to which the Constitution was committed for revision and amendment, should tear up and cast away its first principles? Was it made the business of the Convention to deny "that all men are born equally free," by making political rights depend upon the skin in which a man is born? Or to divide what our fathers bled to unite, to wit, TAXATION and REPRESENTATION? We will not allow ourselves for one moment to suppose, that the majority of the people of Pennsylvania are not too respectful of the rights and too liberal towards the feelings of others as well as too much enlightened to their own interests, to deprive of the right of suffrage a single individual who may safely be trusted with it. And we cannot believe that you have found among those who bear the burdens of taxation any who have proved, by their abuse of the right, that it is not safe in their hands. This is a question, fellow-citizens, in which we plead *your* cause as well as our own. It is the safeguard of the strongest that he lives under a government which is obliged to respect the voice of the weakest. When you have taken from an individual his right to vote, you have made the government, in regard to him, a mere despotism; and you have taken a step towards making it a despotism to all.—To your women and children, their inability to vote at the polls may be no evil, because they are united by the consanguinity and affection with those who can do it. To foreigners and paupers the want of the right may be tolerable because a little time or labor will make it theirs. They are candidates for the privilege, and hence substantially enjoy its benefits. But when a distinct class of the community, already sufficiently the objects of prejudice, are wholly, and for ever, disfranchised and excluded, to the remotest posterity, from the possibility of a voice in regard to the laws under which they are to live—it is the same thing as if their abode were transferred to the dominions of the Russian Autocrat, or of the Grand Turk. They have lost their check upon oppression, their wherewith to but friends, their panoply of manhood; in short, they are thrown upon the mercy of a despotic majority. Like every other despot, this despot majority, will believe in the mildness of its own sway; but who will the more willingly submit to it for that? . . .

By the careful inquiry of a committee appointed by the "Pennsylvania Society for Promoting the Abolition of Slavery," it has been ascertained that the colored population of Philadelphia and its suburbs, numbering 18,768 souls, possess at the present time, of real and personal estate, not less than $1,350,000. They have paid for taxes during the last year $3,232.83, for house, water, and ground rent, $166,963.50. This committee estimate the income of the holders of real estate occupied by the colored people, to be $7\frac{1}{2}$ per cent on a capital of about $2,000,000. Here is an addition to the wealth of their white brethren. But the rents and taxes are not all; to pay them, the colored people must be employed in labor, and here is another profit to the whites, for no man employs another unless he can make his labor profitable to himself. For a similar reason, a profit is made by all the whites who sell to colored people the necessaries or luxuries of life. Though the aggregate amount of the wealth derived by the whites from our people can only be conjectured, its importance is worthy of consideration by those who would make it less by lessening our motive to accumulate for ourselves....

That we are not neglectful of our religious interests, nor of the education of our children, is shown by the fact that there are among us in Philadelphia, Pittsburg, York, West Chester, and Columbia, 22 churches, 48 clergymen, 26 day schools, 20 Sabbath schools, 125 Sabbath school teachers, 4 literary societies, 2 public libraries, consisting of about 800 volumes, besides 8,333 volumes in private libraries, 2 tract societies, 2 Bible societies, and 7 temperance societies.

In other parts of the State we are confident our condition will compare very favorably with that in Philadelphia, although we are not furnished with accurate statistics.

Our fathers shared with yours the trials and perils of the wilderness. Among the facts which illustrate this, it is well known that the founder of your capital, from whom it bears the name of Harrisburg, was rescued by a *colored man*, from a party of Indians, who had captured, and bound him to the stake for execution. In gratitude for this act, he *invited colored persons* to settle in his town, and offered them land on favorable terms. When our common country has been invaded by a foreign foe, colored men have hazarded their lives in its defence. Our fathers fought by the side of yours in the struggle which made us an independent republic.

Questions

1. What evidence do the free blacks present to establish that they are worthy of the right to vote?

2. How do the protesters link their claims to the legacy of the American Revolution?

CHAPTER 11

The Peculiar Institution

66. Frederick Douglass on the Desire for Freedom (1845)

Source: **Narrative of the Life of Frederick Douglass, an American Slave** *(Boston, 1845), pp. 39–43.*

No American of the nineteenth century spoke more eloquently or effectively against slavery and racial inequality than Frederick Douglass. Born into slavery in 1818, he became a major figure in the crusade for abolition, the drama of emancipation, and the effort during Reconstruction to give meaning to black freedom. He was also active in other reform movements, such as the campaign for women's rights.

Douglass experienced slavery in all its variety, from work as a house servant and as a skilled craftsman in a Baltimore shipyard to labor as a plantation field hand. In 1838, having borrowed the free papers of a black sailor, he escaped to the North. He went on to become perhaps the era's most prominent antislavery orator and editor, and wrote three versions of his autobiography. The first, which appeared in 1845, offered an eloquent, brief account of his experiences in slavery and his escape.

I was now about twelve years old, and the thought of being *a slave for life* began to bear heavily upon my heart. Just about this time, I got hold of a book entitled "The Columbian Orator." Every opportunity I got, I used to read this book. Among much of other interesting matter, I found in it a dialogue between a master and his slave. The slave was represented as having run away from his master three times. The dialogue represented the conversation which took place between them, when the slave was retaken the third time. In this dialogue, the whole argument in behalf of slavery was brought forward by the master, all of which was disposed of by the slave. The slave was made to say some very smart as well as impressive things in reply to his master—things which had the desired though unexpected effect; for the conversation resulted in the voluntary emancipation of the slave on the part of the master.

In the same book, I met with one of [British politician Richard B.] Sheridan's mighty speeches on and in behalf of Catholic emancipation. These were choice documents to me. I read them over and over again with unabated interest. They gave tongue to interesting thoughts of my own soul, which had frequently flashed through my mind, and died away for want of utterance. The moral which I gained from the dialogue was the power of truth over the conscience of even a slaveholder. What I got from Sheridan was a bold denunciation of slavery, and a powerful vindication of human rights. The reading of these documents enabled me to utter my thoughts, and to meet the arguments brought forward to sustain slavery; but while they relieved me of one difficulty, they brought on another even more painful than the one of which I was relieved. The more I read, the more I was led to abhor and detest my enslavers. I could regard them in no other light than a band of successful robbers, who had left their homes, and gone to Africa, and stolen us from our homes, and in a strange land reduced us to slavery. I loathed them as being the meanest as well as the most wicked of men. As I read and contemplated the subject, behold! that very discontentment which Master Hugh had predicted would follow my learning to read had already come, to torment and sting my soul to unutterable anguish. As I writhed under it, I would at times feel that learning to read had been a curse rather than a blessing. It had given me a view of my wretched condition, without the remedy. It opened my eyes to the horrible pit, but to no ladder upon which to get out. In moments of agony, I envied my fellow-slaves for their stupidity. I have often wished myself a beast. I preferred the condition of the meanest reptile to my own. Any thing, no matter what, to get rid of thinking! It was this everlasting thinking of my condition that tormented me. There was no getting rid of it. It was pressed upon me by every object within sight or hearing, animate or inanimate. The silver trump of freedom had roused my soul to eternal wakefulness. Freedom now appeared, to disappear no more forever. It was heard in every sound, and seen in every thing. It was ever present to torment me with a sense of my wretched condition. I saw nothing without seeing it, I heard nothing without hearing it, and felt nothing without feeling it. It looked from every star, it smiled in every calm, breathed in every wind, and moved in every storm.

I often found myself regretting my own existence, and wishing myself dead; and but for the hope of being free, I have no doubt but that I should have killed myself, or done something for which I should have been killed. While in this state of mind, I was eager to hear any one speak of slavery. I was a ready listener....

• • •

I went one day down on the wharf of Mr. Waters; and seeing two Irishmen unloading a scow of stone, I went, unasked, and helped them. When we had finished, one of them came to me and asked me if I were a slave. I told him I was. He asked, "Are ye a slave for life?" I told him that I was. The good Irishman seemed to be deeply affected by the statement. He said to the other that it was a pity so fine a little fellow as myself should be a slave for life. He said it was a shame to hold me. They both advised me to run away to the north; that I should find friends there, and that I should be free. I pretended not to be interested in what they said, and treated them as if I did not understand them; for I feared they might be treacherous. White men have been known to encourage slaves to escape, and then, to get the reward, catch them and return them to their masters. I was afraid that these seemingly good men might use me so; but I nevertheless remembered their advice, and from that time I resolved to run away. I looked forward to a time at which it would be safe for me to escape. I was too young to think of doing so immediately; besides, I wished to learn how to write, as I might have occasion to write my own pass. I consoled myself with the hope that I should one day find a good chance. Meanwhile, I would learn to write.

Questions

1. To whom is Douglass addressing his book, and how does the intended audience affect his argument?

2. Why does Douglass so strongly link education with freedom?

---

67. Rise of the Cotton Kingdom (1836)

Source: Fredrick Norcom: "Fredrick Norcom to James C. Johnston, January 24, 1836." #324, Hayes Collection. Southern Historical Collection, Wilson Library, The University of North Carolina at Chapel Hill. Reprinted with permission.

In some ways, the most dynamic feature of the American economy in the first forty years of the nineteenth century was the rise of the Cotton Kingdom. The early industrial revolution, which began in England and soon spread to parts of the North, generated an immense demand for cotton, a crop the Deep South was particularly suited to growing because of climate and soil fertility. Slavery, which many Americans had expected to die out because its major crop, tobacco, exhausted the soil, instead underwent a remarkable period of expansion. Settlers from the older southern states flooded into Alabama, Mississippi, and Louisiana.

The letter that follows was written by Fredrick Norcom, who migrated from North Carolina to Vicksburg, Mississippi, to James Johnson, a planter in Edenton, North Carolina. Norcom describes the feverish speculation in cotton, land, and slaves.

I HAVE MET with I suppose from 50 to 100 men who (many of them are entirely destitute of a common education) five years since could not get credit for a pair of shoes, now worth 100,000 to a million of dollars—I have seen a great number who came here rich, and now immensely rich; I have not seen but one single soul, nor have I heard of three, who have failed—and these were all merchants, who without much Capital went to speculating in Cotton—. It is in truth the only country I ever read or heard of, where a poor man could in two or three years without any aid, become wealthy—A few days of labour and lying out in the woods enabled them to find out a good body of land, and not having the money to enter it for themselves, they would sell their information to those who were too idle, or too rich to undergo the fatigue of hunting for it; by this means they would obtain money enough to enter one section, then two, and so on; soon sell that for ten or twenty times as much as they gave for it, and sometimes would absolutely make what is considered in the old States a fortune in five or six months. . . .

At Pontotoc in the Chickasaw Nation, there was 4 to 5 millions of dollars lying last summer to be employed in land; at the sales in December at Columbus, there was more than 5 millions, how much at the other land offices I have not heard.

All the lands obtained from the Choctaw Indians in 1832 have now been offered for sale; the greater part of the choice land of course was taken up the first year or two, and that now sells from $50–75 to 100 per acre, according to location—the second rate is selling from 20 to 40 per acre, and the third rate of which there is much yet remaining, is selling from 8 to 20 per acre—you can thus see how easy it was to get rich here—a little labour would raise $800—that will enter a section of land, to sell that for 10, to $20,000, and lay that out again and get in return 10 or 20 for one, is an easy and rapid mode of getting rich. . . . The demand for all species of property here is great, constant and increasing—I cannot ascertain what amount of property has been sold in any one county. More than 6,000 Negroes and 10,000 horses and mules have been sold in Yazoo County alone, and from 1st Sept. up to this time (and I am told it so continues until April) there are Negroes by the hundred in every little Log-Village for sale....

I know of no point in the world with four times its population which sells so many goods, Negroes and provisions &c and if things go on at this rate long, we must soon have 20,000 population; goods are lying here in store in quantities, waiting for stores to be built, and all species of houses are going up as if by Magic weekly: property bought in the edge of Town twelve months since for $200 per acre sold for $4,000 per acre last week—. All species of labour here cost three times as much as at Edenton, and as a general rule most every thing costs about four times as much as in the old States, except Negroes—prime man and woman together sell for $2,000—the ordinary mode of selling here is man and wife.

Questions

1. How does Norcom's letter suggest the interconnection between the fate of Native Americans and the opportunities open to white migrants to Mississippi?

2. What were likely to have been the effect on slaves of the speculative process described in the letter?

68. William Sewall, The Results of British Emancipation (1860)

Source: William G. Sewall, The Ordeal of Free Labor in the British West Indies *(New York, 1861), pp. 311–17.*

By 1850, slavery was on the road to abolition in most of the Western Hemisphere. The British had abolished slavery in their Caribbean colonies in 1833, the French in 1848. The newly independent nations of Spanish America had adopted plans for gradual emancipation.

Only in the United States, Brazil, Cuba, and Puerto Rico did slavery survive.

Americans followed carefully the results of emancipation elsewhere in the hemisphere, and its aftermath became part of debate over slavery. Was abolition a success or failure? Defenders of slavery in the American South pointed to the decline in sugar production in the key British island of Jamaica as proof that blacks would not work productively except as slaves. Abolitionists insisted that the planters had failed to adapt to the system of free labor, and that the lives of the former slaves had improved in numerous ways. On the eve of the Civil War, William G. Sewall published a series of articles in the *New York Times* reporting on conditions in the British West Indies and defending the abolition of slavery there. His account appeared as a book the following year.

EMANCIPATION WAS AN isolated experiment in each of the different colonies. Precedents and rules of action for one were no precedents or rules of action for another. Here there were obstacles to overcome and difficulties to surmount which there did not exist, or existed only in a mitigated form. Each colony was a field of battle upon which the banners of free labor and slave labor were flung to the winds; and while in some, where resistance was feeble, all trace of the contest has disappeared, and prosperity has revived, in others, where resistance was strong and determined, the exhaustion that follows a long war and a long reign of oppression weighs heavily upon a dispirited people. Let us not be deceived. Let us not misinterpret the true meaning of Jamaica's desolation at the present time. Let no one be so mad as to believe that it is the work of freedom.... Let no one question the victory, though its choicest fruits are yet to be reaped. Let no one doubt that freedom, when it overturned a despotism and crushed a monopoly, unshackled, at the same time, the commerce, the industry, and the intelligence of the islands, and laid the foundations of permanent prosperity....

If free labor be tested by any other gauge than that of sugar-production, its success in the West Indies is established beyond all cavil and beyond all peradventure. If the people merit any consideration whatever—if their independence, their comfort, their industry, their education, form any part of a country's prosperity—then the West Indies are a hundred-fold more prosperous now than they were in the most flourishing times of slavery. If peace be an element of prosperity—if it be important to enjoy uninterrupted tranquility and be secure from servile war and insurrection—then the West Indies have now an advantage that they never possessed before it was given them by emancipation.

If a largely-extended commerce be an indication of prosperity, then all the West Indies, Jamaica alone excepted, have progressed under a system of free labor, although that system hitherto has been but imperfectly developed....

One of the most natural and legitimate results of emancipation was to allow every man to do what seemed to him best—to achieve independence if he could—to pursue, in any case, the path of industry most agreeable to his tastes, and most conducive to his happiness. When we look at the vast political and social structure that has been demolished—the new and grander edifice that has been erected—the enemies that have been vanquished—the prejudices that have been uprooted—the education that has been sown broadcast, the ignorance that has been removed—the industry that has been trained and fostered—we can not pause to criticize defects, for we are amazed at the progress of so great a revolution within the brief space of twenty-five years....

I have endeavored to show—and I hope successfully—that the experiment of free labor in the West Indies has established its superior economy, as well as its possibility. Not a single island fails to demonstrate that the Creoles of African descent, in all their avocations and in all their pursuits, work, under a free system, for proper remuneration, though their labor is often ignorantly wasted and misdirected. That arises from want of education, want of training, want of good example.

Questions

1. Why does Sewall consider emancipation in the British West Indies a success, despite the decline in sugar production in Jamaica?

2. What lessons do you think Sewall believes Americans should learn from the experience of British emancipation?

---

69. Rules of Highland Plantation (1838)

Source: Bennet H. Barrow: "Rules of Highland Plantation," Plantation Life in the Florida Parishes of Louisiana, 1836–1846, as reflected in the Diary of Bennet H. Barrow, *ed. Edwin Adams David. Copyright © 1943, Columbia University Press. Reprinted with permission of the publisher.*

Southern planters published numerous articles on how best to manage slave labor. Many insisted that treating their slaves kindly would result in a more efficient workforce. A wealthy Louisiana slaveholder, Bennet H. Barrow considered himself a model of planter paternalism who, by his own standards, treated his slaves well. An advocate of rigorous plantation discipline, he drew up a series of strict rules, which he recommended that other owners follow. The rules illustrated that even the most well-intended owners claimed complete authority over the lives of their slaves. Inadvertently, the rules also revealed planters' fears about disobedience and resistance among their slaves.

No Negro shall leave the place at any time without my permission.... No Negro shall be allowed to marry out of the plantation.

No Negro shall be allowed to sell anything without my express permission. I have ever maintained the doctrine that my Negroes have no time whatever, that they are always liable to my call without questioning for a moment the propriety, of it. I adhere to this on the grounds of expediency and right. The very security of the plantation requires that a general and uniform control over the people of it should be exercised. Who are to protect the plantation from the intrusions of ill designed persons when everybody is abroad?... To render this part of the rule justly applicable, however, it would be necessary that such a settled arrangement should exist on the plantation to make it unnecessary for a negro to leave it—or to have a good plea for doing so. You must therefore make him as comfortable at home as possible, affording him what is essentially necessary for his happiness—you must provide for him yourself and by that means create in him a habit of perfect dependence on you. Allow it once to be understood by a Negro that he is to provide for himself, and you that moment give him an undeniable claim on you for a portion of his time to make this provision, and should you from necessity, or any other cause, encroach upon his time, disappointment and discontent are seriously felt.

If I employ a laborer to perform a certain quantum of work per day and I agree to pay him a certain amount for the performance of said work, when he has accomplished it I of course have no further claim on him for his time or services—but how different is it with a slave.... If I furnish my negro with every necessary of life, without the least care on his part—if I support him in sickness, however long it may be, and pay all his expenses, though he does nothing—if I maintain him in his old age, ... am I not entitled to an exclusive right in his time?

No rule that I have stated is of more importance than that relating to Negroes marrying out of the plantation.... It creates a feeling of independence, from being, of right, out of the control of the masters for a time.

Never allow any man to talk to your Negroes, nothing more injurious.

Questions

1. Why does Barrow think that slaves have greater obligations to their owners than free laborers do to their employers?

2. Why does Barrow think it so important to prevent "any man" from speaking with his slaves?

70. Slavery and the Bible (1850)

Source: De Bow's Review, *Vol. 9 (September 1850), pp. 281–86.*

White southerners developed an elaborate set of arguments defending slavery in the period before the Civil War. They insisted that slaves were better off than free laborers in the North and that blacks were inherently liable to lapse into "barbarism" if freed from the supervision of paternalistic whites. One pillar of proslavery thought was the idea that the institution was sanctioned by the Bible, as in this essay from the influential southern magazine *De Bow's Review.* So common had the biblical defense of slavery become by 1850 that the editor prefaced the essay with the following comment: "This paper has been handed us for publication, and, as it contains a summary of the Bible argument for slavery, we give it place, though the subject is growing hacknied [that is, so familiar as to be lacking in any originality]." Nonetheless, De Bow decided to publish it.

A VERY LARGE PARTY in the United states believe that holding slaves is morally wrong; this party founds its belief upon precepts taught in the Bible, and takes that book as the standard of morality and religion. We, also, look to the same book as our guide in the same matters; yet, we think it right to hold slaves—do hold them, and have held and used them from childhood.

As we come to such opposite conclusions from the same foundation, it may be well to consider, whether the Bible teaches us anything whatever, in regard to slavery; if so, what is it and how is it taught.

The anti-slavery party maintain, that the Bible teaches nothing *directly* upon the subject, but, that it establishes rules and principles of action, from which they infer, that in holding slaves, we are guilty of a moral wrong. This mode of reasoning would be perfectly fair, if the Bible really taught nothing directly upon the subject of slavery; but when that book applies the principles it lays down to the particular subject in controversy, we must take the application to be correct. We think we can show, that the Bible teaches clearly and conclusively that the holding of slaves is right; and if so, no deduction from general principles can make it wrong, if that book is true.

From the earliest period of our time down to the present moment, slavery has existed in some form or under some name, in almost every country of the globe. It existed in every country known, even by name, to any one of the sacred writers, at the time of his writing; yet none of them condemns it in the slightest degree. Would this have been the case had it been wrong in itself? Would not some one of the host of sacred writers have spoken of this alleged crime, in such terms as to show, in a manner not to be misunderstood, that God wished all men to be equal?

Abraham, the chosen servant of God, had his bond servants, whose condition was similar to, or worse than, that of our slaves. He considered them as his property, to be bought and sold as any other property which he owned. In Genesis xvii, 13, 23, 27, we are told that God commanded Abraham to circumcise all his bond-servants, *"bought with his money,"* and that Abraham obeyed God's commandment on this same day. In Genesis xx, 14, we are told that Abimelech took sheep and oxen, and *men servants* and *women servants*, and gave them to Abraham. In chapter xii, verse 14, we are told that Abraham possessed sheep and oxen, and he asses, and men servants and maid servants, and she asses, and camels. Also, in Genesis xxvi, 14, Isaac is said to have had possessions of flocks and herds, and a great store of servants. In other places in Genesis, they are spoken of, but always as property....

Paul wrote an epistle to Philemon, a Christian, a disciple of his, and a slaveholder. He sent it to him by Onesimus, also a convert, a slave of Philemon, who was a fugitive. In it, he prays Philemon to charge the fault of Onesimus to him, saying he would repay it, unless Philemon forgave it for his sake.

Now, had the holding of slaves been a crime, Paul's duty to Philemon would have required him to instruct Philemon, that he had no rights over Onesimus, but that the attempt to hold him in servitude was criminal; and his duty to Onesimus would have been, in such case, to send him to some foreign free country, whereby he might have escaped from oppression. But Paul sent him back. Our northern friends think that they manage these matters better than Paul did.

We find, then, that both the Old and New Testaments speak of slavery—that they do not condemn the relation, but, on the contrary, expressly allow it or create it; and they give commands and exhortations, which are based upon its legality and propriety. It can not, then, be wrong.

What we have written is founded solely upon the Bible, and can have no force, unless it is taken for truth. If that book is of divine origin, the holding of slaves is right: as that which God has permitted, recognized and commanded, cannot be inconsistent with his will.

Questions

1. Why do white southerners feel that it is important to show that the Bible sanctions slavery?

2. How do you think the author's understanding of the relationship of slavery and the Bible differs from that of the slaves, most of whom also considered themselves Christians?

---

71. Letter by a Fugitive Slave (1840)

Source: Joseph Taper: Excerpts from "Letter from Joseph Taper to Joseph Long, November 11, 1840" in the Joseph Long Papers located in the Rare Book, Manuscript, and Special Collections Library, Duke University. Reprinted by permission.

No one knows how many slaves succeeded in escaping from bondage before the Civil War. Some who managed to do so settled in northern cities like Boston, Cincinnati, and New York. But because federal law required that fugitives be returned to slavery, many continued northward until they reached Canada.

One successful fugitive was Joseph Taper, a slave in Frederick County, Virginia, who in 1837 ran away to Pennsylvania with his wife and children. Two years later, learning that a "slave catcher" was in the neighborhood, the Tapers fled to Canada. In 1840, Taper wrote to a white acquaintance in Virginia recounting some of his experiences. The biblical passage to which Taper refers reads: "And I will come near to you to judgment; and I will be a swift witness against the sorcerers, and against the adulterers, and against false swearers, and against those that oppress the hireling in his wages, the widow, and the fatherless, and that turn aside the stranger from his right, and fear not me, saith the Lord of hosts."

———————

DEAR SIR,

I now take the opportunity to inform you that I am in a land of liberty, in good health.... I have paid 50 dollars rent this year: next year I expect to build. The Queen of England has granted 50 acres of land to every colored man who will accept of the gift, and become an actual settler. Also a yoke of oxen and plough, for every two families. This is a very great encouragement to those who have come here for the liberty which God had designed for them....

Since I have been in the Queen's dominions I have been well contented, Yes well contented for Sure, man is as God intended he should be. That is, all are born free and equal. This is a wholesome law, not like the Southern laws which puts man made in the image of God, on level with brutes. O, what will become of the people, and where will they stand in the day of Judgment. Would that the 5th verse of the 3d chapter of Malachi were written as with the bar of iron, and the point of a diamond upon every oppressor's heart that they might repent of this evil, and let the oppressed go free....

We have good schools, and all the colored population supplied with schools. My boy Edward who will be six years next January, is now reading, and I intend keeping him at school until he becomes a good scholar.

I have enjoyed more pleasure within one month here than in all my life in the land of bondage.... My wife and self are sitting by a good comfortable fire happy, knowing that there are none to molest [us] or make [us] afraid. God save Queen Victoria. The Lord bless her in this life, and crown her with glory in the world to come is my prayer,

Yours With much respect
most obt, Joseph Taper

Questions

1. How does Taper's letter reverse the rhetoric, common among white Americans, which saw the United States as a land of freedom and the British empire as lacking in liberty?

2. What aspects of life in Canada does Taper emphasize as elements of his new freedom?

---

72. Solomon Northup, The New Orleans Slave Market (1853)

Source: Solomon Northup, Twelve Years a Slave *(Auburn, NY: Derby and Miller, 1853), pp. 78–82.*

The ending of the slave trade from Africa in 1808 stimulated the rapid expansion of the domestic slave trade within the United States. More than two million slaves were sold between 1820 and 1860, a majority to local buyers but hundreds of thousands from older states to "importing" states of the Lower South. The public slave market of New Orleans was one great center of the slave trade, where slaves were sold to man the plantations of the expanding Cotton Kingdom.

A free black resident of New York State, Solomon Northup was kidnaped in 1841 while in Washington, DC, and sold as a slave. After twelve years, during which he labored on plantations in Louisiana, he managed to contact friends in the North who arranged for his release. His memoir, published in 1853, became one of the most widely read accounts of slavery by someone who had experienced it. In the twenty-first century it became the basis for an Academy Award–winning film. In this passage, Northup describes a sale at the New Orleans slave market.

THE VERY AMIABLE, pious-hearted Mr. Theophilus Freeman, partner or consignee of James H. Burch, and keeper of the slave pen in New-Orleans, was out among his animals early in the morning. With an occasional kick of the older men and women, and many a sharp crack of the whip about the ears of the younger slaves, it was not long before they were all astir, and wide awake. Mr. Theophilus Freeman bustled about in a very industrious manner, getting his property ready for the sales-room, intending, no doubt, to do that day a rousing business.

In the first place we were required to wash thoroughly, and those with beards, to shave. We were then furnished with a new suit each, cheap, but clean. The men had hat, coat, shirt, pants and shoes; the women frocks of calico, and handkerchiefs to bind about their heads. We were now conducted into a large room in the front part of the building to which the yard was attached, in order to be properly trained, before the admission of customers. The men were arranged on one side of the room, the women on the other. The tallest was placed at the head of the row, then the next tallest, and so on in the order of their respective heights. Emily was at the foot of the line of women. Freeman charged us to remember our places; exhorted us to appear smart and lively,—sometimes threatening, and again, holding out various inducements. During the day he exercised us in the art of "looking smart," and of moving to our places with exact precision.…

Next day many customers called to examine Freeman's "new lot." The latter gentleman was very loquacious, dwelling at much length upon our several good points and qualities. He would make us hold up our heads, walk briskly back and forth, while customers would feel of our hands and arms and bodies, turn us about, ask us what we could do, make us open our mouths and show our teeth, precisely as a jockey examines a horse which he is about to barter for or purchase. Sometimes a man or woman was taken back to the small house in the yard, stripped, and inspected more minutely. Scars upon a slave's back were considered evidence of a rebellious or unruly spirit, and hurt his sale.

One old gentleman, who said he wanted a coachman, appeared to take a fancy to me. From his conversation with Burch, I learned he was a resident in the city. I very much desired that he would buy me, because I conceived it would not be difficult to make my escape from New-Orleans on some northern vessel. Freeman asked him fifteen hundred dollars for me. The old gentleman insisted it was too much, as times were very hard. Freeman, however, declared that I was sound and healthy, of a good constitution, and intelligent. He made it a point to enlarge upon my musical attainments. The old gentleman argued quite adroitly that there was nothing extraordinary about the nigger, and finally, to my regret, went out, saying he would call again. During the day, however, a number of sales were made. David and Caroline were purchased together by a Natchez planter. They left us, grinning broadly, and in the most happy state of mind, caused by the fact of their not being separated. Lethe was sold to a planter of Baton Rouge, her eyes flashing with anger as she was led away.

The same man also purchased Randall. The little fellow was made to jump, and run across the floor, and perform many other feats, exhibiting his activity and condition. All the time the trade was going on, Eliza was crying aloud, and wringing her hands. She besought the man not to buy him, unless he also bought her self and Emily. She promised, in that case, to be the most faithful slave that ever lived. The man answered that he could not afford it, and then Eliza burst into a paroxysm of grief, weeping plaintively. Freeman turned round to her, savagely, with his whip in his uplifted hand, ordering her to stop her noise, or he would flog her. He would not have such work—such snivelling; and unless she ceased that minute, he would take her to the yard and give her a hundred lashes. Yes, he would take the nonsense out of her pretty quick—if he didn't, might he be d—d. Eliza shrunk before him, and tried to wipe away her tears, but it was all in vain. She wanted to be with her children, she said, the little time she had to live. All the frowns and threats of Freeman, could not wholly silence the afflicted mother. She kept on begging and beseeching them, most piteously not to separate the three. Over and over again she told them how she loved her boy. A great many times she repeated her former promises—how very faithful and obedient she would be; how hard she would labor day and night, to the last moment of her life, if he would only buy them all together. But it was of no avail; the man could not afford it. The bargain was agreed upon, and Randall must go alone. Then Eliza ran to him; embraced him passionately; kissed him again and again; told him to remember her—all the while her tears falling in the boy's face like rain.

Freeman damned her, calling her a blubbering, bawling wench, and ordered her to go to her place, and behave herself; and be somebody. He swore he wouldn't stand such stuff but a little longer. He would soon give her something to cry about, if she was not mighty careful, and that she might depend upon.

The planter from Baton Rouge, with his new purchases, was ready to depart.

"Don't cry, mama. I will be a good boy. Don't cry," said Randall, looking back, as they passed out of the door.

What has become of the lad, God knows. It was a mournful scene indeed. I would have cried myself if I had dared.

Questions

1. What aspects of the buying and selling of slaves does Northup single out for condemnation?

2. What light does Northup's account shed on the biblical arguments in defense of slavery in document 70 above?

CHAPTER 12

An Age of Reform, 1820–1840

73. Robert Owen, "The First Discourse on a New System of Society" (1825)

Source: Robert Owen, The First Discourse on a New System of Society, as Delivered in the Hall of Representatives, at Washington, on the 25th of February, 1825 *(London, 1825), pp. 3–15.*

The increasing economic inequality and intense economic competition promoted by the market revolution led some Americans to create their own miniature societies based on equality and harmony. Through their efforts, the words "socialism" and "communism," meaning societies in which productive property is owned by the community rather than private individuals, entered the language of politics.

The most important secular communitarian (meaning a person who plans or lives in a cooperative community) was Robert Owen, a British factory owner. In 1824, he purchased the Harmony community in Indiana originally founded by the Protestant religious leader George Rapp, and renamed it New Harmony. Early in 1825, Owen addressed a gathering of notable Americans in the hall of the House of Representatives—one of the few foreign citizens ever to speak there—and outlined his vision of "a new system of society."

THE RESULT OF ... [my] reading, reflection, experiments, and personal communication, has been to leave an irresistible impression on my mind, that society is in error; that the notions on which all its institutions are founded are not true; that they necessarily generate deception and vice; and that the practices which proceed from them are destructive of the happiness of human life.

The reflections which I am enabled to make upon the facts which the history of our race presented to me, led me to conclude that the great object intended to be attained, by the various institutions of every age and country, was, or ought to be, to secure happiness for the greatest number of human beings. That this object could be obtained only, first, by a proper training and education from birth, of the physical and mental powers of each individual; second, by arrangements to enable each individual to procure in the best manner at all times, a full supply of those things which are necessary and the most beneficial for human nature; and third, that all individuals should be so united and combined in a social system, as to give to each the greatest benefit from society....

• • •

Man, through ignorance, has been, hitherto, the tormentor of man.

He is here, in a nation deeming itself possessed of more privileges than all other nations, and which pretensions, in many respects, must be admitted to be true. Yet, even here, where the laws are the most mild, and consequently the least unjust and irrational, individuals are punished even to death, for actions which are the natural and necessary effects arising from the injurious circumstances which the government and society, to which they belong, unwisely permit to exist; while other individuals are almost as much injured by being as unjustly rewarded for performing actions for which, as soon as they shall become rational beings, they must be conscious they cannot be entitled to a particle of merit....

• • •

My desire now is to introduce into these States, and through them to the world at large, a new social system, formed in practice of an entire new combination of circumstances, all of them having a direct moral, intellectual, and beneficial tendency, fully adequate to effect the most important improvements throughout society. This system has been solely derived from the facts relative to our common nature, which I have previously explained.

In this new social arrangement, a much more perfect system of liberty and equality will be introduced than has yet any where existed, or been deemed attainable in practice. Within it there will be no privileged thoughts or belief; every one will be at full liberty to express the genuine impressions which the circumstances around them have made on their minds as well as all their own undisguised reflections thereon, and then no motive will exist for deception or insincerity of any kind....

The degrading and pernicious practices in which we are now trained, of buying cheap and selling dear, will be rendered wholly unnecessary; for so long as this principle shall govern the transactions of men, nothing really great or noble can be expected from mankind....

• • •

In the new system, union and co-operation will supersede individual interest, and the universal counteraction of each other's objects; and, by the change, the powers of one man will obtain for him the advantages of many, and all will become as rich as they will desire. The very imperfect experiments of the Moravians, Shakers, and Harmonites, give sure proof of the gigantic superiority of union over division, for the creation of wealth. But these associations have been hitherto subject to many disadvantages, and their progress and success have been materially counteracted by many obstacles which will not exist under a system, founded on a correct knowledge of the constitution of our nature....

Under this system, real wealth will be too easily obtained in perpetuity and full security to be much longer valued as it is now by society, for the distinctions which it makes between the poor and rich. For, when the new arrangements shall be regularly organized and completed, a few hours daily, of healthy and desirable employment, chiefly applied to direct modern mechanical and other scientific improvements, will be amply sufficient to create a full supply, at all times, of the best of every thing for every one, and then all things will be valued according to their intrinsic worth, will be used beneficially, and nothing will be wasted or abused....

• • •

This is a revolution from a system in which individual reward and punishment has been the universal practice, to one, in which individual reward and punishment will be unpracticed and unknown, except as a grievous error of a past wretched system. On this account, my belief has long been, that wherever society should be fully prepared to admit of one experiment on the new system, it could not fail to be also prepared to admit the principle from which it has been derived, and to be ready for all the practice which must emanate from the principle; and, in consequence, that the change could not be one of slow progression, but it must take place at once, and make an immediate, and almost instantaneous resolution in the minds and manners of the society in which it shall be introduced—unless we can imagine that there are human beings who prefer sin and misery to virtue and happiness....

It is to effect this change that I am here this night; that, if possible, a mortal blow shall be now given to the fundamental error which, till now, has governed this wretched world, and inflicted unnumbered cruelties and miseries upon its inhabitants. The time has passed, within the present hour, when this subject can be no longer mentioned or hidden from the public mind of this country. It must now be open to the most free discussion, and I well know what will be the result....

Questions

1. What does Owen see as the greatest "errors" of society in the 1820s?

2. How does he plan to increase the enjoyment of "liberty and equality"?

74. Philip Schaff on Freedom as Self-Restraint (1855)

Source: Philip Schaff, America. A Sketch of the Political, Social, and Religious Character of the United States of North America *(New York, 1855), pp. 43–47.*

Numerous reform movements arose in the United States in the decades before the Civil War, promising to liberate Americans from social injustice and from evils like drink, poverty, or slavery. The reformers did not propose that individuals should simply follow their own desires without restraint. Their definition of the free individual was the person who internalized the practice of self-control.

Philip Schaff, a Swiss-German minister who emigrated to Pennsylvania in 1843 to teach at a small college and later wrote a "sketch" of American society for a European audience, offered perceptive comments on reformers' understanding of freedom. "True national freedom, in the American view," Schaff observed, was "anything but an absence of restraint." Rather, it "rests upon a moral groundwork, upon the virtue of self-possession and self-control in individual citizens." As an example, Schaff offered the temperance movement, which sought to convince Americans to renounce intoxicating liquor. The conflict between freedom as following a moral code (imposed, if necessary, by the government) and freedom as choosing without outside interference how to conduct one's life would be repeated in many subsequent eras of American history.

THE WHOLE ANGLO-AMERICAN conception of freedom is specifically different from the purely negative notion which prevails amongst the radicals and revolutionists on the continent of Europe. With the American, freedom is anything but a mere absence of restraint, an arbitrary, licentious indulgence, every one following his natural impulse, as the revolutionists would have it. It is a rational, moral self-determination, hand in hand with law, order, and authority. True national freedom, in the American view, rests upon a moral groundwork, upon the virtue of self-possession and self-control in individual citizens. He alone is worthy of this great blessing and capable of enjoying it, who holds his passions in check; is master of his sensual nature; obeys natural laws, not under pressure from without, but from inward impulse, cheerfully and joyfully. But the negative and hollow liberalism, or rather the radicalism, which undermines the authority of law and sets itself against Christianity and the church, necessarily dissolves all social ties, and ends in anarchy; which then passes very easily into the worst and most dangerous form of despotism.

These sound views of freedom, in connection with the moral earnestness and the Christian character of the nation, form the basis of the North American republic, and can alone secure its permanence. We also find there, indeed, beyond all question, utterly unsound and dangerous radical tendencies; in the political elections all wild passions, falsehood, calumny, bribery, and wickedness of all sorts, are let loose; and even the halls of the legislatures and of Congress are frequently disgraced by the misconduct of unprincipled demagogues, so that multitudes of the best citizens, disgusted with the wire-pulling and mean selfishness of self-styled friends of the people, shrink from any active participation in politics, or discharge their duty as citizens by nothing more, at most, than their vote at the ballot-box. But on the whole, there prevails undeniably among the people a sound conservative tone, which exerts a constant influence in favor of right and order; and it is an imposing spectacle, when immediately after the election of a president or governor, a universal calm at once succeeds the furious storm of party strife, and the conquered party patiently submits to the result, never dreaming of such a thing as asserting its real or supposed rights in any violent way. Any dissatisfaction—for such certainly has place there as well as elsewhere—reaches never to the republican form of government, but only to the manner of its exercise, not to the constitution of the land, but only to the measures of the dominant party; and it seeks redress of its wrong always in a lawful, constitutional way. So far as this goes, it may well be asserted, that the North American Union, with all the fluctuation and insecurity of

its affairs in particular instances—which is to be expected in so new
a country—stands in general more firmly on its feet, and is safer from
violent revolutions, than any country on the continent of Europe.

A very characteristic proof of our assertion, that American freedom is different in principle from radicalism and licentiousness, and
rests entirely on the basis of self-control and self-restraint, is presented in the really sublime temperance movement, particularly in
the "Maine liquor law," as it is called. This law wholly forbids, not
directly the drinking—for this would be an infringement of personal liberty,—but the manufacture and sale of all intoxicating
drinks, including even wine and beer, except for medicinal, mechanical, and sacramental purposes. This law was first introduced a few
years ago in the predominantly Puritanical, New England State of
Maine, and has since been extended to several other states by a popular majority; and even in the great States of New York, Pennsylvania, and Ohio, the most zealous efforts are now making by public
addresses, by tracts and periodicals, and other means of agitation, to
secure the election of legislators favorable to the temperance cause,
who will strike at the root of the terrible evil, and remove even the
temptation to drunkenness. Even last fall, shortly before the election, I was personal witness of the zeal and earnestness, with which
the agents of the temperance society, ministers and laymen, can-
vassed the countries of Pennsylvania, and spreading their tent under
the open heaven, after a solemn introduction by singing and prayer,
eloquently described the horrible consequences, temporal and eternal, of intemperance, and demonstrated to the people by the most
convincing arguments, the duty of using their elective franchise in a
way demanded by the public weal, in the consciousness of their high
responsibility to God and the world.

It must be granted that this Maine temperance law, *in itself considered*, goes too far, and is to be ranked with radical legislation....

• • •

Yet, think of the "Maine liquor law" as we may,—and we would
here neither advocate nor condemn it,—we must admire the moral

energy and self-denial of a free people, which would rather renounce an enjoyment in itself lawful, than see it drive thousands of weak persons to bodily and spiritual ruin.

To those, who see in America only the land of unbridled radicalism and of the wildest fanaticism for freedom, I take the liberty to put the modest question: In what European state would the government have the courage to enact such a prohibition of the traffic in all intoxicating drinks, and the people the self-denial to submit to it?

Questions

1. How does Schaff believe Christianity influences American understandings of freedom?

2. Why does Schaff have reservations about the "Maine law" prohibiting the manufacture and sale of liquor?

---

75. David Walker's Appeal (1829)

Source: Walker's Appeal, in Four Articles, . . . to the Coloured Citizens of the World . . . (3rd ed.: Boston, 1830), pp. 3–5, 9, 22–24.

A pioneering document of militant abolitionism, David Walker's *Appeal to the Coloured Citizens of the World* condemned the hypocrisy of a nation that proclaimed its belief in liberty yet every day violated its professed principles. Born free in North Carolina, Walker moved to Boston, where he became a used clothing dealer and an outspoken critic of slavery. At a time when most opponents of slavery called for a peaceful, gradual end to the institution and the "colonization" outside of the country of those who became free, Walker insisted that blacks had as much right to live in the United States as whites and spoke of the possibility of armed struggle against slavery. Walker also challenged racism by invoking the achievements of ancient civilizations in Africa, and he urged black Americans to identify with the black republic of Haiti, an early example of internationalism in African-American thought. When free black sailors were found carrying copies of Walker's pamphlet, southern states issued a reward for his arrest or death. Walker died, apparently of natural causes, in 1830, but his words inspired a generation of black abolitionists.

HAVING TRAVELED OVER a considerable portion of these United States, and having, in the course of my travels, taken the most accurate observations of things as they exist—the result of my observations has warranted the full and unshaken conviction, that we, (coloured people of these United States) are the most degraded, wretched, and abject set of beings that ever lived since the world began; and I pray God that none like us ever may live again until time shall be no more. They tell us of the Israelites in Egypt, the Helots in Sparta, and of the Roman Slaves, which last were made up from almost every nation under heaven, whose sufferings under those ancient and heathen nations, were, in comparison with ours, under this enlightened and Christian nation, no more than a cipher—or, in other words, those heathen nations of antiquity, had but little more among them than the name and form of slavery; while wretchedness and endless miseries were reserved . . . to be poured out upon our fathers, ourselves and our children, by Christian Americans! . . . I appeal to Heaven for my motive in writing—who knows that my object is, if possible, to awaken in the breasts of my afflicted, degraded and slumbering brethren, a spirit of inquiry and investigation respecting our miseries and wretchedness in this Republican Land of Liberty!!!!!! . . .

My beloved brethren:—The Indians of North and of South America—the Greeks—the Irish, subjected under the king of Great Britain—the Jews, that ancient people of the Lord—the inhabitants of the islands of the sea—in fine, all the inhabitants of the earth, (except however, the sons of Africa) are called men, and of course are, and ought to be free. But we, (coloured people) and our children are brutes!! and of course are, and ought to be SLAVES to the American people and their children forever!! to dig their mines and work their farms; and thus go on enriching them, from one generation to another with our blood and our tears!!!! ...

When we take a retrospective view of the arts and sciences—the wise legislators—the Pyramids, and other magnificent buildings—the turning of the channel of the river Nile, by the sons of Africa ..., among whom learning originated, and was carried thence into Greece, where it was improved upon and refined. Thence among the Romans, and all over the then enlightened parts of the world, and it has been enlightening the dark and benighted minds of men from then, down to this day. I say, when I view retrospectively, the renown of that once mighty people, the children of our great progenitor I am indeed cheered. Yea further, when I view that mighty son of Africa, Hannibal, one of the greatest generals of antiquity, who defeated and cut off so many thousands of the white Romans or murderers, and who carried his victorious arms, to the very gate of Rome, and I give it as my candid opinion, that had Carthage been well united and had given him good support, he would have carried that cruel and barbarous city by storm. But they were disunited, as the coloured people are now, in the United States of America, the reason our natural enemies are enabled to keep their feet on our throats.

Beloved brethren—here let me tell you, and believe it, that the Lord our God, as true as he sits on his throne in heaven, and as true as our Savior died to redeem the world, will give you a Hannibal, and when the Lord shall have raised him up, and given him to you for your possession, O my suffering brethren! remember the divisions and consequent sufferings of Carthage and of Hayti. ... But what need have I to refer to antiquity, when Hayti, the glory of the blacks and terror of tyrants, is enough to convince the most avaricious and stupid of wretches?

Questions

1. Why does Walker address his pamphlet to "the coloured citizens of the world" and not just the United States?

2. What lessons does Walker think black Americans should learn from the history of the ancient world and that of Haiti?

76. Frederick Douglass on the Fourth of July (1852)

Source: Frederick Douglass, My Bondage and My Freedom *(New York, 1855), pp. 441–45.*

The greatest oration on American slavery and American freedom was delivered in Rochester, New York, in 1852 by Frederick Douglass. Speaking just after the annual Independence Day celebration, Douglass posed the question, "What, to the American slave, is your 4th of July?" He answered that July Fourth festivities revealed the hypocrisy of a nation that proclaimed its belief in liberty yet daily committed "practices more shocking and bloody" than any other country on earth. Like other abolitionists, however, Douglass also laid claim to the founders' legacy. The Revolution had proclaimed "the great principles of political freedom and of natural justice, embodied in [the] Declaration of Independence," from which subsequent generations had tragically strayed. Only by abolishing slavery and freeing the ideals of the Declaration from the bounds of race could the United States, he believed, recapture its original mission.

Fellow-citizens, pardon me, allow me to ask, why am I called upon to speak here to-day? What have I, or those I represent, to do with your national independence? Are the great principles of political freedom and of natural justice, embodied in that Declaration of

Independence, extended to us? and am I, therefore, called upon to bring our humble offering to the national altar, and to confess the benefits and express devout gratitude for the blessings resulting from your independence to us?

Would to God, both for your sakes and ours, that an affirmative answer could be truthfully returned to these questions! Then would my task be light, and my burden easy and delightful. For *who* is there so cold, that a nation's sympathy could not warm him? Who so obdurate and dead to the claims of gratitude, that would not thankfully acknowledge such priceless benefits? Who so stolid and selfish, that would not give his voice to swell the hallelujahs of a nation's jubilee, when the chains of servitude had been torn from his limbs? I am not that man. In a case like that, the dumb might eloquently speak, and the "lame man leap as an hart."

But, such is not the state of the case. I say it with a sad sense of the disparity between us. I am not included within the pale of this glorious anniversary! Your high independence only reveals the immeasurable distance between us. The blessings in which you, this day, rejoice, are not enjoyed in common. The rich inheritance of justice, liberty, prosperity and independence, bequeathed by your fathers, is shared by you, not by me. The sunlight that brought life and healing to you, has brought stripes and death to me. This Fourth [of] July is *yours*, not *mine*. You may rejoice, *I* must mourn. To drag a man in fetters into the grand illuminated temple of liberty, and call upon him to join you in joyous anthems, were inhuman mockery and sacrilegious irony. Do you mean, citizens, to mock me, by asking me to speak to-day? If so, there is a parallel to your conduct. And let me warn you that it is dangerous to copy the example of a nation whose crimes, towering up to heaven, were thrown down by the breath of the Almighty, burying that nation in irrecoverable ruin! I can to-day take up the plaintive lament of a peeled and woesmitten people!

• • •

Fellow-citizens; above your national, tumultuous joy, I hear the mournful wail of millions whose chains, heavy and grievous yesterday, are, today, rendered more intolerable by the jubilee shouts that reach them. If I do forget, if I do not faithfully remember those bleeding children of sorrow this day, "may my right hand forget her cunning, and may my tongue cleave to the roof of my mouth!" To forget them, to pass lightly over their wrongs, and to chime in with the popular theme, would be treason most scandalous and shocking, and would make me a reproach before God and the world. My subject, then fellow-citizens, is AMERICAN SLAVERY. I shall see, this day, and its popular characteristics, from the slave's point of view. Standing, there, identified with the American bondman, making his wrongs mine, I do not hesitate to declare, with all my soul, that the character and conduct of this nation never looked blacker to me than on this 4th of July! Whether we turn to the declarations of the past, or to the professions of the present, the conduct of the nation seems equally hideous and revolting. America is false to the past, false to the present, and solemnly binds herself to be false to the future. Standing with God and the crushed and bleeding slave on this occasion, I will, in the name of humanity which is outraged, in the name of liberty which is fettered, in the name of the constitution and the Bible, which are disregarded and trampled upon, dare to call in question and to denounce, with all the emphasis I can command, everything that serves to perpetuate slavery—the great sin and shame of America! "I will not equivocate; I will not excuse"; I will use the severest language I can command; and yet not one word shall escape me that any man, whose judgement is not blinded by prejudice, or who is not at heart a slaveholder, shall not confess to be right and just.

For the present, it is enough to affirm the equal manhood of the negro race. Is it not astonishing that, while we are ploughing, planting and reaping, using all kinds of mechanical tools, erecting houses, constructing bridges, building ships, working in metals of brass, iron, copper, silver and gold; that, while we are reading, writing and cyphering, acting as clerks, merchants and secretaries, having among us lawyers, doctors, ministers, poets, authors, editors, orators and teachers; that, while we are engaged in all manner of enterprises common to other men, digging gold in California, capturing the whale in the Pacific, feeding sheep and cattle on the hillside, living, moving, acting, thinking, planning, living in families as husbands, wives and children, and, above all, confessing and worshipping the Christian's God, and looking hopefully for life and immortality beyond the grave, we are called upon to prove that we are men!

Would you have me argue that man is entitled to liberty? that he is the rightful owner of his own body? You have already declared it. Must I argue the wrongfulness of slavery? Is that a question for Republicans? Is it to be settled by the rules of logic and argumentation, as a matter beset with great difficulty, involving a doubtful application of the principle of justice, hard to be understood? How should I look to-day, in the presence of Americans, dividing, and subdividing a discourse, to show that men have a natural right to freedom? speaking of it relatively, and positively, negatively, and affirmatively. To do so, would be to make myself ridiculous, and to offer an insult to your understanding. There is not a man beneath the canopy of heaven, that does not know that slavery is wrong *for him.*

What, am I to argue that it is wrong to make men brutes, to rob them of their liberty, to work them without wages, to keep them ignorant of their relations to their fellow men, to beat them with sticks, to flay their flesh with the lash, to load their limbs with irons, to hunt them with dogs, to sell them at auction, to sunder their families, to knock out their teeth, to burn their flesh, to starve them into obedience and submission to their masters? Must I argue that a system thus marked with blood, and stained with pollution, is *wrong?* No! I will not. I have better employments for my time and strength, than such arguments would imply.

What, then, remains to be argued? Is it that slavery is not divine; that God did not establish it; that our doctors of divinity are mistaken? There is blasphemy in the thought. That which is inhuman, cannot be divine! *Who* can reason on such a proposition? They that can, may; I cannot. The time for such argument is past.

At a time like this, scorching irony, not convincing argument, is needed. O! had I the ability, and could I reach the nation's ear, I would, to-day, pour out a fiery stream of biting ridicule, blasting reproach, withering sarcasm, and stern rebuke. For it is not light that is needed, but fire; it is not the gentle shower, but thunder. We need the storm, the whirlwind, and the earthquake. The feeling of the nation must be quickened; the conscience of the nation must be roused; the propriety of the nation must be startled; the hypocrisy of the nation must be exposed; and its crimes against God and man must be proclaimed and denounced.

What, to the American slave, is your 4th of July? I answer: a day that reveals to him, more than all other days in the year, the gross injustice and cruelty to which he is the constant victim. To him, your celebration is a sham; your boasted liberty, an unholy license; your national greatness, swelling vanity; your sounds of rejoicing are empty and heartless; your denunciations of tyrants, brass fronted impudence; your shouts of liberty and equality, hollow mockery; your prayers and hymns, your sermons and thanksgivings, with all your religious parade, and solemnity, are, to him, mere bombast, fraud, deception, impiety, and hypocrisy—a thin veil to cover up crimes which would disgrace a nation of savages. There is not a nation on the earth guilty of practices, more shocking and bloody, than are the people of these United States, at this very hour.

Go where you may, search where you will, roam through all the monarchies and despotisms of the old world, travel through South America, search out every abuse, and when you have found the last, lay your facts by the side of the everyday practices of this nation, and you will say with me, that, for revolting barbarity and shameless hypocrisy, America reigns without a rival.

Questions

1. What does Douglass hope to accomplish by accusing white Americans of injustice and hypocrisy?

2. What evidence does Douglass present to disprove the idea of black inferiority?

77. Catharine Beecher on the "Duty of American Females" (1837)

Source: Catharine E. Beecher, Essay on Slavery and Abolitionism, with Reference to the Duty of American Females *(Philadelphia, 1837), pp. 5–6, 27, 41, 101–08, 128.*

The abolitionist movement enabled women to carve out a place in the public sphere. Women attended antislavery meetings and circulated petitions to Congress. Most prominent during the 1830s were Angelina and Sarah Grimké, the daughters of a South Carolina slaveowner. The sisters had been converted to Quakerism and abolitionism while visiting Philadelphia. They began to deliver popular lectures that offered a scathing condemnation of slavery from the perspective of those who had witnessed its evils firsthand. In 1836, Angelina Grimké wrote *Appeal to the Christian Women of the South,* urging them to take a stand against slavery.

The sight of women lecturing in public to mixed male-female audiences and taking part in public debate on political questions aroused considerable criticism. The prominent writer Catharine Beecher responded to Grimké's essay by reprimanding her for stepping outside "the domestic and social sphere," urging her to accept the fact that "heaven" had designated man "the superior" and woman "the subordinate."

My dear friend:

Your public address to Christian females at the South has reached me, and I have been urged to aid in circulating it at the North. I have also been informed, that you contemplate a tour, during the ensuing year, for the purpose of exerting your influence to form Abolition Societies among ladies of the non-slave-holding States.

Our acquaintance and friendship give me a claim to your private ear; but there are reasons why it seems more desirable to address you, who now stand before the public as an advocate of Abolition measures, in a more public manner.

The object I have in view, is to present some reasons why it seems unwise and inexpedient for ladies of the non-slave-holding States to unite themselves in Abolition Societies; and thus, at the same time, to exhibit the inexpediency of the course you propose to adopt....

Now Abolitionists are before the community, and declare that all slavery is sin, which ought to be immediately forsaken; and that it is their object and intention to promote the *immediate emancipation* of all the slaves in this nation.... [R]eproaches, rebukes, and sneers, were employed to convince the whites that their prejudices were sinful....

[T]he severing of the Union by the present mode of agitating the question ... may be one of the results, and, if so, what are the probabilities for a Southern republic that has torn itself off for the purpose of excluding foreign interference, and for the purpose of perpetuating slavery? ...

Heaven has appointed to one sex the superior, and to the other the subordinate station, and this without any reference to the character or conduct of either. It is therefore as much for the dignity as it is for the interest of females, in all respects to conform to the duties of this relation.... But while woman holds a subordinate relation in society to the other sex, it is not because it was designed that her duties or her influence should be any the less important, or all-pervading. But it was designed that the mode of gaining influence and of exercising power should be altogether different and peculiar....

Woman is to win every thing by peace and love; by making herself so much respected, esteemed and loved, that to yield to her opinions and to gratify her wishes, will be the free-will offering of the heart. But this is to be all accomplished in the domestic and social circle.... But the moment woman begins to feel the promptings of ambition, or the thirst for power, her aegis of defence is gone. All the sacred protection of religion, all the generous promptings of chivalry, all the poetry of romantic gallantry, depend upon woman's retaining her place as dependent and defenceless, and making no claims, and maintaining no right but what are the gifts of honour, rectitude and love.

A woman may seek the aid of co-operation and combination among her own sex, to assist her in her appropriate offices of piety, charity, maternal and domestic duty; but whatever, in any measure, throws a woman into the attitude of a combatant either for herself or others—whatever binds her in a party conflict—whatever obliges her in any way to exert coercive influences, throws her out of her appropriate sphere. . . .

If it is asked, "May not woman appropriately come forward as a suppliant for a portion of her sex who are bound in cruel bondage?" It is replied, that, the rectitude and propriety of any such measure, depend entirely on its probable results. If petitions from females will operate to exasperate; if they will be deemed obtrusive, indecorous, and unwise, by those to whom they are addressed; . . . if they will be the opening wedge, that will eventually bring females as petitioners and partisans into every political measure that may tend to injure and oppress their sex . . . then it is neither appropriate nor wise, nor right, for a woman to petition for the relief of oppressed females. . . .

In this country, petitions to congress, in reference to the official duties of legislators, seem, IN ALL CASES, to fall entirely without the sphere of female duty. Men are the proper persons to make appeals to the rulers whom they appoint, and if their female friends, by arguments and persuasions, can induce them to petition, all the good that can be done by such measures will be secured. But if females cannot influence their nearest friends, to urge forward a public measure in this way, they surely are out of their place, in attempting to do it themselves. . . .

It is allowed by all reflecting minds, that the safety and happiness of this nation depends upon having the *children* educated, and not only intellectually, but morally and religiously. There are now nearly two millions of children and adults in this country who cannot read, and who have no schools of any kind. To give only a small supply of teachers to these destitute children, who are generally where the population is sparse, will demand *thirty thousand teachers* at the moment and an addition of *two thousand every year.* Where is this army of teachers to be found? Is it at all probable that the other sex will afford even a moderate portion of this supply? ... Men will be educators in the college, in the high school, in some of the most honourable and lucrative common schools, but the *children*, the *little children* of this nation must, to a wide extent, be taught by females, or remain untaught.... And as the value of education rises in the public mind ... women will more and more be furnished with those intellectual advantages which they need to fit them for such duties.

The result will be, that America will be distinguished above all other nations, for well-educated females and for the influence they will exert on the general interests of society. But if females, as they approach the other sex, in intellectual elevation, begin to claim, or to exercise in any manner, the peculiar prerogatives of that sex, education will prove a doubtful and dangerous blessing. But this will never be the result. For the more intelligent a woman becomes, the more she can appreciate the wisdom of that ordinance that appointed her subordinate station.

But it may be asked, is there nothing to be done to bring this national sin of slavery to an end? Must the internal slave-trade, a trade now ranked as piracy among all civilized nations, still prosper in our bounds? Must the very seat of our government stand as one of the chief slave-markets of the land; and must not Christian females open their lips, nor lift a finger, to bring such a shame and sin to an end? To this it may be replied, that Christian females may, and can say and do much to bring these evils to an end; and the present is a time and an occasion when it seems most desirable that they should know, and appreciate, and *exercise* the power which they do possess for so desirable an end....

In the present aspect of affairs among us, when everything seems to be tending to disunion and distraction, it surely has become the duty of every female instantly to relinquish the attitude of a partisan, in every matter of clashing interests, and to assume the office of a mediator, and an advocate of peace. And to do this, it is not necessary that a woman should in any manner relinquish her opinion as to the evils or the benefits, the right or the wrong, of any principle of practice. But, while quietly holding her own opinions, and calmly avowing them, when conscience and integrity make the duty imperative, every female can employ her influence, not for the purpose of exciting or regulating public sentiment, but rather for the purpose of promoting a spirit of candour, forbearance, charity, and peace.

Questions

1. How does Beecher think women should exert power within American society?

2. Why does she believe that the abolitionist movement is dangerous?

78. Angelina Grimké on Women's Rights (1837)

Source: The Liberator, *August 2, 1837.*

In response to Catharine Beecher's criticism, Angelina Grimké wrote a series of twelve letters forthrightly defending the right of women to take part in political debate. The final one addressed the question of women's rights directly. "I know nothing," she wrote, "of men's rights and women's rights." "My doctrine," she declared, "is that whatever is morally right for man to do, it is morally right for woman to do." The Grimké sisters soon retired from the fray, after Angelina married the abolitionist Theodore Weld. But their writings helped to spark the movement for women's rights that arose in the 1840s.

SINCE I ENGAGED in the investigation of the rights of the slave, I have necessarily been led to a better understanding of my own; for I have found the Anti-Slavery cause to be the high school of morals in our land—the school in which human rights are more fully investigated, and better understood and taught, than in any other benevolent enterprise. Here one great fundamental principle is disinterred, which, as soon as it is uplifted to public view, leads the mind into a thousand different ramifications, into which the rays of this central light are streaming with brightness and glory. Here we are led to examine why human beings have any rights. It is because they are moral beings; the rights of all men, from the king to the slave, are built upon their moral nature: and as all men have this moral nature, so all men have essentially the same rights. These rights may be plundered from the slave, but they cannot be alienated: his right and title to himself is as perfect now, as is that of Lyman Beecher: they are written in his moral being, and must remain unimpaired as long as that being continues.

Now it naturally occurred to me, that if rights were founded in moral being, then the circumstance of sex could not give to man higher rights and responsibilities, than to woman. To suppose that it did, would be to deny the self-evident truth, "that the physical constitution is the mere instrument of the moral nature." To suppose that it did, would be to break up utterly the relations of the two natures, and to reverse their functions, exalting the animal nature into a monarch, and humbling the moral into a slave; "making the former a proprietor, and the latter its property." When I look at human beings as moral beings, all distinction in sex sinks to insignificance and nothingness; for I believe it regulates rights and responsibilities no more than the color of the skin or the eyes. My doctrine then is, that whatever it is morally right for man to do, it is morally right for woman to do. Our duties are governed, not by difference of sex, but by the diversity of our relative connections in life, and the variety of gifts and talents committed to our care, and the different eras in which we live.

This regulation of duty by the mere circumstance of sex, rather than by the fundamental principle of moral being, has led to all that multifarious train of evils flowing out of the anti-christian doctrine of masculine and feminine virtues. By this doctrine, man has been converted into the warrior, and clothed in sternness, and those other kindred qualities, which, in the eyes of many, belong to his character as a man; whilst woman has been taught to lean upon an arm of flesh, to sit as a soul arrayed "in gold and pearls, and costly array," to be admired for her personal charms, and caressed and humored like a spoiled child, or converted into a mere drudge to suit the convenience of her lord and master. This principle has spread desolation over the whole moral world, and brought into all the diversified relations of life, "confusion and every evil work." It has given to man a charter for the exercise of tyranny and selfishness, pride and arrogance, lust and brutal violence. It has robbed woman of essential rights, the right to think and speak and act on all great moral questions, just as men think and speak and act; the right to share their responsibilities, dangers, and toils; the right to fulfill the great end of her being, as a help meet for man, as a moral, intellectual and immortal creature, and of glorifying God in her body and her spirit which are His. Hitherto, instead of being a help meet to man, in the highest, noblest sense of the term, as a companion, a co-worker, an equal; she has been a mere appendage of his being, and instrument of his convenience and pleasure, the pretty toy, with which he wiled away his leisure moments, or the pet animal whom he humored into playfulness and submission. Woman, instead of being regarded as the equal of man, has uniformly been looked down upon as his inferior, a mere gift to fill up the measure of his happiness. In the poetry of "romantic gallantry," it is true, she has been called the "last best gift of God to man;" but I believe I speak forth the words of truth and soberness when I affirm, that woman never was given to man. She was created, like him, in the image of God, and crowned with glory and honor; created only a little lower than the angels,—not, as is too generally presumed, a little lower than man; on her brow, as well as on his, was placed the "diadem of beauty," and in her hand the scepter of universal dominion....

Measure her rights and duties by the sure, unerring standard of moral being, not by the false rights and measures of a mere circumstance of her human existence, and then will it become a self-evident truth, that whatever it is morally right for a man to do, it is morally right for a woman to do. I recognize no rights but human rights—I know nothing of men's rights and women's rights; for in Christ Jesus, there is neither male or female; and it is my solemn conviction, that, until this important principle of equality is recognized and carried out into practice, that vain will be the efforts of the church to do anything effectual for the permanent reformation of the world. Woman was the first transgressor, and the first victim of power. In all the heathen nations, she has been the slave of man, and no Christian nation has ever acknowledged her rights. Nay more, no Christian Society has ever done so either, on the broad and solid basis of humanity. I know that in some few denominations, she is permitted to preach the gospel; but this is not done from a conviction of her equality as a human being, but of her equality in spiritual gifts—for we find that woman, even in these Societies, is not allowed to make the Discipline by which she is to be governed. Now, I believe it is her right to be consulted in all the laws and regulations by which she is to be governed, whether in Church or State, and that the present arrangement of Society, on those points, are a violation of human rights, an usurpation of power over her, which is working mischief, great mischief, in the world. If Ecclesiastical and Civil governments are ordained of God, then I contend that woman has just as much right to sit in solemn counsel in Conventions, Conferences, Associations, and General Assemblies, as man—just as much right to sit upon the throne of England, or in the Presidential chair of the United States, as man....

• • •

I believe the discussion of Human Rights at the North has already been of immense advantage to this country. It is producing the happiest influence upon the minds and hearts of those who are engaged in it; ... Indeed, the very agitation of the question, which it involved, has been highly important. Never was the heart of man so expanded; never were its generous sympathies so generally and so perseveringly excited. These sympathies, thus called into existence, have been useful preservatives of national virtue. I therefore do wish very much to promote the Anti-Slavery excitement at the North, because I believe it will prove a useful preservative of national virtue....

The discussion of the wrongs of slavery has opened the way for the discussion of other rights, and the ultimate result will most certainly be "the breaking of every yoke," the letting the oppressed of every grade and description go free—an emancipation far more glorious than any the world has ever yet seen, an introduction into that liberty wherewith Christ hath made his people free....

Questions

1. Why does Angelina Grimké call the abolitionist movement the nation's foremost "school [of] human rights"?

2. What role does she think the difference between the sexes should play in determining a person's rights and obligations?

79. Declaration of Sentiments of the Seneca Falls Convention (1848)

Source: Elizabeth Cady Stanton et al., eds., A History of Woman Suffrage *(Rochester, NY, 1881–1922), Vol. 1, pp. 70–74.*

The Seneca Falls convention of 1848 marked the beginning of the seventy-year struggle for women's suffrage. Elizabeth Cady Stanton, a veteran of

the antislavery crusade, was the principal author of the Declaration of
Sentiments adopted at Seneca Falls, the town in upstate New York where
she lived. Modeled on the Declaration of Independence, the document
added "women" to Jefferson's axiom, "all men are created equal." And in
place of Jefferson's list of injustices committed by George III, Stanton condemned the "injuries and usurpations on the part of man toward woman."
The first to be listed was denying her the right to vote. As Stanton told
the convention, only the vote would make woman "free as man is free,"
since in a democratic society, freedom was impossible without the ballot.
The vote, however, was hardly the only issue raised at the convention.
Equal rights became the rallying cry of the early movement for women's
rights, and equal rights meant claiming access to all the prevailing definitions of American freedom.

WHEN, IN THE course of human events, it becomes necessary for
one portion of the family of man to assume among the people of the
earth a position different from that which they have hitherto occupied, but one to which the laws of nature and of nature's God entitle
them, a decent respect to the opinions of mankind requires that
they should declare the causes that impel them to such a course.

We hold these truths to be self-evident: that all men and women
are created equal; that they are endowed by their Creator with certain
inalienable rights; that among these are life, liberty, and the pursuit
of happiness; that to secure these rights governments are instituted,
deriving their just powers from the consent of the governed. Whenever any form of government becomes destructive of these ends, it
is the right of those who suffer from it to refuse allegiance to it, and
to insist upon the institution of a new government, laying its foundation on such principles, and organizing its powers in such form,
as to them shall seem most likely to effect their safety and happiness.
Prudence, indeed, will dictate that governments long established
should not be changed for light and transient causes; and accordingly
all experience hath shown that mankind are more disposed to suffer,
while evils are sufferable, than to right themselves by abolishing

the forms to which they were accustomed. But when a long train of abuses and usurpations, pursuing invariably the same object evinces a design to reduce them under absolute despotism, it is their duty to throw off such government, and to provide new guards for their future security. Such has been the patient sufferance of the women under this government, and such is now the necessity which constrains them to demand the equal station to which they are entitled.

The history of mankind is a history of repeated injuries and usurpations on the part of man toward woman, having in direct object the establishment of an absolute tyranny over her. To prove this, let facts be submitted to a candid world.

He has never permitted her to exercise her inalienable right to the elective franchise.

He has compelled her to submit to laws, in the formation of which she had no voice.

He has withheld from her rights which are given to the most ignorant and degraded men—both natives and foreigners.

Having deprived her of this first right of a citizen, the elective franchise, thereby leaving her without representation in the halls of legislation, he has oppressed her on all sides.

He has made her, if married, in the eye of the law, civilly dead.

He has taken from her all right in property, even to the wages she earns.

He has made her, morally, an irresponsible being, as she can commit many crimes with impunity, provided they be done in the presence of her husband. In the covenant of marriage, she is compelled to promise obedience to her husband, he becoming, to all intents and purposes, her master—the law giving him power to deprive her of her liberty, and to administer chastisement.

He has so framed the laws of divorce, as to what shall be the proper causes, and in case of separation, to whom the guardianship of the children shall be given, as to be wholly regardless of the happiness of women—the law, in all cases, going upon a false supposition of the supremacy of man, and giving all power into his hands.

After depriving her of all rights as a married woman, if single, and the owner of property, he has taxed her to support a government which recognizes her only when her property can be made profitable to it.

He has monopolized nearly all the profitable employments, and from those she is permitted to follow, she receives but a scanty remuneration. He closes against her all the avenues to wealth and distinction which he considers most honorable to himself. As a teacher of theology, medicine, or law, she is not known.

He has denied her the facilities for obtaining a thorough education, all colleges being closed against her.

He allows her in Church, as well as State, but a subordinate position, claiming Apostolic authority for her exclusion from the ministry, and, with some exceptions, from any public participation in the affairs of the Church.

He has created a false public sentiment by giving to the world a different code of morals for men and women, by which moral delinquencies which exclude women from society, are not only tolerated, but deemed of little account in man.

He has usurped the prerogative of Jehovah himself, claiming it as his right to assign for her a sphere of action, when that belongs to her conscience and to her God.

He has endeavored, in every way that he could, to destroy her confidence in her own powers, to lessen her self-respect, and to make her willing to lead a dependent and abject life.

Now, in view of this entire disfranchisement of one-half the people of this country, their social and religious degradation—in view of the unjust laws above mentioned, and because women do feel themselves aggrieved, oppressed, and fraudulently deprived of their most sacred rights, we insist that they have immediate admission to all the rights and privileges which belong to them as citizens of the United States.

In entering upon the great work before us, we anticipate no small amount of misconception, misrepresentation, and ridicule; but we shall use every instrumentality within our power to effect our object. We shall employ agents, circulate tracts, petition the State and National legislatures, and endeavor to enlist the pulpit and the press in our behalf. We hope this Convention will be followed by a series of Conventions embracing every part of the country.

Questions

1. What are the key demands, other than the right to vote, put forward by the Seneca Falls Convention?

2. How does the Declaration seem to define freedom for women?

CHAPTER 13

A House Divided, 1840–

80. John L. O'Sullivan, Manifest Destiny (1845)

Source: John L. O'Sullivan, "Annexation," United States Magazine, and Democratic Review, Vol. 17 (July/August 1845), pp. 5–10.

The expansionist spirit of the 1840s was captured in the phrase "manifest destiny," coined by John L. O'Sullivan, a New York journalist. O'Sullivan employed it to suggest that the United States had a divinely appointed mission to occupy all of North America. This right to the continent was provided by the nation's mission to extend the area of freedom. In the excerpt that follows, O'Sullivan defends the annexation of Texas, and suggests that California, then a province of Mexico, would be the next area to be absorbed into the United States, linked to the rest of the country by a new transcontinental road. O'Sullivan foresees the day when one government will control the entire North American continent. The spirit of manifest destiny would soon help to justify the Mexican War and, half a century later, the annexation of Puerto Rico and the Philippines as a result of the Spanish-American War.

―――――

IT IS TIME now for all opposition to annexation of Texas to cease.... Texas is now ours. Already before these records are written, her convention has undoubtedly ratified the acceptance, by her congress, of our proffered invitation into the Union; and made the requisite changes in her already republican form of constitution to apt it to its future federal relations. Her star and stripe may already be said to have taken their place in the glorious blazon of our common nationality; and the sweep of our eagle's wing already includes within its circuit the wide extent of her fair and fertile land.

She is no longer to us a mere geographical space—a certain combination of coast, plain, mountain, valley, forest, and stream. She is no longer to us a mere country on the map.... It is time when all should cease to treat her as alien, and even adverse ... and cease ... thwarting our policy and hampering our power, limiting our greatness and checking the fulfillment of our manifest destiny to overspread the continent allotted by Providence for the free development of our yearly multiplying millions.

• • •

It is wholly untrue, and unjust to ourselves, the pretense that the annexation has been a measure of spoliation, unrightful and unrighteous of military conquest under forms of peace and law of territorial aggrandizement at the expense of justice....

The independence of Texas was complete and absolute. It was an independence, not only in fact, but of right.... If Texas became peopled with an American population, it was by no contrivance of our government, but on the express invitation of that of Mexico herself; accompanied with such guaranties of state independence, and the maintenance of a federal system analogous to our own.... She was released, rightfully and absolutely released, from all Mexican allegiance, or duty of cohesion to the Mexican political body, by acts and fault of Mexico herself, and Mexico alone. There was never a clearer case. It was not revolution; it was resistance to revolution: and resistance under such circumstances as left independence the necessary resulting state, caused by the abandonment of those with whom her former federal association had existed.

Nor is there any just foundation for the charge that annexation is a great pro-slavery measure calculated to increase and perpetuate that institution. Slavery had nothing to do with it. Opinions were

and are greatly divided, both at the North and South, as to the influence to be exerted by it on slavery and the slave states. . . .

Every new slave state in Texas will make at least one free state from
among those in which that institution now exists—to say nothing
of those portions of Texas on which slavery cannot spring and grow—
to say nothing of the far more rapid growth of new states in the free
West and Northwest, as these fine regions are overspread by the
emigration fast flowing over them from Europe, as well as from
the Northern and Eastern states of the Union as it exists. . . .

California will, probably, next fall away from the loose adhesion
which, in such a country as Mexico, holds a remote province in a
slight equivocal kind of dependence on the metropolis. Imbecile and
distracted, Mexico never can exert any real government authority
over such a country. . . .

In the case of California this is now impossible. The Anglo-Saxon
foot is already on its borders. Already the advance guard of the irresistible army of Anglo-Saxon emigration has begun to pour down
upon it, armed with the plough and the rifle, and marking its trail
with schools and colleges, courts and representative halls, mills and
meetinghouses. A population will soon be in actual occupation of
California, over which it will be idle for Mexico to dream of dominion.
They will necessarily become independent. All this without agency
of our government, without responsibility of our people. . . .

And they will have a right to independence—to self-government—
to the possession of the homes conquered from the wildness of their
own labors and dangers, sufferings and sacrifices—a better and a
truer right than the artificial title of sovereignty in Mexico, a thousand miles distant, inheriting from Spain a title good only against
those who have none better. Their right to independence will be the
natural right of self-government belonging to any community strong
enough to maintain it. . . . This will be their title to independence;
and by this title, there can be no doubt that the population now fast
streaming down upon California will both assert and maintain that
independence.

Whether they will attach themselves to our Union or not is not to be predicted with any certainty. Unless the projected railroad across the continent to the Pacific be carried into effect, perhaps they may not; though even in that case, the day when the empires of the Atlantic and Pacific would again flow together into one, as soon as their inland border should approach each other. But that great work, colossal as appears the plan on its first suggestion, cannot remain long unbuilt.

Its [the transcontinental railroad] necessity for this very purpose of binding and holding together in its iron clasp our fast settling Pacific region with that of the Mississippi Valley, the natural facility of the route, the ease with which any amount of labor for the construction can be drawn in from the overcrowded populations of Europe, to be paid in the lands made valuable by the progress of the work itself and its immense utility, to the whole commerce of the world with the whole eastern coast of Asia, alone almost sufficient for the support of such a road—these considerations give assurance that the day cannot be distant which shall witness the conveyance of representatives from Oregon and California to Washington [D.C.] within less time than a few years ago was devoted to a similar journey by those from Ohio; while the magnetic telegraph will enable the editors of the *San Francisco Union*, the *Astoria Evening Post*, or the *Nootka Morning News*, to set up in type the first half of the President's inaugural before the echoes of the latter half shall have died away beneath the lofty porch of the Capitol, as spoken from his lips.

Away, then, with all idle French talk of balances of power on the American continent. There is no growth in Spanish America! Whatever progress of population may be in British Canada, is only for their own early severance of their present colonial relation to the little island 3,000 miles across the Atlantic; soon to be followed by annexation, and destined to swell the still accumulating momentum of our progress.

And whosoever may hold the balance, though they should cast into the opposite scale all the bayonets and cannon, not only of

France and England, but of Europe entire, how would it kick the beam against the simple, solid weight of the 250, or 300 million, and American millions destined to gather beneath the flutter of the stars and stripes, in the fast hastening year of the Lords 1845!

Questions

1. What connection does O'Sullivan see between manifest destiny and the idea of American freedom?

2. What does O'Sullivan mean when he describes America's destiny to rule the entire continent as "manifest"?

---

81. A Protest against Anti-Chinese Prejudice (1852)

Source: **Daily Alta California** *(San Francisco), May 5, 1852.*

The discovery of gold in California in 1848 unleashed a massive influx of migrants hoping to make their fortunes. The non-Indian population, under 15,000 in 1848, rose to over 360,000 by 1860. Prospectors came to the gold fields from all over the world—the eastern states, Europe, Latin America, and Asia. Nearly 25,000 Chinese landed between 1849 and 1852, most of them young men who had signed long-term labor contracts and went to work for the state's mines and railroads. Anti-Chinese sentiment quickly developed and in 1852 the state's governor, Democrat John Bigler, proposed that the legislature restrict Chinese immigration (even though the Constitution gives power over immigration to the federal government). In response, Norman Asing, a naturalized American citizen and leader of the Chinese community of San Francisco, issued an eloquent appeal for equal rights for the Chinese.

SIR: I AM a Chinaman, a republican, and a lover of free institutions; am much attached to the principles of the government of the United States, and therefore take the liberty of addressing you as the chief of the government of this State. Your official position gives you a great opportunity of good and evil.... The effect of your late message has been thus far to prejudice the public mind against my people, to enable those who wait the opportunity to hunt them down, and rob them of the rewards of their toil. You may not have meant that this should be the case, but you can see what will be the result of your propositions.

I am not much acquainted with your logic, that by excluding population from this State you enhance its wealth. I have always considered that population was wealth; particularly a population of producers, of men who by the labor of their hands or intellect, enrich the warehouses or the granaries of the country with the products of nature and art. You are deeply convinced you say "that to enhance the prosperity and preserve the tranquility of this State, Asiatic immigration must be checked." This, your Excellency, is but one step towards a retrograde movement of the government, which, on reflection, you will discover; and which the citizens of this country ought never to tolerate. It was one of the principal causes of quarrel between you (when colonies) and England; when the latter pressed laws against emigration, you looked for immigration; it came, and immigration made you what you are—your nation what it is. It transferred you at once from childhood to manhood and made you great and respectable throughout the nations of the earth. I am sure your Excellency cannot, if you would, prevent your being called the descendant of an immigrant, for I am sure you do not boast of being a descendant of the red man. But your further logic is more reprehensible. You argue that this is a republic of a particular race—that the Constitution of the United States admits of no asylum to any other than the pale face. This proposition is false in the extreme, and you know it. The declaration of your independence, and all the acts of your government, your people, and your history are all against you....

We would beg to remind you that when your nation was a wilderness, and the nation from which you sprung barbarous, we exercised most of the arts and virtues of civilized life; that we are possessed of a language and a literature, and that men skilled in science and the arts are numerous among us; that the productions of our manufactories, our sail, and workshops, form no small share of the commerce of the world; and that for centuries, colleges, schools, charitable institutions, asylums, and hospitals, have been as common as in your own land. That our people cannot be reproved for their idleness, and that your historians have given them due credit for the variety and richness of their works of art, and for their simplicity of manners, and particularly their industry. And we beg to remark, that so far as the history of our race in California goes, it stamps with the test of truth the fact that we are not the degraded race you would make us. We came amongst you as mechanics or traders, and following every honorable business of life. . . .

I am a naturalized citizen, your Excellency, of Charleston, South Carolina, and a Christian, too; and so hope you will stand corrected in your assertion "that none of the Asiatic class" as you are pleased to term them, have applied for benefits under our naturalization act. I could point out to you numbers of citizens, all over the whole continent, who have taken advantage of your hospitality and citizenship, and I defy you to say that our race have ever abused that hospitality or forfeited their claim on this or any of the governments of South America, by an infringement on the laws of the countries into which they pass. You find us peculiarly peaceable and orderly. It does not cost your state much for our criminal prosecution. We apply less to your courts for redress, and so far as I know, there are none who are a charge upon the state, as paupers.

Questions

1. Why does Asing argue that the governor's proposal violates the Constitution and the principles of the Declaration of Independence?

2. How does he invoke the history of China to bolster his criticism of the idea of excluding Chinese immigrants from the United States?

82. Henry David Thoreau, "Resistance to Civil Government" (1849)

Source: Henry David Thoreau, "Resistance to Civil Government," in **Aesthetic Papers** *(Boston, 1849), pp. 189–200.*

The Mexican-American War of 1846–1848 was the first American conflict to be fought primarily on foreign soil and the first in which American troops occupied a foreign capital. It resulted in the absorption by the United States of about one-third of the territory of Mexico—the present-day states of Arizona, California, New Mexico, Nevada, and Utah.

Inspired by the expansionist fervor of manifest destiny, a majority of Americans supported the war. But a significant minority in the North feared that far from expanding the "empire of liberty," the real aim of the administration of James K. Polk was to acquire new land for the expansion of slavery. In Massachusetts, Henry David Thoreau was imprisoned in 1846 for refusing to pay taxes as a protest against the war. (He spent one night in jail, after which a relative paid the tax and he was released.) Defending his action, Thoreau wrote an essay on civil disobedience. The essay would inspire such later advocates of nonviolent resistance to unjust laws as Mohandas K. Gandhi and Martin Luther King Jr.

I HEARTILY ACCEPT THE MOTTO,—"That government is best which governs least" and I should like to see it acted up to more rapidly and systematically. Carried out, it finally amounts to this, which also I believe,—"That government is best which governs not at all;" and when men are prepared for it, that will be the kind of government which they will have. Government is at best but an expedient; but most governments are usually, and all governments are sometimes, inexpedient....

This American government,—what is it but a tradition, though a recent one, endeavoring to transmit itself unimpaired to posterity; but each instant losing some of its integrity? It has not the vitality and force of a single living man; for a single man can bend it to his will.... *It* does not keep the country free. *It* does not settle the West. *It* does not educate. The character inherent in the American people has done all that has been accomplished; and it would have done somewhat more, if the government had not sometimes got in its way. For government is an expedient by which men would fain succeed in letting one another alone; and, as has been said, when it is most expedient, the governed are most let alone by it....

But, to speak practically and as a citizen, unlike those who call themselves no-government men, I ask for, not at once no government, but *at once* a better government. Let every man make known what kind of government would command his respect, and that will be one step toward obtaining it.

After all, the practical reason why, when the power is once in the hands of the people, a majority are permitted, and for a long period continue, to rule, is not because they are most likely to be in the right, nor because this seems fairest to the minority, but because they are physically the strongest. But a government in which the majority rule in all cases cannot be based on justice, even as far as men understand it.... Must the citizen ever for a moment, or in the least degree, resign his conscience to the legislator? Why has every man a conscience, then? I think that we should be men first, and subjects afterward. It is not desirable to cultivate a respect for the law, so much as for the right. The only obligation which I have a right to assume, is to do at any time what I think right....

How does it become a man to behave toward this American government to-day? I answer that he cannot without disgrace be associated with it. I cannot for an instant recognize that political organization as my government which is the *slave's* government also.

All men recognize the right of revolution; that is, the right to refuse allegiance to and to resist the government, when its tyranny or its inefficiency are great and unendurable. But almost all say that such is not the case now.... But when ... oppression and robbery are organized, I say, let us not have such a machine any longer. In other words, when a sixth of the population of a nation which has undertaken to be the refuge of liberty are slaves, and a whole country is unjustly overrun and conquered by a foreign army, and subjected to military law, I think that it is not too soon for honest men to rebel and revolutionize. What makes this duty the more urgent is the fact, that the country so overrun is not our own, but ours is the invading army....

Practically speaking, the opponents to a reform in Massachusetts are not a hundred thousand politicians at the South, but a hundred thousand merchants and farmers here, who are more interested in commerce and agriculture than they are in humanity, and are not prepared to do justice to the slave and to Mexico, *cost what it may*. I quarrel not with far-off foes, but with those who, near at home, co-operate with, and do the bidding of those far away, and without whom the latter would be harmless. We are accustomed to say, that the mass of men are unprepared; but improvement is slow, because the few are not materially wiser or better than the many. It is not so important that many should be as good as you, as that there be some absolute goodness somewhere; for that will leaven the whole lump. There are thousands who are *in opinion* opposed to slavery and to the war, who yet in effect do nothing to put an end to them; who, esteeming themselves children of Washington and Franklin, sit down with their hands in their pockets, and say that they know not what to do, and do nothing; who even postpone the question of freedom to the question of free-trade, and quietly read the prices-current along with the latest advices from Mexico, after dinner, and, it may be, fall asleep over them both....

Unjust laws exist: shall we be content to obey them, or shall we endeavor to amend them, and obey them until we have succeeded, or shall we transgress them at once? Men generally, under such a government as this, think that they ought to wait until they have persuaded the majority to alter them. They think that, if they should resist, the remedy would be worse than the evil. But it is the fault of the government itself that the remedy *is* worse than the evil. *It* makes it worse. Why is it not more apt to anticipate and provide for reform? Why does it not cherish its wise minority? Why does it cry and resist before it is hurt? Why does it not encourage its citizens to be on the alert to point out its faults, and *do* better than it would have them? Why does it always crucify Christ, and excommunicate Copernicus and Luther, and pronounce Washington and Franklin rebels?

As for adopting the ways which the State has provided for remedying the evil, I know not of such ways. They take too much time, and a man's life will be gone. I have other affairs to attend to. I came into this world, not chiefly to make this a good place to live in, but to live in it, be it good or bad. A man has not every thing to do, but something; and because he cannot do *every thing*, it is not necessary that he should do *something* wrong. It is not my business to be petitioning the governor or the legislature any more than it is theirs to petition me; and, if they should not hear my petition, what should I do then? But in this case the State has provided no way: its very Constitution is the evil. . . .

I do not hesitate to say, that those who call themselves abolitionists should at once effectually withdraw their support, both in person and property, from the government of Massachusetts, and not wait till they constitute a majority of one, before they suffer the right to prevail through them. I think that it is enough if they have God on their side, without waiting for that other one. Moreover, any man more right than his neighbors, constitutes a majority of one already.

Under a government which imprisons any unjustly, the true place for a just man is also a prison. The proper place to-day, the only place which Massachusetts has provided for her freer and less desponding spirits, is in her prisons, to be put out and locked out of the State by her own act, as they have already put themselves out by their principles. It is there that the fugitive slave, and the Mexican prisoner on parole, and the Indian come to plead the wrongs of his race, should find them; on that separate, but more free and honorable ground, where the State places those who are not *with* her but *against* her,—the only house in a slave-state in which a free man can abide with honor. If any think that their influence would be lost there, and their voices no longer afflict the ear of the State, that they would not be as an enemy within its walls, they do not know by how much truth is stronger than error, nor how much more eloquently and effectively he can combat injustice who has experienced a little in his own person. Cast your whole vote, not a strip of paper merely, but your whole influence. A minority is powerless while it conforms to the majority; it is not even a minority then; but it is irresistible when it clogs by its whole weight. If the alternative is to keep all just men in prison, or give up war and slavery, the State will not hesitate which to choose. If a thousand men were not to pay their tax-bills this year, that would not be a violent and bloody measure, as it would be to pay them, and enable the State to commit violence and shed innocent blood. This is, in fact, the definition of a peaceable revolution, if any such is possible. . . .

The authority of government, even such as I am willing to submit to,—for I will cheerfully obey those who know and can do better than I, and in many things even those who neither know nor can do so well,—is still an impure one: to be strictly just, it must have the sanction and consent of the governed. It can have no pure right over my person and property but what I concede to it. The progress from an absolute to a limited monarchy, from a limited monarchy to a democracy, is a progress toward a true respect for the individual. Is a democracy, such as we know it, the last improvement possible in government? Is it not possible to take a step further towards recognizing and organizing the rights of man? There will never be a really free and enlightened State, until the State comes to recognize the individual as a higher and independent power, from which all its own power and authority are derived, and treats him accordingly. I please myself with imagining a State at last which can afford to be just to all men, and to treat the individual with respect as a neighbor; which even would not think it inconsistent with its own repose, if a few were to live aloof from it, not meddling with it, nor embraced by it, who fulfilled all the duties of neighbors and fellow-men. A State which bore this kind of fruit, and suffered it to drop off as fast as it ripened, would prepare the way for a still more perfect and glorious State, which also I have imagined, but not yet anywhere seen.

Questions

1. What does Thoreau see as the relationship between government and freedom?

2. How does he justify an individual's deciding to break the law?

---

83. William Henry Seward, "The Irrepressible Conflict" (1858)

Source: The Irrepressible Conflict: A Speech by William H. Seward, Delivered at Rochester, Monday, Oct. 25, 1858 *(New York, 1858), pp. 1–6.*

As the controversy over the expansion of slavery intensified during the 1850s, a new political party, the Republican Party, rose to dominance in the North. The party's appeal rested on the idea of "free labor." Republicans glorified the North as the home of progress, opportunity, and freedom.

One of the most powerful statements of the Republican outlook was delivered in 1858 by William H. Seward, a senator from New York. Seward described the nation's division into free and slave societies as an "irrepressible conflict" between two fundamentally different social systems. Although Seward condemned slavery as immoral, his essential argument had to do with economic development and national unity. The market revolution, he argued, was drawing the entire nation closer together in a web of transportation and commerce, thus heightening the tension between freedom and slavery. The United States, he predicted, "must and will, sooner or later, become either entirely a slaveholding nation, or entirely a free-labor nation."

OUR COUNTRY IS a theater, which exhibits, in full operation, two radically different political systems; the one resting on the basis of servile or slave labor, the other on the basis of voluntary labor of freemen.

The laborers who are enslaved are all Negroes, or persons more or less purely of African derivation. But this is only accidental. The principle of the system is, that labor in every society, by whomsoever performed, is necessarily unintellectual, groveling and base; and that the laborer, equally for his own good and for the welfare of the State, ought to be enslaved. The white laboring man, whether native or foreigner, is not enslaved, only because he cannot, as yet, be reduced to bondage....

• • •

One of the chief elements of the value of human life is freedom in the pursuit of happiness. The slave system is not only intolerant, unjust, and inhuman, toward the laborer, whom, only because he is a laborer, it loads down with chains and converts into merchandise, but is scarcely less severe upon the freeman, to whom, only because he is a laborer from necessity, it denies facilities for employment, and whom it expels from the community because it cannot enslave and convert him into merchandise also. It is necessarily improvident and ruinous, because, as a general truth, communities prosper and flourish or droop and decline in just the degree that they practice or neglect to practice the primary duties of justice and humanity. The free-labor system conforms to the divine law of equality, which is written in the hearts and consciences of men, and therefore is always and everywhere beneficent.

The slave system is one of constant danger, distrust, suspicion, and watchfulness. It debases those whose toil alone can produce wealth and resources for defense, to the lowest degree of which human nature is capable, to guard against mutiny and insurrection, and thus wastes energies which otherwise might be employed in national development and aggrandizement.

The free-labor system educates all alike, and by opening all the fields of industrial employment, and all the departments of authority, to the unchecked and equal rivalry of all classes of men, at once secures universal contentment, and brings into the highest possible activity all the physical, moral, and social energies of the whole State. In States where the slave system prevails, the masters, directly or indirectly, secure all political power, and constitute a ruling aristocracy. In States where the free-labor system prevails, universal suffrage necessarily obtains, and the State inevitably becomes, sooner or later, a republic or democracy....

• • •

The two systems are at once perceived to be incongruous. But they are more than incongruous—they are incompatible. They never have permanently existed together in one country, and they never can. It would be easy to demonstrate this impossibility, from the irreconcilable contrast between their great principles and characteristics. But the experience of mankind has conclusively established it....

Hitherto, the two systems have existed in different States, but side by side within the American Union. This has happened because the Union is a confederation of States. But in another aspect the United States constitute only one nation. Increase of population, which is filling the States out to their very borders, together with a new and extended network of railroads and other avenues, and an internal commerce which daily becomes more intimate, is rapidly bringing the States into a higher and more perfect social unity or consolidation. Thus, these antagonistic systems are continually coming into closer contact, and collision results.

Shall I tell you what this collision means? . . . It is an irrepressible conflict between opposing and enduring forces, and it means that the United States must and will, sooner or later, become either entirely a slaveholding nation, or entirely a free-labor nation. Either the cotton and rice fields of South Carolina and the sugar plantations of Louisiana will ultimately be filled by free labor, and Charleston and New Orleans become marts for legitimate merchandise alone, or else the rye-fields and wheat-fields of Massachusetts and New York must again be surrendered by their farmers to slave culture and to the production of slaves, and Boston and New York become once more markets for trade in the bodies and souls of men. . . .

Thus far, the course of that contest has not been according to the humane anticipations and wishes [of the founding fathers]. In the field of federal policies, Slavery, deriving unlooked-for advantages from commercial changes, and energies unforeseen from the facilities of combination between members of the slaveholding class and between that class and other property classes, early rallied, and has at length made a stand, not merely to retain its original defensive position, but to extend its sway throughout the whole Union. . . . This is a Constitution of Freedom. It is being converted into a Constitution of Slavery.

Questions

1. How does Seward expand the antislavery argument beyond the moral appeal of the abolitionists?

2. To whom does Seward seem to be addressing his remarks?

84. Texas Declaration of Independence (1836)

Source: Texas State Library and Archives Commission.

In the 1820s, some 7,000 emigrants from the United States emigrated to Texas, then part of Mexico, whose government at first welcomed them to the sparsely settled region. But as the number of emigrants grew, the Mexican government became alarmed and sought to discourage newcomers. When the settlers demanded greater autonomy, the Mexican government sent an army to impose central authority. In response, a convention of representatives from American settlements on March 2, 1836, declared Texas an independent nation. Like the revolutionaries of 1776, they issued a Declaration explaining their action. Sixty men signed the Declaration; three had been born in Mexico, the remainder in the United States. Texas would win the war and remain independent until 1845, when it was annexed to the United States.

WHEN A GOVERNMENT has ceased to protect the lives, liberty and property of the people, from whom its legitimate powers are derived, and for the advancement of whose happiness it was instituted, and so far from being a guarantee for the enjoyment of those inestimable and inalienable rights, becomes an instrument in the hands of evil rulers for their oppression.

When the Federal Republican Constitution of their country, which they have sworn to support, no longer has a substantial existence, and the whole nature of their government has been forcibly changed, without their consent, from a restricted federative republic, composed of sovereign states, to a consolidated central military despotism, in which every interest is disregarded but that of the army and the priesthood, both the eternal enemies of civil liberty, the everready minions of power, and the usual instruments of tyrants.

When, long after the spirit of the constitution has departed, moderation is at length so far lost by those in power, that even the semblance of freedom is removed, and the forms themselves of the constitution discontinued, and so far from their petitions and remonstrances being regarded, the agents who bear them are thrown into dungeons, and mercenary armies sent forth to force a new government upon them at the point of the bayonet.

When, in consequence of such acts of malfeasance and abdication on the part of the government, anarchy prevails, and civil society is dissolved into its original elements. In such a crisis, the first law of nature, the right of self-preservation, the inherent and inalienable rights of the people to appeal to first principles, and take their political affairs into their own hands in extreme cases, enjoins it as a right towards themselves, and a sacred obligation to their posterity, to abolish such government, and create another in its stead, calculated to rescue them from impending dangers, and to secure their future welfare and happiness.

Nations, as well as individuals, are amenable for their acts to the public opinion of mankind. A statement of a part of our grievances is therefore submitted to an impartial world, in justification of the hazardous but unavoidable step now taken, of severing our political connection with the Mexican people, and assuming an independent attitude among the nations of the earth.

The Mexican government, by its colonization laws, invited and induced the Anglo-American population of Texas to colonize its wilderness under the pledged faith of a written constitution, that they should continue to enjoy that constitutional liberty and republican government to which they had been habituated in the land of their birth, the United States of America.

In this expectation they have been cruelly disappointed, inasmuch as the Mexican nation has acquiesced in the late changes made in the government by General Antonio Lopez de Santa Anna, who having overturned the constitution of his country, now offers us the cruel alternative, either to abandon our homes, acquired by so many privations, or submit to the most intolerable of all tyranny, the combined despotism of the sword and the priesthood....

It has failed to establish any public system of education, although possessed of almost boundless resources, (the public domain), and although it is an axiom in political science, that unless a people are educated and enlightened, it is idle to expect the continuance of civil liberty, or the capacity for self government. . . .

It denies us the right of worshipping the Almighty according to the dictates of our own conscience, by the support of a national religion, calculated to promote the temporal interest of its human functionaries, rather than the glory of the true and living God.

It has demanded us to deliver up our arms, which are essential to our defence, the rightful property of freemen, and formidable only to tyrannical governments.

It has invaded our country both by sea and by land, with intent to lay waste our territory, and drive us from our homes; and has now a large mercenary army advancing, to carry on against us a war of extermination.

It has, through its emissaries, incited the merciless savage, with the tomahawk and scalping knife, to massacre the inhabitants of our defenseless frontiers. . . .

These, and other grievances, were patiently borne by the people of Texas, until they reached that point at which forbearance ceases to be a virtue. We then took up arms in defence of the national constitution. We appealed to our Mexican brethren for assistance. Our appeal has been made in vain. Though months have elapsed, no sympathetic response has yet been heard from the Interior. We are, therefore, forced to the melancholy conclusion, that the Mexican people have acquiesced in the destruction of their liberty, and the substitution therfore of a military government; that they are unfit to be free, and incapable of self government. . . .

We, therefore, the delegates with plenary powers of the people of Texas, in solemn convention assembled, appealing to a candid world for the necessities of our condition, do hereby resolve and declare, that our political connection with the Mexican nation has forever ended, and that the people of Texas do now constitute a free,

Sovereign, and independent republic, and are fully invested with all
the rights and attributes which properly belong to independent
nations; and, conscious of the rectitude of our intentions, we fear-
lessly and confidently commit the issue to the decision of the
Supreme arbiter of the destinies of nations.

Questions

1. In what ways is this Declaration similar to the American Declaration of
Independence?

2. What seems to be the attitude of the Texas revolutionaries toward other
elements of Texas society (Mexicans, Native Americans, and slaves)?

85. The Lincoln-Douglas Debates (1858)

Source: **Political Debates between Honorable Abraham Lincoln and
Honorable Stephen Douglas, in the Celebrated Campaign of 1858
(Columbus, Ohio, 1860), pp. 71, 75, 178–82, 204, 209, 234, 238.**

Americans' divisions over slavery were brought into sharp focus in 1858
in the election campaign that pitted Illinois senator Stephen A. Douglas,
the North's most prominent Democratic leader, against the then little-
known Abraham Lincoln.

The Lincoln-Douglas debates, held in seven Illinois towns and attended
by tens of thousands of listeners, remain classics of American political
oratory. Clashing definitions of freedom lay at their heart. To Lincoln,
freedom meant opposition to slavery. Douglas insisted that the essence of
freedom lay in local self-government. A large, diverse nation could survive only by respecting the right of each locality to determine its own
institutions. He attempted to portray Lincoln as a dangerous radical
whose positions threatened to degrade white Americans by reducing
them to equality with blacks.

Douglas was reelected. But the campaign created Lincoln's national reputation.

. . .

DOUGLAS: Do you desire to strike out of our state constitution that clause which keeps slaves and free negroes out of the state, and allow the free negroes to flow in, and cover your prairies with black settlements? Do you desire to turn this beautiful state into a free negro colony, in order that when Missouri abolishes slavery she can send one hundred thousand emancipated slaves into Illinois, to become citizens and voters, on an equality with yourselves? If you desire negro citizenship, if you desire to allow them to come into the state and settle with the white man, if you desire them to vote on an equality with yourselves, and to make them eligible to office, to serve on juries, and to adjudge your rights, then support Mr. Lincoln and the Black Republican party, who are in favor of the citizenship of the negro. For one, I am opposed to negro citizenship in any and every form. I believe this government was made on the white basis. I believe it was made by white men, for the benefit of white men and their posterity for ever, and I am in favor of confining citizenship to white men, men of European birth and descent, instead of conferring it upon negroes, Indians and other inferior races.

Mr. Lincoln, following the example and lead of all the little Abolition orators, who go around and lecture in the basements of schools and churches, reads from the Declaration of Independence, that all men were created equal, and then asks how can you deprive a negro of that equality which God and the Declaration of Independence awards to him. He and they maintain that negro equality is guaranteed by the laws of God, and that it is asserted in the Declaration of Independence. If they think so, of course they have a right to say so, and so vote. I do not question Mr. Lincoln's conscientious belief that the negro was made his equal, and hence is his brother, (laughter), but for my own part, I do not regard the negro as my equal, and positively deny that he is my brother or any kin to me whatever.

• • •

LINCOLN: Now gentlemen, I don't want to read at any greater length, but this is the true complexion of all I have ever said in regard to the institution of slavery and the black race. This is the whole of it, and anything that argues me into his idea of perfect social and political equality with the negro, is but a specious and fantastic arrangement of words, by which a man can prove a horse chestnut to be a chestnut horse. I will say here, while upon this subject, that I have no purpose directly or indirectly to interfere with the institution of slavery in the states where it exists. I believe I have no lawful right to do so, and I have no inclination to do so. I have no purpose to introduce political and social equality between the white and the black races. There is a physical difference between the two, which in my judgment will probably forever forbid their living together upon the footing of perfect equality, and inasmuch as it becomes a necessity that there must be a difference, I, as well as Judge Douglas, am in favor of the race to which I belong, having the superior position. I have never said anything to the contrary, but I hold that notwithstanding all this, there is no reason in the world why the negro is not entitled to all the natural rights enumerated in the Declaration of Independence, the right to life, liberty and the pursuit of happiness. I hold that he is as much entitled to these as the white man. I agree with Judge Douglas he is not my equal in many respects—certainly not in color, perhaps not in moral or intellectual endowment. But in the right to eat the bread, without leave of anybody else, which his own hand earns, *he is my equal and the equal of Judge Douglas, and the equal of every living man.*

• • •

DOUGLAS: He tells you that I will not argue the question whether slavery is right or wrong. I tell you why I will not do it. I hold that under the Constitution of the United States, each state of this Union has a right to do as it pleases on the subject of slavery. In Illinois we have exercised that sovereign right by prohibiting slavery within our own limits. I approve of that line of policy. We have performed our whole duty in Illinois. We have gone as far as we have a right to go under the Constitution of our common country. It is none of our business whether slavery exists in Missouri or not. Missouri is a sovereign state of this Union, and has the same right to decide the slavery question for herself that Illinois has to decide it for herself. ("Good.") Hence I do not choose to occupy the time allotted to me discussing a question that we have no right to act upon.

• • •

LINCOLN: The real issue in this controversy—the one pressing upon every mind—is the sentiment on the part of one class that looks upon the institution of slavery *as a wrong*, and of another class that *does not* look upon it as a wrong. The sentiment that contemplates the institution of slavery in this country as a wrong is the sentiment of the Republican party. It is the sentiment around which all their actions—all their arguments circle—from which all their propositions radiate. They look upon it as being a moral, social and political wrong; and while they contemplate it as such, they nevertheless have due regard for its actual existence among us, and the difficulties of getting rid of it in any satisfactory way and to all the constitutional obligations thrown about it. Yet having a due regard for these, they desire a policy in regard to it that looks to its not creating any more danger. They insist that it should as far as may be, *be treated* as a wrong, and one of the methods of treating it as a wrong is to *make provision that it shall grow no larger.* They also desire a policy that looks to a peaceful end of slavery at sometime, as being wrong....

That is the real issue. That is the issue that will continue in this country when these poor tongues of Judge Douglas and myself shall be silent. It is the eternal struggle between these two principles—right and wrong—throughout the world. They are the two principles that have stood face to face from the beginning of time; and will ever continue to struggle. The one is the common right of humanity and the other the divine right of kings. It is the same principle in whatever shape it develops itself. It is the same spirit that says, "You work and toil and earn bread, and I'll eat it." [Loud applause.] No matter in what shape it comes, whether from the mouth of a king who seeks to bestride the people of his own nation and live by the fruit of their labor, or from one race of men as an apology for enslaving another race, it is the same tyrannical principal. I was glad to express my gratitude at Quincy, and I re-express it here to Judge Douglas—*that he looks to no end of the institution of slavery.* That will help the people to see where the struggle really is. It will hereafter place with us all men who really do wish the wrong may have an end. And whenever we can get rid of the fog which obscures the real question—when we can get Judge Douglas and his friends to avow a policy looking to its perpetuation—we can get out from among them that class of men and bring them to the side of those who treat it as a wrong. Then there will soon be an end of it, and that end will be its "ultimate extinction." Whenever the issue can be distinctly made, and all extraneous matter thrown out so that men can fairly see the real difference between the parties, this controversy will soon be settled, and it will be done peaceably too.

• • •

Questions

1. How do Douglas and Lincoln differ in their views on what rights black Americans ought to enjoy?

2. What is Douglas's response to antislavery criticism of slavery in the southern states?

86. South Carolina Ordinance of Secession (1860)

Source: Frank H. Moore, ed., The Rebellion Record (New York, 1861–1868), Vol. 1, pp. 3–5.

In the three months that followed Abraham Lincoln's election as president in November 1860, seven states seceded from the Union. First to act was South Carolina, the state with the highest percentage of slaves in its population and a long history of political radicalism. On December 20, 1860, the legislature unanimously voted to leave the Union. In justifying the right to secede, the legislature issued an *Ordinance of Secession*. It restated the compact theory of the Constitution that had become more and more central to southern political thought during the three decades since the nullification controversy and placed the issue of slavery squarely at the center of the crisis. Rather than accept permanent minority status in a nation governed by their opponents, South Carolina's leaders boldly struck for their region's independence. At stake, they believed, was not a single election but an entire way of life based on slavery.

THE STATE OF South Carolina having resumed her separate and equal place among nations, deems it due to herself, to the remaining United States of America, and to the nations of the world, that she should declare the immediate causes which have led to this act.

In 1787, Deputies were appointed by the States to revise the Articles of Confederation; and on 17th September, 1787, these Deputies recommended, for the adoption of the States, the Articles of Union, known as the Constitution of the United States....

Thus was established by compact between the States, a Government with defined objects and powers, limited to the express words of the grant.... We hold that the Government thus established is subject to the two great principles asserted in the Declaration of Independence; and we hold further, that the mode of its formation

subjects it to a third fundamental principle, namely, the law of compact. We maintain that in every compact between two or more parties, the obligation is mutual; that the failure of one of the contracting
parties to perform a material part of the arrangement, entirely
releases the obligation of the other, and that, where no arbiter is provided, each party is remitted to his own judgment to determine the
fact of failure, with all its consequences.

• • •

We affirm that the ends for which this Government was instituted have been defeated, and the Government itself has been made
destructive of them by the action of the non-slaveholding States.
Those States have assumed the right of deciding upon the propriety
of our domestic institutions, and have denied the rights of property
established in fifteen of the States and recognized by the Constitution; they have denounced as sinful the institution of Slavery; they
have permitted the open establishment among them of societies,
whose avowed object is to disturb the peace of and eloin [take away]
the property of the citizens of other States. They have encouraged and
assisted thousands of our slaves to leave their homes; and those who
remain, have been incited by emissaries, books, and pictures, to servile insurrection.

For twenty-five years this agitation has been steadily increasing,
until it has now secured to its aid the power of the common Government. Observing the *forms* of the Constitution, a sectional party has
found within that article establishing the Executive Department,
the means of subverting the Constitution itself. A geographical line
has been drawn across the Union, and all the States north of that
line have united in the election of a man to the high office of President of the United States whose opinions and purposes are hostile
to Slavery. He is to be intrusted with the administration of the common Government, because he has declared that "Government cannot endure permanently half slave, half free," and that the public
mind must rest in the belief that Slavery is in the course of ultimate
extinction.

This sectional combination for the subversion of the Constitution has been aided, in some of the States, by elevating to citizenship persons who, by the supreme law of the land are incapable of becoming citizens; and their votes have been used to inaugurate a new policy, hostile to the South, and destructive of its peace and safety.

On the 4th of March next this party will take possession of the Government. It has announced that the South shall be excluded from the common territory, that the Judicial tribunal shall be made sectional, and that a war must be waged against Slavery until it shall cease throughout the United States.

The guarantees of the Constitution will then no longer exist; the equal rights of the States will be lost. The Slaveholding States will no longer have the power of self-government, or self-protection, and the Federal Government will have become their enemy.

Sectional interest and animosity will deepen the irritation; and all hope of remedy is rendered vain, by the fact that the public opinion at the North has invested a great political error with the sanctions of a more erroneous religious belief.

We, therefore, the people of South Carolina, by our delegates in Convention assembled, appealing to the Supreme Judge of the world for the rectitude of our intentions, have solemnly declared that the Union heretofore existing between this State and the other States of North America is dissolved, and that the State of South Carolina has resumed her position among the nations of the world as a separate and independent state, with full power to levy war, conclude peace, contract alliances, establish commerce, and to do all other acts and things which independent States may of right do.

Questions

1. Why do secessionists place so much emphasis on the growth of antislavery public opinion in the North?

2. What appears to be the main motivation for South Carolina's secession?

CHAPTER 14

A New Birth of Freedom: The Civil War, 1861–1865

87. Alexander H. Stephens, The Cornerstone of the Confederacy (1861)

Source: Frank H. Moore, ed., The Rebellion Record, Vol. 1 (New York: G.P. Putnam, 1861–1868), pp. 45–46.

Alexander H. Stephens, one of Georgia's most prominent political leaders, opposed secession in the winter of 1860–1861, but once his state acted, agreed to serve as the vice president of the Confederacy. In March 1861, he delivered a speech in Savannah that laid out his explanation for the dissolution of the Union and argued that the Confederate Constitution represented a significant improvement over that of the United States. After the war, Stephens would write a long book arguing that the Civil War was caused not by slavery but by a constitutional question—the South's insistence on preserving state sovereignty against an overly powerful national government. In his 1861 speech, however, he forthrightly identified the defense of slavery and of white supremacy as the fundamental motivation of the Confederacy, the "cornerstone" of the new southern nation. Apparently, Stephens's speech embarrassed Confederate president Jefferson Davis, who hoped to gain recognition from European powers by downplaying the role of slavery in the secession movement.

WE ARE PASSING through one of the greatest revolutions in the annals of the world. Seven States have within the last three months thrown off an old government and formed a new. This revolution has been signally marked, up to this time, by the fact of its having been accomplished without the loss of a single drop of blood.

This new constitution. or form of government, constitutes the subject to which your attention will be partly invited. In reference to it, I make this first general remark: it amply secures all our ancient rights, franchises, and liberties. All the great principles of Magna Charta are retained in it. No citizen is deprived of life, liberty, or property, but by the judgment of his peers under the laws of the land. The great principle of religious liberty, which was the honor and pride of the old constitution, is still maintained and secured. All the essentials of the old constitution, which have endeared it to the hearts of the American people, have been preserved and perpetuated.... So, taking the whole new constitution, I have no hesitancy in giving it as my judgment that it is decidedly better than the old.

Allow me briefly to allude to some of these improvements. The question of building up class interests, or fostering one branch of industry to the prejudice of another under the exercise of the revenue power, which gave us so much trouble under the old constitution, is put at rest forever under the new. We allow the imposition of no duty with a view of giving advantage to one class of persons, in any trade or business, over those of another. All, under our system, stand upon the same broad principles of perfect equality. Honest labor and enterprise are left free and unrestricted in whatever pursuit they may be engaged....

But not to be tedious in enumerating the numerous changes for the better, allow me to allude to one other though last, not least. The new constitution has put at rest, forever, all the agitating questions relating to our peculiar institution African slavery as it exists amongst us the proper status of the negro in our form of civilization. This was the immediate cause of the late rupture and present revolution. Jefferson in his forecast, had anticipated this, as the "rock upon which the old Union would split." He was right. What was conjecture with him, is now a realized fact. But whether he fully comprehended the great truth upon which that rock stood and stands, may be doubted. The prevailing ideas entertained by him and most of the leading statesmen at the time of the formation of the old constitution, were that the enslavement of the African was in violation of the laws of nature; that it was wrong in principle, socially, morally, and politically. It was an evil they knew not well how to deal with, but the general opinion of the men of that day was that, somehow or other in the order of Providence, the institution would be evanescent and pass away. This idea, though not incorporated in the constitution, was the prevailing idea at that time. The constitution, it is true, secured every essential guarantee to the institution while it should last, and hence no argument can be justly urged against the constitutional guarantees thus secured, because of the common sentiment of the day. Those ideas, however, were fundamentally wrong. They rested upon the assumption of the equality of races. This was an error. It was a sandy foundation, and the government built upon it fell when the "storm came and the wind blew."

Our new government is founded upon exactly the opposite idea; its foundations are laid, its cornerstone rests, upon the great truth that the negro is not equal to the white man; that slavery, subordination to the superior race, is his natural and normal condition. This, our new government, is the first, in the history of the world, based upon this great physical, philosophical, and moral truth. This truth has been slow in the process of its development, like all other truths in the various departments of science. It has been so even amongst us. Many who hear me, perhaps, can recollect well, that this truth was not generally admitted, even within their day. The errors of the past generation still clung to many as late as twenty years ago. Those at the North, who still cling to these errors, with a zeal above knowledge, we justly denominate fanatics.... They assume that the negro is equal, and hence conclude that he is entitled to equal privileges

and rights with the white man.... I recollect once of having heard a
gentleman from one of the northern States, of great power and ability, announce in the House of Representatives, with imposing effect,
that we of the South would be compelled, ultimately, to yield upon
this subject of slavery, that it was as impossible to war successfully
against a principle in politics, as it was in physics or mechanics. That
the principle would ultimately prevail. That we, in maintaining
slavery as it exists with us, were warring against a principle, a principle founded in nature, the principle of the equality of men. The reply
I made to him was, that upon his own grounds, we should, ultimately, succeed, and that he and his associates, in this crusade
against our institutions, would ultimately fail. The truth announced,
that it was as impossible to war successfully against a principle in
politics as it was in physics and mechanics, I admitted; but told him
that it was he, and those acting with him, who were warring against
a principle. They were attempting to make things equal which the
Creator had made unequal....

   As I have stated, the truth of this principle may be slow in development, as all truths are and ever have been, in the various branches
of science. It was so with the principles announced by Galileo it was
so with Adam Smith and his principles of political economy....
Now, they are universally acknowledged. May we not, therefore,
look with confidence to the ultimate universal acknowledgment of
the truths upon which our system rests? It is the first government
ever instituted upon the principles in strict conformity to nature,
and the ordination of Providence, in furnishing the materials of
human society. Many governments have been founded upon the
principle of the subordination and serfdom of certain classes of the
same race; such were and are in violation of the laws of nature. Our
system commits no such violation of nature's laws. With us, all of
the white race, however high or low, rich or poor, are equal in the eye
of the law. Not so with the negro. Subordination is his place. He, by
nature, or by the curse against Canaan, is fitted for that condition
which he occupies in our system.... by experience we know that it is

best, not only for the superior, but for the inferior race, that it should be so. It is, indeed, in conformity with the ordinance of the Creator. It is not for us to inquire into the wisdom of His ordinances, or to question them. For His own purposes, He has made one race to differ from another, as He has made "one star to differ from another star in glory." The great objects of humanity are best attained when there is conformity to His laws and decrees, in the formation of governments as well as in all things else. Our confederacy is founded upon principles in strict conformity with these laws. This stone which was rejected by the first builders "is become the chief of the corner" the real "corner-stone" in our new edifice.

Questions

1. What argument does Stephens offer for the idea that blacks are innately suited for the condition of slaves?

2. Why does Stephens believe the U.S. Constitution is fundamentally flawed?

---

88. Marcus M. Spiegel, Letter of a Civil War Soldier (1864)

Source: Marcus M. Spiegel: Reprinted from A Jewish Colonel in the Civil War: Marcus M. Spiegel of the Ohio Volunteers, *edited by Jean Powers Soman and Frank L. Byrne, by permission of the University of Nebraska Press. © 1985 by The Kent State University Press. © 1994 by Jean P. Soman.*

Born into a Jewish family in Germany in 1829, Marcus Spiegel took part in the failed German revolution of 1848. In the following year, he emigrated to Ohio, where he married the daughter of a local farmer. He enlisted in the Union army in 1861. He went to war, he wrote to his brother-in-law, to defend "the flag that was ever ready to protect you and me and every one who sought its protection from oppression." Spiegel rose to the rank of colonel in the 120th Ohio Infantry and saw action in Virginia, Mississippi, and Louisiana. He was an ardent Democrat, who shared the era's racist attitudes and thought Lincoln's Emancipation Proclamation a serious mistake. Yet, as the Union army penetrated the heart of the Deep South, Spiegel became increasingly antislavery. Spiegel died in a minor engagement in Louisiana in May 1864, one of the hundreds of thousands of Americans to perish in the Civil War.

—————

PLAQUEMINE LA JAN 22/64

My dear Wife, my sweet Cary!

• • •

... You must not expect any news inasmuch as this [is] as monotonous a place as ever Millersburg can be. We are living here right on the Mississippi River and with exception of three or four Steamboats landing here every day which are called Coast Packets and travel from Baton Rouge to New Orleans and back, we have no news. When I first came here we had four Regiments of Infantry, three Batteries of Artillery and one Company of Cavelery. Since then two Regiments of Infantry, the 22nd and 7th Kentucky and two Batteries have been moved to Baton Rouge where they got up a big scare the other day.

This leaves us the 42nd-Ohio and the 120th Ohio, one Battery and one Company of Cavelery, sufficient to hold this place against all marauding forces they can bring; we are building a very large and formidable Fort here. The weather here is beautiful, just like our June; it is very warm and the air is mild, wholesome and refreshing. I wish to God you could be here. Colonel L. A. Sheldon of the 42nd Ohio is in command here; you know if you remember what I think of him; he commanded our Brigade last year at Chickasaw and Arkansas Post. Yet he is a very clever man and extremely kind to me. He has his wife here; she is from Lorain County; a regular build

Western Reserve Yankee Girl. I do not see her often, though very much pressed to call. I saw her twice in four weeks.

Dr. Stanton, Adjutand, Uncle Josey, Sinsheimer and myself spend most of our time together. There was a report yesterday that there were a lot of Rebels twelve miles from here, so I started out with a Company of Cavelery. Uncle Josey and Doctor Stanton and my friend Lieutenant Miller (whom you saw at home) acted as volunteer Aids, but we found "nary Reb" after a hard ride. I managed to get four dozend Eggs and we came home. We are living in a House all together (i.e. field and Staff); our boy does the cooking for our Mess. Uncle Josey's business does not go very well just now; there are so very few troops here and they have no money and the lines are closed.

I have at present twelve Sergeants in Ohio on the recruiting Service; I do not know how well or whether at all, they succeed. It takes so long somehow to hear from Ohio and the North generally that we do not know what is going on. In New Orleans they have news once a week at least but here it is very irregular.

Captain Moffit sent in his resignation Papers about three months ago and a few days ago they came back accepted. I am very sorry for them indeed. Since I am here I have learned and seen more of what the horrors of Slavery was than I ever knew before and I am glad indeed that the signs of the times show, towards closing out the accursed institution. You know it takes me long to say anything that sounds antidemocratic and it goes hard, but whether I stay in the Army or come home, I am [in] favor of doing away with the institution of Slavery. I am willing for the Planters to hire them and in favor of making the negro work at all events; inasmuch as he is naturally lazy and indolent, but never hereafter will I either speak or vote in favor of Slavery; this is no hasty conclusion but a deep conviction. Yet I never mean hereafter to be a politician, but quietly as a good citizen doing duty to my God, my family, my Country and myself.

Charley has left here about a week ago; I think however he is yet in New Orleans. You must write me a long, long letter and many of them and ask me ten thousand questions in every one and I will take them up one by one and answer them. This is the tirest place I ever was at, during my Soldier life, but the boys are so comfortable and feel so very well that I am not at all anxious to leave here. We had a negro woman cooking for us when Uncle Josey, Charley and Sinsheimer messed with us, but it is so far for them and they left us and we discharged our Cook and have only our boy. One of my men who deserted in Covington and was brought up by the Provost Marshal was tried by a Court Marshal and sentenced to forfeit all his pay and condemned for six months hard labor on Fort Espararox [Esperanza], Texas, with a Ball and Chain on his right leg, a very very hard sentence indeed; I would rather they would have shot him, for death is not so hard as degradation.

I am well and hearty and if I had my dear, dear little family here I would not wish anything better, but as it is my heart is ever yearning for home, home with all its blessings. I hope you are comfortable during this extreme awful cold weather, such as I see by the Papers you must have had; it makes me tremble to think you had to be there without me God grant all was right.

Hamlin must continue to be a good and obedient boy. It is about getting to be a youth and he must endeavor to learn well and make a man so he can aid and assist his father and mother when they get old. I hope soon to be at home when I can teach him and help him along....

Questions

1. What do you think Spiegel means by "the horrors of slavery"?

2. Why does he say that his new antislavery viewpoint "goes hard"?

89. Samuel S. Cox Condemns Emancipation (1862)

Source: Congressional Globe, *37th Congress, 2nd Session, Appendix,* pp. 242–49.

The abolition of slavery seems so inevitable a result of the American Civil War that it is difficult to realize how much controversy it aroused at the time, in both the Union and the Confederacy. In 1862, as the Lincoln administration slowly moved toward ending slavery, most northern Democrats expressed bitter opposition. Some of their arguments are illustrated in this June speech in Congress by Samuel S. Cox of Ohio. Cox supported the war effort but insisted that its goal must be the restoration of the Union "as it was"—that is, with slavery intact. Cox marshaled many arguments against emancipation, including the claims that it would disrupt the nation's economy, violate the Constitution, and alienate many white soldiers. He also invoked racist fears of an influx into the North of emancipated slaves who, he claimed, would lower wages by competing with white laborers and become a drain on public resources. Cox's speech was circulated as a campaign document in the congressional elections of 1862 when, partly because of fear of the consequences of emancipation, Democrats made strong gains in the northern states.

———

THERE IS SOMETHING needed in making successful civil war besides raising money and armies. You must keep the confidence and spirit of the people. It must not only be animated by a noble passion at the outset, but it must be sustained by confidence in the cause. . . . Is there a member here who dare say that Ohio troops will fight successfully or fight at all, if the result shall be the flight and movement of the black race by millions northward to their own State? . . .

Is it the policy here, as it would seem to be, . . . to [convert] the war into a St. Domingo-insurrection, turning the South into one utter desolation? . . . We want no more poetry about striking off chains and bidding the oppressed go. Plain people want to know whether the chains will not be put upon white limbs, and *whither* the oppressed are to go. If the industry of the North is to be fettered with their support; if they are to go to Ohio and the North, we want to know it. Nay, we want, if we can, to stop it. . . .

Slavery may be an evil, it may be wrong for southern men to use unpaid labor, but what will be the condition of the people of Ohio when the free jubilee shall have come in its ripe and rotten maturity? If slavery is bad, the condition of the State of Ohio, with an unrestrained black population . . . will be far worse. . . . The free negroes will become equal, or will continue unequal to the whites. Equality is a condition which is self-protective, wanting nothing, asking nothing, able to take care of itself. It is an absurdity to say that two races as dissimilar as black and white, of different origin, of unequal capacity, can succeed in the same society when placed in competition. There is no such example in history of the success of two separate races under such circumstances. . . .

Prejudice, stronger than all principles, though not always stronger than lust, has imperatively separated the whites from the blacks. In the school-house, the church, or the hospital, the black man must not seat himself beside the white; even in death and at the cemetery the line of distinction is drawn. To abolish slavery the North must go still further and forget that fatal prejudice of race which governs it, and which makes emancipation so illusory. To give men their liberty, to open to them the gates of the city, and then say, "there, you shall live among yourself, you shall marry among yourselves, you shall form a separate society in society," is to create a cursed caste, and replace slaves by pariahs.

Questions

1. Why does Cox feel that emancipating slaves endangers the liberties of white northerners?

2. What status does he anticipate for the slaves if they are freed?

90. Abraham Lincoln, The Gettysburg Address (1863)

Source: Abraham Lincoln: Letters and Addresses *(New York, 1903), pp. 289–90.*

Probably the most famous single speech in American history, Abraham Lincoln's Gettysburg Address was delivered in November 1863 at the dedication of a military cemetery at the site of the Civil War's greatest battle. In fewer than 270 words, which took only three minutes to deliver, Lincoln distilled his conception of the war's meaning and displayed his genius for linking the conflict with the deepest beliefs of northern society. At Gettysburg, he identified the nation's mission with the principle that "all men are created equal," spoke of the war as bringing about a "new birth of freedom" through the emancipation of the slaves, and defined the essence of democratic government. The sacrifices of Union soldiers, he declared, would ensure that "government of the people, by the people, for the people, shall not perish from the earth."

The speech also illustrated how the Civil War brought into being a new American nation-state. In his inaugural address in 1861, Lincoln had used the word "Union" twenty times, while making no mention of the "nation." But Union does not appear at all in the Gettysburg Address, while Lincoln referred five times to the "nation."

———

FOUR SCORE AND seven years ago our fathers brought forth on this continent, a new nation, conceived in liberty, and dedicated to the proposition that all men are created equal.

Now we are engaged in a great civil war, testing whether that nation, or any nation so conceived and so dedicated, can long endure. We are met on a great battle-field of that war. We have come to dedicate a portion of that field, as a final resting place for those who here gave their lives that that nation might live. It is altogether fitting and proper that we should do this.

But, in a larger sense, we can not dedicate—we can not consecrate—
we can not hallow—this ground. The brave men, living and dead, who
struggled here, have consecrated it, far above our poor power to add
or detract. The world will little note, nor long remember what we say
here, but it can never forget what they did here. It is for us the living,
rather, to be dedicated here to the unfinished work which they who
fought here have thus far so nobly advanced. It is rather for us to be
here dedicated to the great task remaining before us—that from these
honored dead we take increased devotion to that cause for which they
gave the last full measure of devotion—that we here highly resolve
that these dead shall not have died in vain—that this nation, under
God, shall have a new birth of freedom—and that government of the
people, by the people, for the people, shall not perish from the earth.

Questions

1. Why does Lincoln date the foundation of the nation from 1776 (the date
of the Declaration of Independence) rather than 1787, when the Constitution was written?

2. Why does Lincoln consider the Civil War a "new birth of freedom"?

91. Frederick Douglass on Black Soldiers (1863)

Source: **Men of Color, to Arms,** *Broadside, Rochester, March 21, 1863.*

At the beginning of the Civil War, the Union army refused to accept
northern black volunteers. But as casualty rolls expanded, pressure
mounted to allow blacks to serve. Although preliminary steps to enlist
combat troops were taken in a few parts of the South in 1862, only after
the Emancipation Proclamation of January 1, 1863, did the recruitment of
black soldiers begin in earnest.

Some black units won considerable fame, among them the 54th Massachusetts Volunteers, a company of free blacks from throughout the North commanded by Robert Gould Shaw, a young reformer from a prominent Boston family. In March 1863, Frederick Douglass called on northern blacks to volunteer for this unit. "Liberty won by white men would lose half its luster," he wrote. Douglass realized that by serving in the army, black men would be placing the question of postwar black citizenship on the nation's agenda.

WHEN FIRST THE rebel cannon shattered the walls of Sumter and drove away its starving garrison, I predicted that the war then and there inaugurated would not be fought out entirely by white men. Every month's experience during these dreary years has confirmed that opinion. A war undertaken and brazenly carried on for the perpetual enslavement of colored men, calls logically and loudly for colored men to help suppress it. Only a moderate share of sagacity was needed to see that the arm of the slave was the best defense against the arm of the slaveholder. Hence with every reverse to the national arms, with every exulting shout of victory raised by the slaveholding rebels, I have implored the imperiled nation to unchain against her foes, her powerful black hand. Slowly and reluctantly that appeal is beginning to be heeded. Stop not now to complain that it was not heeded sooner. It may or it may not have been best that it should not. This is not the time to discuss that question. Leave it to the future. When the war is over, the country is saved, peace is established, and the black man's rights are secured, as they will be, history with an impartial hand will dispose of that and sundry other questions. Action! Action! not criticism, is the plain duty of this hour. Words are now useful only as they stimulate to blows. The office of speech now is only to point out when, where, and how to strike to the best advantage. There is no time to delay. The tide is at its flood that leads on to fortune. From East to West, from North to South, the sky is written all over, "Now or never."

Liberty won by white men would lose half its luster. "Who would be free themselves must strike the blow." "Better even die free, than to live slaves." This is the sentiment of every brave colored man amongst us. There are weak and cowardly men in all nations. We have them amongst us. They tell you this is the "white man's war"; that you will be "no better off after than before the war"; that the getting of you into the army is to "sacrifice you on the first opportunity." Believe them not; cowards themselves, they do not wish to have their cowardice shamed by your brave example. Leave them to their timidity, or to whatever motive may hold them back. I have not thought lightly of the words I am now addressing you. The counsel I give comes of close observation of the great struggle now in progress, and of the deep conviction that this is your hour and mine. In good earnest then, and after the best deliberation, I now for the first time during this war feel at liberty to call and counsel you to arms. By every consideration which binds you to your enslaved fellow-countrymen, and the peace and welfare of your country; by every aspiration which you cherish for the freedom and equality of yourselves and your children; by all the ties of blood and identity which make us one with the brave black men now fighting our battles in Louisiana and in South Carolina, I urge you to fly to arms, and smite with death the power that would bury the government and your liberty in the same hopeless grave. I wish I could tell you that the State of New York calls you to this high honor. For the moment her constituted authorities are silent on the subject. They will speak by and by, and doubtless on the right side; but we are not compelled to wait for her. We can get at the throat of treason and slavery through the State of Massachusetts. She was first in the War of Independence; first to break the chains of her slaves; first to make the black man equal before the law; first to admit colored children to her common schools, and she was first to answer with her blood the alarm cry of the nation, when its capital was menaced by rebels. You know her patriotic governor, and you know Charles Sumner. I need not add more.

Massachusetts now welcomes you to arms as soldiers. She has but a small colored population from which to recruit. She has full leave of the general government to send one regiment to the war, and she has undertaken to do it. Go quickly and help fill up the first colored regiment from the North. I am authorized to assure you that you will receive the same wages, the same rations, the same equipments, the same protection, the same treatment, and the same bounty, secured to the white soldiers. You will be led by able and skillful officers, men who will take especial pride in your efficiency and success. They will be quick to accord to you all the honor you shall merit by your valor, and see that your rights and feelings are respected by other soldiers. I have assured myself on these points, and can speak with authority. More than twenty years of unswerving devotion to our common cause may give me some humble claim to be trusted at this momentous crisis. I will not argue. To do so implies hesitation and doubt, and you do not hesitate. You do not doubt. The day dawns; the morning star is bright upon the horizon! The iron gate of our prison stands half open. One gallant rush from the North will fling it wide open, while four millions of our brothers and sisters shall march out into liberty. The chance is now given you to end in a day the bondage of centuries, and to rise in one bound from social degradation to the plane of common equality with all other varieties of men. Remember Denmark Vesey of Charleston; remember Nathaniel Turner of Southampton; remember Shields Green and Copeland, who followed noble John Brown, and fell as glorious martyrs for the cause of the slave. Remember that in a contest with oppression, the Almighty has no attribute which can take sides with oppressors. The case is before you. This is our golden opportunity. Let us accept it, and forever wipe out the dark reproaches unsparingly hurled against us by our enemies. Let us win for ourselves the gratitude of our country, and the best blessings of our posterity through all time. The nucleus of this first regiment is now in camp at Readville, a short distance from Boston. I will undertake to forward to Boston all per-

sons adjudged fit to be mustered into the regiment, who shall apply
to me at any time within the next two weeks.

Questions

1. Why does Douglass believe that black service in the Union army will
lead to an expansion of blacks' rights in the postwar world?

2. What does Douglass mean when he writes that black soldiers will "wipe
out the dark reproaches" directed at blacks "by our enemies"?

———

92. Letter by the Mother of a Black Soldier (1863)

Source: Ira Berlin et al., eds., Freedom: A Documentary History of
Emancipation, 1861–1867, *Series 2 (New York, 1982), pp. 582–83.*

Within the Union army, black soldiers were anything but equal to white.
Serving in segregated units and ineligible, until the end of the war, to rise
to the rank of commissioned officers, they were initially paid less than
white soldiers. Even more alarming, the Confederacy announced that it
would treat captured black soldiers not as prisoners of war but as fugitives
who would be remanded to slavery.

One of the more remarkable letters of the Civil War era was written to
President Lincoln by Hannah Johnson, the mother of a black soldier.
Although, as she notes, she had enjoyed but a "poor education," Mrs. Johnson eloquently advised the president to insist that black prisoners be
treated the same as white and resist pressures to rescind the Emancipation
Proclamation. The fact that she felt she had a sympathetic recipient in the
White House illustrates the enormous changes American society was
undergoing as a result of the Civil War. Mrs. Johnson did not know that
the day before she wrote the letter, Lincoln had ordered that, for every

captured black soldier enslaved, a Confederate prisoner would be put to hard labor for the duration of the war.

Excellent Sir

My good friend says I must write to you and she will send it[.] My son went in the 54th regiment. I am a colored woman and my son was strong and able to fight for his country and the colored people have as much to fight for as any. My father was a Slave and escaped from Louisiana before I was born morn forty years agone[.] I have but poor edication but I never went to schol, but I know just as well as any what is right between man and man. Now I know it is right that a colored man should go and fight for his country, and so ought to a white man. I know that a colored man ought to run no greater risques than a white, his pay is no greater his obligation to fight is the same. So why should not our enemies be compelled to treat him the same, Made to do it.

My son fought at Fort Wagoner but thank God he was not taken prisoner, as many were[.] I thought of this thing before I let my boy go but then they said Mr. Lincoln will never let them sell our colored soldiers for slaves, if they do he will get them back quck[.] he will rettallyate and stop it. Now Mr. Lincoln dont you think you oght to stop this thing and make them do the same by the colored men they have lived in idleness all their lives on stolen labor and made savages of the colored people, but they now are so furious because they are proving themselves to be men, such as have come away and got some edication. It must not be so. You must put the rebels to work in State prisons to making shoes and things, if they sell our colored soldiers, till they let them all go. And give their wounded the same treatment. it would seem cruel, but their [is] no other way, and a just man must do hard things sometimes, that shew him to be a great man. They tell me some do you will take back the Proclamation, don't do it. When

you are dead and in Heaven, in a thousand years that action of yours
will make the Angels sing your praises I know it. Ought one man to
own another, law for or not, who made the law, surely the poor slave
did not. so it is wicked, and a horrible Outrage, there is no sense in it,
because a man has lived by robbing all his life and his father before
him, should he complain because the stolen things found on him are
taken. Robbing the colored people of their labor is but a small part
of the robbery[.] their souls are almost taken, they are made bruits of
often. You know all about this[.]

Will you see that the colored men fighting now, are fairly treated.
You ought to do this, and do it at once, Not let the thing run along
meet it quickly and manfully, and stop this, mean cowardly cruelty.
We poor oppressed ones, appeal to you, and ask fair play.

Yours for Christs sake
Hannah Johnson

Questions

1. What is Mrs. Johnson's opinion of slavery and slaveholders?

2. How would you describe the tone Mrs. Johnson adopts in writing to the
president?

---

93. Abraham Lincoln, Address at Sanitary Fair, Baltimore (1864)

Source: Abraham Lincoln: Letters and Addresses *(New York, 1903), pp. 295–96.*

Never was freedom's contested nature more evident than during the
Civil War. Both sides fought in the name of freedom. "We all declare for
liberty," Lincoln observed in a speech in Baltimore in 1864, "but in using
the same *word* we do not all mean the same *thing*." He went on to explain

the differences between the two sides' understandings of this word. Lincoln noted that Maryland, a slave state before the Civil War, had just adopted a new constitution abolishing slavery. And he announced his intention to investigate reports (later confirmed) that Confederate forces had massacred a number of black Union soldiers after they surrendered at Fort Pillow, Tennessee. The advance of emancipation and the service of black troops, for Lincoln, embodied "the advance of liberty."

THE WORLD HAS never had a good definition of the word liberty, and the American people, just now, are much in want of one. We all declare for liberty; but in using the same word we do not all mean the same thing. With some the word liberty may mean for each man to do as he pleases with himself, and the product of his labor; while with others the same word may mean for some men to do as they please with other men, and the product of other men's labor. Here are two, not only different, but incompatible things, called by the same name, liberty. And it follows that each of the things is, by the respective parties, called by two different and incompatible names—liberty and tyranny.

The shepherd drives the wolf from the sheep's throat, for which the sheep thanks the shepherd as his liberator, while the wolf denounces him for the same act, as the destroyer of liberty, especially as the sheep was a black one. Plainly, the sheep and the wolf are not agreed upon a definition of the word liberty; and precisely the same difference prevails to-day among us human creatures, even in the North, and all professing to love liberty. Hence we behold the process by which thousands are daily passing from under the yoke of bondage hailed by some as the advance of liberty, and bewailed by others as the destruction of all liberty. Recently, as it seems, the people of Maryland have been doing something to define liberty, and thanks to them that, in what they have done, the wolf's dictionary has been repudiated.

It is not very becoming for one in my position to make speeches at great length; but there is another subject upon which I feel that I ought to say a word.

A painful rumor—true, I fear—has reached us of the massacre by the rebel forces at Fort Pillow, in the west end of Tennessee, on the Mississippi River, of some three hundred colored soldiers and white officers, who had just been overpowered by their assailants. There seems to be some anxiety in the public mind whether the government is doing its duty to the colored soldier, and to the service, at this point. At the beginning of the war, and for some time, the use of colored troops was not contemplated; and how the change of purpose was wrought I will not now take time to explain. Upon a clear conviction of duty I resolved to turn that element of strength to account; and I am responsible for it to the American people, to the Christian world, to history, and in my final account to God. Having determined to use the negro as a soldier, there is no way but to give him all the protection given to any other soldier. The difficulty is not in stating the principle, but in practically applying it. It is a mistake to suppose the government is indifferent to this matter, or is not doing the best it can in regard to it. We do not to-day know that a colored soldier, or white officer commanding colored soldiers, has been massacred by the rebels when made a prisoner. We fear it,—believe it, I may say,—but we do not know it. To take the life of one of their prisoners on the assumption that they murder ours, when it is short of certainty that they do murder ours, might be too serious, too cruel, a mistake. We are having the Fort Pillow affair thoroughly investigated; and such investigation will probably show conclusively how the truth is. If after all that has been said it shall turn out that there has been no massacre at Fort Pillow, it will be almost safe to say there has been none, and will be none, elsewhere. If there has been the massacre of three hundred there, or even the tenth part of three hundred, it will be conclusively proved; and being so proved, the retribution shall as surely come. It will be matter of grave consideration

in what exact course to apply the retribution; but in the supposed
case it must come.

Questions

1. What does Lincoln identify as the essential difference between northern and southern definitions of freedom?

2. What is the purpose of Lincoln's metaphor about the wolf and the sheep
and their differing views of liberty?

94. Mary Livermore on Women and the War (1883)

*Source: Mary A. Livermore, **What Shall We Do with Our Daughters?**
(Boston, 1883), pp. 10–16.*

The Civil War opened new doors of opportunity for northern women.
Some took advantage of the wartime labor shortage to move into jobs in
factories and into previously largely male professions like nursing.
Hundreds of thousands of northern women took part in organizations
that gathered money and medical supplies for soldiers and sent books,
clothing, and food to the freedmen. Women played a leading role in organizing sanitary fairs—grand bazaars that raised money for soldiers' aid.
The suffrage movement suspended operations during the war to devote
itself to the Union and emancipation. But from the ranks of this wartime
mobilization came many of the leaders of the postwar movement for
women's rights. Mary Livermore, the wife of a Chicago minister, toured
military hospitals to assess their needs, cared for injured and dying soldiers, and organized two sanitary fairs. She emerged from the war with a
deep resentment against women's legal and political subordination and
organized her state's first woman suffrage convention. Looking back on
her experience two decades later, Livermore concluded that the spirit of

the age was emancipating women no less than slaves and creating new opportunities in education, employment, and the law.

———

THE CONTEMPTUOUS OPINION entertained of woman in the past has found expression, not alone in literature, but also in unjust laws and customs. "In marriage she has been a serf; as a mother she has been robbed of her children; in public instruction she has been ignored; in labor she has been a menial, and then inadequately compensated; civilly she has been a minor, and politically she has had no existence. She has been the equal of man only when punishment, and the payment of taxes, were in question."

Born and bred for generations under such conditions of hindrance, it has not been possible for women to rise much above the arbitrary standards of inferiority persistently set before them. Here and there through the ages some woman endowed with phenomenal force of character has towered above the mediocrity of her sex, hinting at the qualities imprisoned in the feminine nature. It is not strange that these instances have been rare: it is strange, indeed, that women have held their own during these ages of degradation....

• • •

Humanity has moved forward to an era where wrong and slavery are being displaced, and reason and justice are being recognized as the rule of life. Science is extending immeasurably the bounds of knowledge and power; art is refining life, giving to it beauty and grace; literature bears in her hands whole ages of comfort and sympathy; industry, aided by the hundred-handed elements of nature, is increasing the world's wealth; and invention is economizing its labor. The age looks steadily to the redressing of wrong, to the righting of every form of error and injustice; and a tireless and prying philanthropy, which is almost omniscient, is one of the most hopeful characteristics of the time....

• • •

It could not be possible in such an era but that women should share in the justice and kindliness with which the time is fraught. A great wave is lifting them to higher levels. The leadership of the world is being taken from the hands of the brutal and low, and the race is groping its way to a higher ideal than once it knew. It is the evolution of this tendency that is lifting women out of their subject condition, that is emancipating them from the seclusion of the past, and adding to the sum total of the world's worth and wisdom, by giving to them the cultivation human beings need. The demand for their education,—technical and industrial, as well as intellectual,— and for their civil and political rights, is being urged each year by an increasing host, and with more emphatic utterance.

Colleges, professional schools, and universities, closed against them for ages, are opening to them. They are invited to pursue the same course of study as their brothers, and are graduated with the same diplomas. Trades, businesses, remunerative vocations, and learned professions seek them; and even the laws, which are the last to feel the change in public opinion,—usually dragging a whole generation behind,—even these are being annually revised and amended, and then they fail to keep abreast of the advancing civilization.

All this is but prefatory, and prophetic of the time when, for women, law will be synonymous with justice, and no opportunity for knowledge or effort will be denied them on the score of sex....

• • •

It is for our young women that the great changes of the time promise the most: it is for our daughters,—the fair, bright girls, who are the charm of society and the delight of home; the sources of infinite comfort to fathers and mothers, and the sources of great anxiety also. What shall we do with them,—and what shall they do with and for themselves?

> "New occasions teach new duties,
> Time makes ancient good uncouth,"

and the training of fifty years ago is not sufficient for the girls of today. The changed conditions of life which our young women confront compel greater care and thought on the part of those charged with their education than has herefore been deemed necessary. They are to be weighted with heavy duties, and to assume heavier responsibilities; for the days of tutelage seem to be ended for civilized women, and they are to think and act for themselves.

Questions

1. How does Livermore explain the inequality in status and achievement between men and women?

2. How does Livermore understand freedom for women?

CHAPTER 15

"What Is Freedom?":
Reconstruction, 1865–1877

95. Petition of Black Residents of Nashville (1865)

Source: Newspaper clipping enclosed in Col. R. D. Mussey to Capt. C. P. Brown, January 23, 1865, Letters Received, ser. 925, Department of the Cumberland, U.S. Army Continental Commands, National Archives.

At the request of military governor Andrew Johnson, Lincoln exempted Tennessee from the Emancipation Proclamation of 1863 (although many slaves in the state gained their freedom by serving in the Union army). In January 1865, a state convention was held to complete the work of abolition. A group of free blacks of Nashville sent a petition to the delegates, asking for immediate action to end slavery and granting black men the right to vote (which free blacks had enjoyed in the state until 1835). The document emphasized their loyalty to the Union, their natural right to freedom, and their willingness to take on the responsibilities of citizenship. The document offers a revealing snapshot of black consciousness at the dawn of Reconstruction.

To the Union Convention of Tennessee Assembled in the Capitol at Nashville, January 9th, 1865:

We the undersigned petitioners, American citizens of African descent, natives and residents of Tennessee, and devoted friends of the great National cause, do most respectfully ask a patient hearing of your honorable body in regard to matters deeply affecting the future condition of our unfortunate and long suffering race.

First of all, however, we would say that words are too weak to tell how profoundly grateful we are to the Federal Government for the good work of freedom which it is gradually carrying forward; and for the Emancipation Proclamation which has set free all the slaves in some of the rebellious States, as well as many of the slaves in Tennessee.

After two hundred years of bondage and suffering a returning sense of justice has awakened the great body of the American people to make amends for the unprovoked wrongs committed against us for over two hundred years.

Your petitioners would ask you to complete the work begun by the nation at large, and abolish the last vestige of slavery by the express words of your organic law.

Many masters in Tennessee whose slaves have left them, will certainly make every effort to bring them back to bondage after the reorganization of the State government, unless slavery be expressly abolished by the Constitution.

We hold that freedom is the natural right of all men, which they themselves have no more right to give or barter away, than they have to sell their honor, their wives, or their children.

We claim to be men belonging to the great human family, descended from one great God, who is the common Father of all, and who bestowed on all races and tribes the priceless right of freedom. Of this right, for no offence of ours, we have long been cruelly deprived, and the common voice of the wise and good of all countries, has remonstrated against our enslavement, as one of the greatest crimes in all history.

We claim freedom, as our natural right, and ask that in harmony and co-operation with the nation at large, you should cut up by the roots the system of slavery, which is not only a wrong to us, but the source of all the evil which at present afflicts the State. For slavery, corrupt itself, corrupted nearly all, also, around it, so that it has influenced nearly all the slave States to rebel against the Federal Government, in order to set up a government of pirates under which slavery might be perpetrated.

In the contest between the nation and slavery, our unfortunate people have sided, by instinct, with the former. We have little fortune to devote to the national cause, for a hard fate has hitherto forced us to live in poverty, but we do devote to its success, our hopes, our toils, our whole heart, our sacred honor, and our lives. We will work, pray, live, and, if need be, die for the Union, as cheerfully as ever a white patriot died for his country. The color of our skin does not lesson in the least degree, our love either for God or for the land of our birth.

We are proud to point your honorable body to the fact, that so far as our knowledge extends, not a negro traitor has made his appearance since the begining of this wicked rebellion. . . .

Devoted as we are to the principles of justice, of love to all men, and of equal rights on which our Government is based, and which make it the hope of the world. We know the burdens of citizenship, and are ready to bear them. We know the duties of the good citizen, and are ready to perform them cheerfully, and would ask to be put in a position in which we can discharge them more effectually. We do not ask for the privilege of citizenship, wishing to shun the obligations imposed by it.

Near 200,000 of our brethren are to-day performing military duty in the ranks of the Union army. Thousands of them have already died in battle, or perished by a cruel martyrdom for the sake of the Union, and we are ready and willing to sacrifice more. But what higher order of citizen is there than the soldier? or who has a greater trust confided to his hands? If we are called on to do military duty against the rebel armies in the field, why should we be denied the privilege of voting against rebel citizens at the ballot-box? The latter is as necessary to save the Government as the former. . . .

This is not a Democratic Government if a numerous, law-abiding, industrious, and useful class of citizens, born and bred on the soil, are to be treated as aliens and enemies, as an inferior degraded class, who must have no voice in the Government which they support, protect and defend, with all their heart, soul, mind, and body, both in peace and war.

Questions

1. Why do the petitioners place so much emphasis on their loyalty to the Union cause during the war?

2. What understanding of American history and the nation's future do the petitioners convey?

---

96. Petition of Committee on Behalf of the Freedmen to Andrew Johnson (1865)

Source: Henry Bram et al. to the President of the United States, October 28, 1865, P-27, 1865, Letters Received (series 15), Washington Headquarters, Freedmen's Bureau Papers, National Archives.

By June 1865, some 40,000 freedpeople had been settled on "Sherman land" in South Carolina and Georgia, in accordance with Special Field Order 15. That summer, however, President Andrew Johnson, who had succeeded Lincoln, ordered nearly all land in federal hands returned to its former owners. In October, O. O. Howard, head of the Freedmen's Bureau, traveled to the Sea Islands to inform blacks of the new policy.

Howard was greeted with disbelief and protest. A committee drew up petitions to Howard and President Johnson. Their petition to the president pointed out that the government had encouraged them to occupy the land and affirmed that they were ready to purchase it if given the opportunity. Johnson rejected the former slaves' plea. And, throughout the South, because no land distribution took place, the vast majority of rural freedpeople remained poor and without property during Reconstruction.

EDISTO ISLAND S.C. Oct 28th, 1865.

To the President of these United States. We the freedmen of Edisto Island South Carolina have learned From you through Major General O O Howard commissioner of the Freedmans Bureau. with deep sorrow and Painful hearts of the possibility of government restoring These lands to the former owners. We are well aware Of the many perplexing and trying questions that burden Your mind and do therefore pray to god (the preserver of all and who has through our Late and beloved President (Lincoln) proclamation and the war made Us A free people) that he may guide you in making Your decisions and give you that wisdom that Cometh from above to settle these great and Important Questions for the best interests of the country and the Colored race: Here is where secession was born and Nurtured Here is were we have toiled nearly all Our lives as slaves and were treated like dumb Driven cattle, This is our home, we have made These lands what they are we were the only true and Loyal people that were found in posession of these Lands we have been always ready to strike for Liberty and humanity yea to fight if needs be To preserve this glorious union. Shall not we who Are freedman and have been always true to this Union have the same rights as are enjoyed by Others? Have we broken any Law of these United States? Have we forfieted our rights of property In Land?—If not then! are not our rights as A free people and good citizens of these United States To be considered before the rights of those who were Found in rebellion against this good and just Government (and now being conquered) come (as they Seem) with penitent hearts and beg forgiveness For past offences and also ask if their lands Cannot be restored to them are these rebellious Spirits to be reinstated in their *possessions* And we who have been abused and oppressed For many long years not to be allowed the Privilege of purchasing land But be subject To the will of these large Land owners? God forbid, Land monopoly is injurious to the advancement of the course of freedom, and if Government Does not make some provision by which we as Freedmen can obtain A Homestead, we have Not bettered our condition.

We have been encouraged by Government to take Up these lands in small tracts, receiving Certificates of the same—we have thus far Taken Sixteen thousand (16000) acres of Land here on This Island. We are ready to pay for this land When Government calls for it and now after What has been done will the good and just government take from us all this right and make us Subject to the will of those who have cheated and Oppressed us for many years God Forbid!

We the freedmen of this Island and of the State of South Carolina—Do therefore petition to you as the President of these United States, that some provisions be made by which Every colored man can purchase land and Hold it as his own. We wish to have A home if It be but A few acres without some provision is Made our future is sad to look upon yess our Situation is dangerous we therefore look to you In this trying hour as A true friend of the poor and Neglected race for protection and Equal Rights with the privilege of purchasing A Homestead—A Homestead right here in the Heart of South Carolina.

We pray that God will direct your heart in Making such provision for us as freedmen which Will tend to united these states together stronger Than ever before—May God bless you in the Administration of your duties as the President Of these United States is the humble prayer Of us all.—

In behalf of the Freedmen

　　　　　　　Henry Bram

Committee　Ishmael Moultrie.

　　　　　　　yates. Sampson

Questions

1. How important is it for the petitioners to obtain land on Edisto Island, as opposed to land elsewhere in the country?

2. What do they think is the relationship between owning land and freedom?

97. The Mississippi Black Code (1865)

Source: Walter L. Fleming, ed., Documentary History of Reconstruction *(Cleveland, 1906–1907), Vol. 1, pp. 281–90.*

During 1865, Andrew Johnson put into effect his own plan of Reconstruction, establishing procedures whereby new governments, elected by white voters only, would be created in the South. Among the first laws passed by the new governments were the Black Codes, which attempted to regulate the lives of the former slaves. These laws granted the freedpeople certain rights, such as legalized marriage, ownership of property, and limited access to the courts. But they denied them the right to testify in court in cases that only involved whites, serve on juries or in state militias, or to vote. And in response to planters' demands that the freedpeople be required to work on the plantations, the Black Codes declared that those who failed to sign yearly labor contracts could be arrested and hired out to white landowners. The Black Codes indicated how the white South would regulate black freedom if given a free hand by the federal government. But they so completely violated free labor principles that they discredited Johnson's Reconstruction policy among northern Republicans.

━━━━━━━

Vagrant Law

Sec. 2.... All freedmen, free negroes and mulattoes in this State, over the age of eighteen years, found on the second Monday in January, 1866, or thereafter, with no lawful employment or business, or found unlawfully assembling themselves together, either in the day or night time, and all white persons so assembling themselves with freedmen, free negroes or mulattoes, or usually associating with freedmen, free negroes or mulattoes, on terms of equality, or living in adultery or fornication with a freed woman, free negro or mulatto, shall be deemed vagrants, and on conviction thereof shall be fined in a sum not exceeding, in the case of a freedman, free negro, or mulatto, fifty dollars, and a white man two hundred dollars, and imprisoned at the discretion of the court, the free negro not exceeding ten days, and the white man not exceeding six months....

Sec. 7.... If any freedman, free negro, or mulatto shall fail or refuse to pay any tax levied according to the provisions of the sixth section of this act, it shall be *prima facie* evidence of vagrancy, and it shall be the duty of the sheriff to arrest such freedman, free negro, or mulatto or such person refusing or neglecting to pay such tax, and proceed at once to hire for the shortest time such delinquent tax-payer to any one who will pay the said tax, with accruing costs, giving preference to the employer, if there be one.

CIVIL RIGHTS OF FREEDMEN

Sec. 1.... That all freedmen, free negroes, and mulattoes may sue and be sued, implead and be impleaded, in all the courts of law and equity of this State, and may acquire personal property, and choses in action, by descent or purchase, and may dispose of the same in the same manner and to the same extent that white persons may: *Provided*, That the provisions of this section shall not be so construed as to allow any freedman, free negro, or mulatto to rent or lease any lands or tenements except in incorporated cities or towns....

Sec. 2.... All freedmen, free negroes, and mulattoes may intermarry with each other, in the same manner and under the same regulations that are provided by law for white persons: *Provided*, That the clerk of probate shall keep separate records of the same.

Sec. 3.... All freedmen, free negroes, or mulattoes who do now and have herebefore lived and cohabited together as husband and wife shall be taken and held in law as legally married, and the issue shall be taken and held as legitimate for all purposes; that it shall not be lawful for any freedman, free negro, or mulatto to intermarry with any white person; nor for any white person to intermarry with any freedman, free negro, or mulatto; and any person who shall so intermarry, shall be deemed guilty of felony, and on conviction thereof shall be confined in the State penitentiary for life; and those shall be deemed freedmen, free negroes, and mulattoes who are of pure negro blood, and those descended from a negro to the third generation, inclusive, though one ancestor in each generation may have been a white person.

Sec. 4.... In addition to cases in which freedmen, free negroes, and mulattoes are now by law competent witnesses, freedmen, free negroes, or mulattoes shall be competent in civil cases, when a party or parties to the suit, either plaintiff or plaintiffs, defendant or defendants; also in cases where freedmen, free negroes, and mulattoes is or are either plaintiff or plaintiffs, defendant or defendants, and a white person or white persons, is or are the opposing party or parties, plaintiff or plaintiffs, defendant or defendants. They shall also be competent witnesses in all criminal prosecutions where the crime charged is alleged to have been committed by a white person upon or against the person or property of a freedman, free negro, or mulatto: *Provided*, that in all cases said witnesses shall be examined in open court, on the stand; except, however, they may be examined before the grand jury, and shall in all cases be subject to the rules and tests of the common law as to competency and credibility.

Sec. 5.... Every freedman, free negro, and mulatto shall, on the second Monday of January, one thousand eight hundred and sixty-six and annually thereafter, have a lawful home or employment, and shall have written evidence thereof....

Sec. 6.... All contracts for labor made with freedmen, free negroes, and mulattoes for a longer period than one month shall be in writing, and in duplicate, attested and read to said freedman, free negro, or mulatto by a beat, city or county officer, or two disinterested white persons of the county in which the labor is to be performed, of which each party shall have one; and said contracts shall be taken and held as entire contracts, and if the laborer shall quit the service of the employer before the expiration of his term of service, without good cause, he shall forfeit his wages for that year up to the time of quitting.

Sec. 7.... Every civil officer shall, and every person may, arrest and carry back to his or her legal employer any freedman, free negro, or mulatto who shall have quit the service of his or her employer before the expiration of his or her term of service without good cause.... *Provided*, that said arrested party, after being so returned, may appeal to the justice of the peace or member of the board of police of the county, who, on notice to the alleged employer, shall try summarily whether said appellant is legally employed by the alleged employer, and has good cause to quit said employer; either party shall have the right of appeal to the county court, pending which the alleged deserter shall be remanded to the alleged employer or otherwise disposed of, as shall be right and just; and the decision of the county court shall be final.

CERTAIN OFFENSES OF FREEDMEN

Sec. 1.... That no freedman, free negro or mulatto, not in the military service of the United States government, and not licensed so to do by the board of police of his or her county, shall keep or carry firearms of any kind, or any ammunition, dirk or bowie knife, and on conviction thereof in the county court shall be punished by fine, not exceeding ten dollars, and pay the costs of such proceedings, and all such arms or ammunition shall be forfeited to the informer....

Sec. 2.... Any freedman, free negro, or mulatto committing riots, routs, affrays, trespasses, malicious mischief, cruel treatment to animals, seditious speeches, insulting gestures, language, or acts, or assaults on any person, disturbance of the peace, exercising the function of a minister of the Gospel without a license from some regularly organized church, vending spirituous or intoxicating liquors, or committing any other misdemeanor, the punishment of which is not specifically provided for by law, shall, upon conviction thereof in the county court, be fined not less than ten dollars, and not more than one hundred dollars, and may be imprisoned at the discretion of the court, not exceeding thirty days.

Sec. 3.... If any white person shall sell, lend, or give to any freedman, free negro, or mulatto any fire-arms, dirk or bowie knife, or ammunition, or any spirituous or intoxicating liquors, such person or persons so offending, upon conviction thereof in the county court of his or her county, shall be fined not exceeding fifty dollars, and may be imprisoned, at the discretion of the court, not exceeding thirty days....

Sec. 5.... If any freedman, free negro, or mulatto, convicted of any of the misdemeanors provided against in this act, shall fail or refuse for the space of five days, after conviction, to pay the fine and costs imposed, such person shall be hired out by the sheriff or other officer, at public outcry, to any white person who will pay said fine and all costs, and take said convict for the shortest time.

Questions

1. Why do you think the state of Mississippi required all black persons to sign yearly labor contracts but not white citizens?

2. What basic rights are granted to the former slaves and which are denied to them by the Black Code?

98. A Sharecropping Contract (1866)

Source: Records of the Assistant Commissioner for the State of Tennessee, Bureau of Refugees, Freedmen, and Abandoned Lands, National Archives.

Despite the widespread desire for land, few former slaves were able to acquire farms of their own in the post–Civil War South. Most ended up as sharecroppers, working on white-owned land for a share of the crop at the end of the growing season. Sharecropping was a kind of compromise between blacks' desire for independence from white control and planters' desire for a disciplined labor force. This contract, typical of thousands, originated in Shelby County, Tennessee. The laborers signed with an X, as they were illiterate. Typical of early postwar contracts, it gave the planter the right to supervise the labor of his employees. Later sharecropping contracts afforded former slaves greater autonomy. Families would rent parcels of land, work it under their own direction, and divide the crop with the owner at the end of the year. But as the price of cotton fell continuously after the Civil War, workers found it difficult to profit from the sharecropping system.

THOMAS J. ROSS agrees to employ the Freedmen to plant and raise a crop on his Rosstown Plantation.... On the following Rules, Regulations and Remunerations.

The said Ross agrees to furnish the land to cultivate, and a sufficient number of mules & horses and feed them to make and house said crop and all necessary farming utensils to carry on the same and to give unto said Freedmen whose names appear below one half of all the cotton, corn and wheat that is raised on said place for the year 1866 after all the necessary expenses are deducted out that accrues on said crop. Outside of the Freedmen's labor in harvesting, carrying to market and selling the same and the said Freedmen whose names appear below covenant and agrees to and with said Thomas J. Ross that for and in consideration of one half of the crop before mentioned that they will plant, cultivate, and raise under the management control and Superintendence of said Ross, in good faith, a cotton, corn and oat crop under his management for the year 1866. And we the said Freedmen agrees to furnish ourselves & families in provisions, clothing, medicine and medical bills and all, and every kind of other expenses that we may incur on said plantation for the year 1866 free of charge to said Ross. Should the said Ross furnish us any of the above supplies or any other kind of expenses, during said year, are to settle and pay him out of the net proceeds of our part of the crop the retail price of the county at time of sale or any price we may agree upon. The said Ross shall keep a regular book account, against each and every one or the head of every family to be adjusted and settled at the end of the year.

We furthermore bind ourselves to and with said Ross that we will do good work and labor ten hours a day on an average, winter and summer. The time to run from the time we commence to the time we quit.... We further agree that we will lose all lost time, or pay at the rate of one dollar per day, rainy days excepted. In sickness and women lying in childbed are to lose the time and account for it to the other hands out of his or her part of the crop at the same rates that she or they may receive per annum.

We furthermore bind ourselves that we will obey the orders of said Ross in all things in carrying out and managing said crop for said year and be docked for disobedience. All is responsible for all farming utensils that is on hand or may be placed in care of said Freedmen for the year 1866 to said Ross and are also responsible to said Ross if we carelessly, maliciously maltreat any of his stock for said year to said Ross for damages to be assessed out of our wages for said year.

Samuel (X) Johnson, Thomas (X) Richard, Tinny (X) Fitch, Jessie (X) Simmons, Sophe (X) Pruden, Henry (X) Pruden, Frances (X) Pruden, Elijah (X) Smith

Questions

1. In what ways does the contract limit the freedom of the laborers?

2. What kinds of benefits and risks for the freedpeople are associated with a sharecropping arrangement?

99. Elizabeth Cady Stanton, "Home Life" (ca. 1875)

Source: "Home Life," manuscript, ca. 1875, Elizabeth Cady Stanton Papers, Library of Congress.

Women activists saw Reconstruction as the moment for women to claim their own emancipation. With blacks guaranteed equality before the law

by the Fourteenth Amendment and black men given the right to vote by
the Fifteenth, women demanded that the boundaries of American democracy be expanded to include them as well. Other feminists debated how to
achieve "liberty for married women." In 1875, Elizabeth Cady Stanton
drafted an essay that demanded that the idea of equality, which had "revolutionized" American politics, be extended into private life. Genuine liberty for women, she insisted, required an overhaul of divorce laws (which
generally required evidence of adultery, desertion, or extreme abuse to terminate a marriage) and an end to the authority men exercised over their
wives.

Women's demand for the right to vote found few sympathetic male listeners. Even fewer supported liberalized divorce laws. But Stanton's exten-
sion of the idea of "liberty for women" into the most intimate areas of
private life identified a question that would become a central concern of
later generations of feminists.

WE ARE IN the midst of a social revolution, greater than any political or religious revolution, that the world has ever seen, because it
goes deep down to the very foundations of society.... A question of
magnitude presses on our consideration, whether man and woman
are equal, joint heirs to all the richness and joy of earth and Heaven,
or whether they were eternally ordained, one to be sovereign, the
other slave.... Here is a question with half the human family, and
that the stronger half, on one side, who are in possession of the cita-
del, hold the key to the treasury and make the laws and public sentiment to suit their own purposes. Can all this be made to change base
without prolonged discussion, upheavings, heartburnings, violence
and war? Will man yield what he considers to be his legitimate authority over woman with less struggle than have Popes and Kings their
supposed rights over their subjects, or slaveholders over their slaves?
No, no. John Stuart Mill says the generality of the male sex cannot
yet tolerate the idea of living with an equal at the fireside; and here is
the secret of the opposition to woman's equality in the state and the
church—men are not ready to recognize it in the home. This is the

real danger apprehended in giving woman the ballot, for as long as man makes, interprets, and executes the laws for himself, he holds the power under any system. Hence when he expresses the fear that liberty for woman would upset the family relation, he acknowledges that her present condition of subjection is not of her own choosing, and that if she had the power the whole relation would be essentially changed. And this is just what is coming to pass, the kernel of the struggle we witness to day.

This is woman's transition period from slavery to freedom and all these social upheavings, before which the wisest and bravest stand appalled, are but necessary incidents in her progress to equality. Conservatism cries out we are going to destroy the family. Timid reformers answer, the political equality of woman will not change it. They are both wrong. It will entirely revolutionize it. When woman is man's equal the marriage relation cannot stand on the basis it is to day. But this change will not destroy it; as state constitutions and statute laws did not create conjugal and maternal love, they cannot annual them.... We shall have the family, that great conservator of national strength and morals, after the present idea of man's headship is repudiated and woman set free. To establish a republican form of government [and] the right of individual judgment in the family must of necessity involve discussion, dissension, division, but the purer, higher, holier marriage will be evolved by the very evils we now see and deplore. This same law of equality that has revolutionized the state and the church is now knocking at the door of our homes and sooner or later there too it must do its work. Let us one and all wisely bring ourselves into line with this great law for man will gain as much as woman by an equal companionship in the nearest and holiest relations of life.... So long as people marry from considerations of policy, from every possible motive but the true one, discord and division must be the result. So long as the State provides no education for youth on the questions and throws no safeguards around the formation of marriage ties, it is in honor bound to open wide the door of escape. From a woman's standpoint, I see that marriage as an indissoluble tie is slavery for woman, because law, religion and public sentiment all combine under this idea to hold her true to this relation, whatever it may be and there is no other human slavery that knows such depths of degradations as a wife chained to a man whom she neither loves nor respects, no other slavery so disastrous in its consequences on the race, or to individual respect, growth and development....

• • •

By the laws of several states in this republic made by Christian representatives of the people divorces are granted to day for ... seventeen reasons.... By this kind of legislation in the several states we have practically decided two important points: 1st That marriage is a dissoluble tie that may be sundered by a decree of the courts. 2nd That it is a civil contract and not a sacrament of the church, and the one involves the other....

A legal contract for a section of land requires that the parties be of age, of sound mind, [and] that there be no flaw in the title.... But a legal marriage in many states in the Union may be contracted between a boy of fourteen and a girl of twelve without the consent of parents or guardians, without publication of banns.... Now what person of common sense, or conscience, can endorse laws as wise or prudent that sanction acts such as these. Let the state be logical: if marriage is a civil contract, it should be subject to the laws of all other contracts, carefully made, the parties of age, and all agreements faithfully observed....

Let us now glance at a few of the popular objections to liberal divorce laws. It is said that to make divorce respectable by law, gospel and public sentiment is to break up all family relations. Which is to say that human affections are the result and not the foundation of the canons of the church and statutes of the state.... To open the doors of escape to those who dwell in continual antagonism, to the unhappy wives of drunkards, libertines, knaves, lunatics and tyrants, need not necessarily embitter the relations of those who *are* contented and happy, but on the contrary the very fact of freedom strengthens and purifies the bond of union. When husbands and wives do not own each other as property, but are bound together only by affection, marriage will be a life long friendship and not a heavy yoke, from which both may sometimes long for deliverance. The freer the relations are between human beings, the happier....

• • •

Home life to the best of us has its shadows and sorrows, and because of our ignorance this must needs be.... The day is breaking. It is something to know that life's ills are not showered upon us by the Good Father from a kind of Pandora's box, but are the results of causes that we have the power to control. By a knowledge and observance of law the road to health and happiness opens before [us]: a joy and peace that passeth all understanding shall yet be ours and Paradise regained on earth. When marriage results from a true union of intellect and spirit and when Mothers and Fathers give to their holy offices even that preparation of soul and body that the artist gives to the conception of his poem, statue or landscape, then will marriage, maternity and paternity acquire a new sacredness and dignity and a nobler type of manhood and womanhood will glorify the race!!

Questions

1. How does Stanton define the "social revolution" the United States underwent after the Civil War?

2. How does Stanton believe that individual freedom within the family can be established?

─────

100. Frederick Douglass, "The Composite Nation" (1869)

Source: Philip S. Foner and Daniel Rosenberg, eds., Racism, Dissent, and Asian Americans from 1850 to the Present *(Westport, Conn., 1993), pp. 217–30.*

Another group that did not share fully in the expansion of rights inspired by the Civil War and Reconstruction was Asian-Americans. Prejudices against Asians were deeply entrenched, especially on the West Coast, where most immigrants from Asia lived. When the radical Republican Charles Sumner, senator from Massachusetts, moved to allow Asians to become naturalized citizens (a right that had been barred to them since 1790), senators from California and Oregon objected vociferously, and the proposal was defeated.

Another advocate of equal rights for Asian-Americans was Frederick Douglass. In his remarkable "Composite Nation" speech, delivered in Boston in 1869, Douglass condemned anti-Asian discrimination and called for giving them all the rights of other Americans, including the right to vote. Douglass's comprehensive vision of a country made up of people of all races and national origins and enjoying equal rights was too radical for the time, but it would win greater and greater acceptance during the twentieth century.

THERE WAS A time when even brave men might look fearfully at the destiny of the Republic. When our country was involved in a tangled network of contradictions; when vast and irreconcilable social forces fiercely disputed for ascendancy and control; when a heavy curse rested upon our very soil, defying alike the wisdom and the virtue of the people to remove it; when our professions were loudly mocked by our practice and our name was a reproach and a by word to a mocking earth; when our good ship of state, freighted with the best hopes of the oppressed of all nations, was furiously hurled against the hard and flinty rocks of derision, and every cord, bolt, beam and bend in her body quivered beneath the shock, there was some apology for doubt and despair. But that day has happily passed away. The storm has been weathered, and the portents are nearly all in our favor.

There are clouds, wind, smoke and dust and noise, over head and around, and there will always be; but no genuine thunder, with destructive bolt, menaces from any quarter of the sky.

The real trouble with us was never our system or form of Government, or the principles under lying it; but the peculiar composition of our people; the relations existing between them and the compromising spirit which controlled the ruling power of the country.

We have for a long time hesitated to adopt and may yet refuse to adopt, and carry out, the only principle which can solve that difficulty and give peace, strength and security to the Republic, *and that is* the principle of absolute *equality*.

We are a country of all extremes, ends and opposites; the most conspicuous example of composite nationality in the world. Our people defy all the ethnological and logical classifications. In races we range all the way from black to white, with intermediate shades which, as in the apocalyptic vision, no man can name a number.

In regard to creeds and faiths, the condition is no better, and no worse. Differences both as to race and to religion are evidently more likely to increase than to diminish.

We stand between the populous shores of two great oceans. Our land is capable of supporting one fifth of all the globe. Here, labor is abundant and here labor is better remunerated than any where else. All moral, social and geographical causes, conspire to bring to us the peoples of all other over populated countries.

Europe and Africa are already here, and the Indian was here before either. He stands to-day between the two extremes of black and white, too proud to claim fraternity with either, and yet too weak to with stand the power of either. Heretofore the policy of our government has been governed by race pride, rather than by wisdom. Until recently, neither the Indian nor the negro has been treated as a part of the body politic. No attempt has been made to inspire either with a sentiment of patriotism, but the hearts of both races have been diligently sown with the dangerous seeds of discontent and hatred.

The policy of keeping the Indians to themselves, has kept the tomahawk and scalping knife busy upon our borders, and has cost us largely in blood and treasure. Our treatment of the negro has slacked humanity, and filled the country with agitation and ill-feeling and brought the nation to the verge of ruin.

Before the relations of these two races are satisfactorily settled, and in spite of all opposition, a new race is making its appearance within our borders, and claiming attention. It is estimated that not less than one-hundred thousand Chinamen are now within the limits of the United States. Several years ago every vessel, large or small, of steam or sail, bound to our Pacific coast and hailing from the Flowery kingdom, added to the number and strength of this element of our population.

Men differ widely as to the magnitude of this potential Chinese immigration. The fact that by the late treaty with China, we bind ourselves to receive immigrants from that country only as the subjects of the Emperor, and by the construction, at least, are bound not to naturalize them, and the further fact that Chinamen themselves have a superstitious devotion to their country and an aversion to permanent location in any other, contracting even to have their bones carried back should they die abroad, and from the fact that many have returned to China, and the still more stubborn that resistance to their coming has increased rather than diminished, it is inferred that we shall never have a large Chinese population in America. This however is not my opinion.

It may be admitted that these reasons, and others, may check and moderate the tide of immigration; but it is absurd to think that they will do more than this. Counting their number now, by the thousands, the time is not remote when they will count them by the millions. The Emperor's hold upon the Chinaman may be strong, but the Chinaman's hold upon himself is stronger.

Treaties against naturalization, like all other treaties, are limited by circumstances. As to the superstitious attachment of the Chinese to China, that, like all other superstitions, will dissolve in the light and heat of truth and experience. The Chinaman may be a bigot, but it does not follow that he will continue to be one, tomorrow. He is a man, and will be very likely to act like a man. He will not be long in finding out that a country which is good enough to live in, is good enough to die in; and that a soil that was good enough to hold his body while alive, will be good enough to hold his bones when he is dead.

Those who doubt a large immigration, should remember that the past furnishes no criterion as a basis of calculation. We live under new and improved conditions of migration, and these conditions are constantly improving. America is no longer an obscure and inaccessible country. Our ships are in every sea, our commerce in every port, our language is heard all around the globe, steam and lightning have revolutionized the whole domain of human thought, changed all geographical relations, make a day of the present seem equal to a thousand years of the past, and the continent that Columbus only conjectured four centuries ago is now the center of the world.

• • •

I have said that the Chinese will come, and have given some reasons why we may expect them in very large numbers in no very distant future. Do you ask, if I favor such immigration, I answer *I would*. Would you have them naturalized, and have them invested with all the rights of American citizenship? *I would*. Would you allow them to vote? *I would*. Would you allow them to hold office? *I would*.

But are there not reasons against all this? Is there not such a law or principle as that of self preservation? Does not every race owe something to itself? Should it not attend to the dictates of common sense? Should not a superior race protect itself from contact with inferior ones? Are not the white people the owners of this continent? Have they not the right to say what kind of people shall be allowed to come here and settle? Is there not such a thing as being more generous than wise? In the effort to promote civilization may we not corrupt and destroy what we have? Is it best to take on board more passengers than the ship will carry?

To all this and more I have one among many answers, altogether satisfactory to me, though I cannot promise that it will be so to you.

I submit that this question of Chinese immigration should be settled upon higher principles than those of a cold and selfish expediency. There are such things in the world as human rights. They rest upon no conventional foundation, but are external, universal, and indestructible. Among these, is the right of locomotion; the right of migration; the right which belongs to no particular race, but belongs alike to all and to all alike. It is the right you assert by staying here, and your fathers asserted by coming here. It is this great right that I assert for the Chinese and the Japanese, and for all other varieties of men equally with yourselves, now and forever. I know of no rights of race superior to the rights of humanity, and when there is a supposed conflict between human and national rights, it is safe to go to the side of humanity. I have great respect for the blue eyes and light haired races of America. They are a mighty people. In any struggle for the good things of this world they need have no fear. They have no need to doubt that they will get their full share.

But I reject the arrogant and scornful theory by which they would limit migratory rights, or any other essential human rights to themselves, and which would make them the owners of this great continent to the exclusion of all other races of men.

I want a home here not only for the negro, the mulatto and the Latin races; but I want the Asiatic to find a home here in the United States, and feel at home here, both for his sake and for ours. Right wrongs no man. If respect is had to majorities, the fact that only one fifth of the population of the globe is white, the other four fifths are colored, ought to have some weight and influence in disposing of this and similar questions. It would be a sad reflection upon the laws of nature and upon the idea of justice, to say nothing of a common Creator, if four-fifths of mankind were deprived of the rights of migration to make room for the one fifth. If the white race may exclude all other races from this continent, it may rightfully do the same in respect to all other lands, islands, capes and continents, and thus have all the world to itself. Thus what would seem to belong to the whole, would become the property only of a part. So much for what is right, now let us see what is wise.

And here I hold that a liberal and brotherly welcome to all who are likely to come to the United States is the only wise policy which this nation can adopt.

• • •

I close these remarks as I began. If our action shall be in accordance with the principles of justice, liberty, and perfect human equality, no eloquence can adequately portray the greatness and grandeur of the future of the Republic.

We shall spread the network of our science and civilization over all who seek their shelter whether from Asia, Africa, or the Isles of the sea. We shall mold them all, each after his kind, into Americans; Indian and Celt, negro and Saxon, Latin and Teuton, Mongolian and Caucasian, Jew and Gentile, all shall here bow to the same law, speak the same language, support the same government, enjoy the same liberty, vibrate with the same national enthusiasm, and seek the same national ends.

Questions

1. What does Douglass mean by the term "composite nationality"?

2. Why does he believe that people should be allowed to move freely from one country to another?

101. Robert B. Elliott on Civil Rights (1874)

Source: Civil Rights. Speech of Hon. Robert B. Elliott, of South Carolina, in the House of Representatives, January 6, 1874 *(Washington, D.C., 1874), pp. 1–8.*

One of the South's most prominent black politicians during Reconstruction, Robert B. Elliott appears to have been born in England and arrived in Boston shortly before the Civil War. He came to South Carolina in 1867, where he established a law office and was elected as a delegate to the state's constitutional convention of 1868. During the 1870s, he served in the legislature and was twice elected to the U.S. House of Representatives.

In January 1874, Elliott delivered a celebrated speech in Congress in support of the bill that became the Civil Rights Act of 1875. The measure outlawed racial discrimination in transportation and places of public accommodation like theaters and hotels. Thanks to the Civil War and Reconstruction, Elliott proclaimed, "equality before the law" regardless of race had been written into the laws and Constitution and had become an essential element of American freedom. Reconstruction, he announced, had "settled forever the political status of my race."

Elliott proved to be wrong. By the turn of the century, many of the rights blacks had gained after the Civil War had been taken away. It would be left to future generations to breathe new life into Elliott's dream of "equal, impartial, and universal liberty."

SIR, IT IS scarcely twelve years since that gentleman [Alexander H. Stephens] shocked the civilized world by announcing the birth of a government which rested on human slavery as its corner-stone. The progress of events has swept away that *pseudo*-government which rested on greed, pride, and tyranny; and the race whom he then ruthlessly spurned and trampled on are here to meet him in debate, and to demand that the rights which are enjoyed by their former oppressors—who vainly sought to overthrow a Government which they could not prostitute to the base uses of slavery—shall be accorded to those who even in the darkness of slavery kept their allegiance true to freedom and the Union: Sir, the gentleman from Georgia has learned much since 1861; but he is still a laggard. Let him put away entirely the false and fatal theories which have so greatly marred an otherwise enviable record. Let him accept, in its fullness and benefi-cence, the great doctrine that American citizenship carries with it every civil and political right which manhood can confer. Let him lend his influence, with all his masterly ability, to complete the proud structure of legislation which makes this nation worthy of the great declaration which heralded its birth, and he will have done that which will most nearly redeem his reputation in the eyes of the world, and best vindicate the wisdom of that policy which has per-mitted him to regain his seat upon this floor. . . .

• • •

Sir, equality before the law is now the broad, universal, glorious rule and mandate of the Republic. No State can violate that. Kentucky and Georgia may crowd their statute-books with retrograde and barbarous legislation; they may rejoice in the odious eminence of their consistent hostility to all the great steps of human progress which have marked our national history since slavery tore down the stars and stripes on Fort Sumter; but, if Congress shall do its duty, if Congress shall enforce the great guarantees which the Supreme Court has declared to be the one pervading purpose of all the recent amendments, then their unwise and unenlightened conduct will fall with the same weight upon the gentlemen from those States who now lend their influence to defeat this bill, as upon the poorest slave who once had no rights which the honorable gentlemen were bound to respect. . . .

No language could convey a more complete assertion of the power of Congress over the subject embraced in the present bill than is expressed [in the Fourteenth Amendment]. If the States do not conform to the requirements of this clause, if they continue to deny to any person within their jurisdiction the equal protection of the laws, or as the Supreme Court had said, "deny equal justice in its courts," then Congress is here said to have power to enforce the constitutional guarantee by appropriate legislation. That is the power which this bill now seeks to put in exercise. It proposes to enforce the constitutional guarantee against inequality and discrimination by appropriate legislation. It does not seek to confer new rights, nor to place rights conferred by State citizenship under the protection of the United States, but simply to prevent and forbid inequality and discrimination on account of race, color, or previous condition of servitude. Never was there a bill more completely within the constitutional power of Congress. Never was there a bill which appealed for support more strongly to that sense of justice and fair-play which has been said, and in the main with justice, to be a characteristic of the Anglo-Saxon race. The Constitution warrants it; the Supreme Court sanctions it; justice demands it.

Sir, I have replied to the extent of my ability to the arguments which have been presented by the opponents of this measure. I have replied also to some of the legal propositions advanced by gentlemen on the other side; and now that I am about to conclude, I am deeply sensible of the imperfect manner in which I have performed the task. Technically, this bill is to decide upon the civil status of the colored American citizen; a point disputed at the very formation of our present Government, when by a short-sighted policy, a policy repugnant to true republican government, one negro counted as three-fifths of a man. The logical result of this mistake of the framers of the Constitution strengthened the cancer of slavery, which finally spread its poisonous tentacles over the southern portion of the body-politic. To arrest its growth and save the nation we have passed through the harrowing operation of intestine war, dreaded at all times, resorted to at the last extremity, like the surgeon's knife, but absolutely necessary to extirpate the disease which threatened with the life of the nation the overthrow of civil and political liberty on this continent. In that dire extremity the members of the race which I have the honor in part to represent—the race which pleads for justice at your hands to-day, forgetful of their inhuman and brutalizing servitude at the South, their degradation and ostracism at the North—flew willingly and gallantly to the support of the national Government. Their sufferings, assistance, privations, and trials in the swamps and in the rice-fields, their valor on the land and on the sea, is a part of the ever-glorious record which makes up the history of a nation preserved, and might, should I urge the claim, incline you to respect and guarantee their rights and privileges as citizens of our common Republic. But I remember that valor, devotion, and loyalty are not always rewarded according to their just deserts, and that after the battle some who have borne the brunt of the fray may, through neglect or contempt, be assigned to a subordinate place, while the enemies in war may be preferred to the sufferers.

The results of the war, as seen in reconstruction, have settled forever the political status of my race. The passage of this bill will determine the civil status, not only of the negro, but of any other class of citizens who may feel themselves discriminated against. It will form the cap-stone of that temple of liberty, begun on this continent under discouraging circumstances, carried on in spite of the sneers of monarchists and the cavils of pretended friends of freedom, until at last it stands in all its beautiful symmetry and proportions, a building the grandest which the world has ever seen, realizing the most sanguine expectations and the highest hopes of those who, in the name of equal, impartial, and universal liberty, laid the foundation stones.

Questions

1. How does Elliott defend the constitutionality of the Civil Rights Bill?

2. Why does Elliott refer to the "cornerstone speech" of Alexander H. Stephens in making his argument?